How the French
Saved America

How the French Saved America

SOLDIERS, SAILORS, DIPLOMATS, LOUIS XVI, AND THE SUCCESS OF A REVOLUTION

TOM SHACHTMAN

St. Martin's Press

New York

www.stmartins.com

The Library of Congress Cataloging-in-Publication Data is available upon request.

ISBN 978-1-250-08087-5 (hardcover)
ISBN 978-1-250-14614-4 (ebook)

Our books may be purchased in bulk for promotional, educational, or business use.
Please contact your local bookseller or the Macmillan Corporate and Premium Sales Department at
1-800-221-7945, extension 5442, or by email at MacmillanSpecialMarkets@macmillan.com.

First Edition: September 2017

10 9 8 7 6 5 4 3 2 1

For Harriet, who helped me through.

In Memoriam
John L. Tishman, 1926–2016
Donald Oresman, 1925–2016

Contents

Prologue

"Matters so delicate that I tremble as I walk." —Achard de Bonvouloir

On December 18, 1775, as the winter solstice approached, darkness arrived early to Philadelphia, capital of the British colony of Pennsylvania, giving cover to the men individually making their ways through the streets to Carpenters' Hall for a rendezvous with a visitor from France touted as bearing an important message for Americans.

Their encounter would take place at a moment of high military and political peril for America. Nine months earlier, hostilities had begun at Lexington and Concord, and since the summer the struggle between the British and Continental troops had become a standoff at Boston. The Continental army was so bereft of cannons, ammunition, and gunpowder that General George Washington was unable to lay a proper siege or launch assaults on British positions. "Our want of powder is inconceivable," Washington wrote that week in December. "A daily waste and no supply administers a gloomy prospect." Washington had sent Colonel Henry Knox to the recently seized former British stronghold of Fort Ticonderoga in upper New York to haul their cannons overland to Boston in order that their eventual presence on the heights above the city might force the British to abandon the metropolis. But at year's end, well before those cannons could possibly arrive in Boston, the enlistment periods of many Continental soldiers would end, and Washington worried that soldiers would then just go home, leaving him too shorthanded to continue the fight.

There was equal political peril, for sentiment in the Second Continental Congress was seriously divided over whether to declare independence. The First Continental Congress, convened in 1774, had avoided any attempt to do so, and in July 1775 the Second had issued the so-called Olive Branch Petition, a plea to King George III to calm the fraternal conflict and find a way to allow the colonies to remain within the Empire. That petition had been answered on August 23, 1775, by A Proclamation for Suppressing Rebellion and Sedition, in which the king declared the colonies to be in open rebellion and their leaders to be "Traitors," and which was followed by an order to close American ports to any would-be suppliers of the rebels. In the fall Congress had sent a second conciliatory petition to the king. By late December 1775 it had received no response, and Congress feared that George III's next message to Parliament would specifically reject it.

Tendrils from the past and imaginings of the future are integral to all clandestine assignations. While Congress awaited the king's likely rejection of their pacific overtures, it had established a Committee of Correspondence to explore with Americans abroad and "friends . . . in other parts of the world" the possibilities of foreign assistance to the rebelling colonies. Immediately after the committee's chartering, its members had renamed it the Committee of Secret Correspondence and closed its records to other congressmen. They did so to protect the overseas agents whom the committee might employ, and to conceal those agents' identities from that fraction of the delegates who continued to resist declaring independence. For the same reason the committee was being very circumspect about this evening's clandestine meeting, convened at their behest.

The walkers' destination was the headquarters of the Library Company, a subscription club founded by Benjamin Franklin and friends in 1731 and moved to Carpenters' Hall in 1773. Franklin, a member of the Committee of Secret Correspondence, was one of the walkers; the most famous American in the world, now sixty-nine and in poor health, he had returned home after fifteen years in London, where he represented the interests of Pennsylvania and Massachusetts. He and the other walkers had arranged for each to arrive at the assignation at slightly different times and by roundabout routes. Their purpose was to avoid alerting the suspicions of the city's British and Tory spies, who might judge treasonous the walkers' participation in the business of this meeting: assessing a potential connection between France and the American colonies that were on the verge of severing their existing connection with Great Britain.

Like Congress as a whole, the Committee of Secret Correspondence was a mix of radicals, centrists, and conservatives; none of the members qualified as a die-hard Loyalist to the Crown, for King George had already branded all those in Congress as traitors for daring to meet without his permission. Franklin, although the oldest of the committee members, was perhaps the most independence-minded; the relative moderate was John Dickinson, the author of the popular *Letters from a Farmer in Pennsylvania*, which argued that forcible resistance to British tyranny was justifiable, but also the author of that Olive Branch Petition to George III. The members also included a rockbound conservative—the ascetic, patrician New York lawyer John Jay, thirty, who was being dragged by events from favoring reconciliation to accepting the need for rebellion.

An inherent difficulty for Americans in seeking a foreign liaison was that they were reluctant suitors. Raised from childhood to be self-reliant, they were also distrustful of even tangential involvement with the shifting alignments and resulting perfidies of the European balance-of-powers system, which over the past century had amply demonstrated its inability to produce peace for more than a dozen years at a time. Congress had concluded only very recently, and with some distaste, that to further resist British subjugation they must seek arms, powder, ammunition, and funds from abroad. Still, few congressmen of any stripe, even the most radical, desired an outright alliance with any foreign nation.

Nor did the European powers have much interest in alliance with the rebelling British colonies, despite a correspondent having told Franklin that *"toute l'Europe nous souhaite le plus heureux succès pour le maintien de nos libertés"* (all Europe wishes you the happiest success in the maintaining of your liberties). It was becoming increasingly clear to the committee, as well as to most of the other congressional delegates and knowledgeable observers, that as the magazine editor Tom Paine was writing, just then, "While we [continue to] profess ourselves the subjects of Britain, we must, in the eyes of foreign nations, be considered as rebels." In a room just a few blocks from Carpenters' Hall, Paine was putting the finishing touches on his pamphlet, *Common Sense*. "Under our present denomination of British subjects we can neither be received nor heard abroad . . . until, by an independence, we take rank with other nations."

Even France and Spain, the countries whose wealth and power were the closest to Great Britain's, worried about reprisals should they openly ally with George III's rebellious subjects. Given the dominance of the Royal Navy their fear was reasonable, and was made more palpable by France and Spain's knowing the relative weakness of their own land forces, which had deteriorated since the end of the Seven Years' War.

Each of the evening walkers to Carpenters' Hall ascended in turn the broad exterior marble steps, strode through large double doors into the building, and mounted the narrow, spiraling staircase to the second floor, where they joined the French émigré Francis Daymon, whose presence there after hours would not be suspect since he was the Library Company's paid librarian. Daymon, Franklin's personal translator, would interpret for the visitor. Candles were lit and shades drawn in the Library Company's book-lined smaller room, the other being unusable because it was crammed with scientific apparatus.

Only Jay, among Franklin's colleagues on the Committee of Secret

Correspondence, would later acknowledge having met the French visitor. Franklin had already become an admirer of Jay, perhaps glimpsing hints of the strength that underlay Jay's cultured and considered persona. Devoted like Franklin to furthering the cause of American freedom, Jay also like Franklin had a close relative who was a Tory, had made his mark in the world primarily with his pen, and did not want the colonies to break with Great Britain unless there was no viable alternative.

Jay remembered the French visitor as an "elderly, lame gentleman, having the appearance of an old, wounded French officer," although the visitor was then only twenty-six and his apparent wounds consisted of a limp and other congenital physical malformations. The visitor had previously been coy, only presenting letters from European merchants indicating that he was an Antwerp-based trader. But in this first meeting with the committee members, recognizing their worry that he might be a British spy or double agent, he announced his true identity—the Chevalier Julien Alexandre Achard de Bonvouloir et Loyauté—and he probably displayed his commission as a brevetted lieutenant, signed by Louis XVI, and expected that the Americans would not know that such brevetted commissions were mostly honorific.

To reach this Philadelphia assignation Bonvouloir had made quite an effort. The idea had come to him during a tour of the colonies earlier that year, when he had met Daymon, who boasted of ties to Franklin. The chevalier had then gone to Boston, where his attempt to volunteer for the Continental forces was rebuffed. That did not deter him, on reaching London, from touting his access to Franklin to the Comte de Guines, France's ambassador to the Court of St James's. Bonvouloir's timing was fortuitous: Guines desperately needed a success to vault him over a troubling lawsuit and to counter the distrust of his boss, the French foreign minister Vergennes. Guines owed his diplomatic career to Queen Marie Antoinette, who liked the way that Guines made her laugh; but of late her protecting hand had faltered.

Guines recommended Bonvouloir to Vergennes as an emissary to sound out America as to its intentions and to present France's own. The foreign minister, ever practical even with his enemies (among them Guines), saw little downside and some potential gain in dispatching to America a low-status, unofficial messenger whose cost to the French crown was trifling. And since Bonvouloir was the black sheep of a noble family, he would be easy to disavow should that become necessary.

Unable due to his birth defects to perform properly in his cavalry regiment, as his forefathers had done with their military assignments and as his brothers were currently doing, Bonvouloir had become so dissolute and indebted that he had accepted a posting to Saint-Domingue, the Haitian haunt of many similarly indebted French officers. In Haiti he had disgraced himself further. Vergennes, seeking more information on the potential messenger, could verify only that Bonvouloir had been a volunteer in Haiti's Régiment du Cap. Nonetheless he allowed Bonvouloir to be dispatched to America after providing strict guidelines for his conduct, including instructions to be memorized, not carried on paper, and on how to communicate using invisible ink.

Meeting with American representatives at the Library Company, Bonvouloir could truthfully say he was there as a private person who was not unconnected at Versailles. As such he conveyed three simple, seemingly straightforward messages: He assured the Americans that France wished them well, had no interest in regaining Canada, and would welcome American vessels in French ports.

France not want Canada?! Most Americans thought that the northernmost Atlantic colony had been viciously wrested from France by Great Britain in the Peace of Paris, signed in 1763. In fact it had actually been traded away by France as too expensive to maintain, but still, Americans in 1775 were incredulous that a European colonial power would neither covet more colonies nor desire the return of an old one as the spoils of a forthcoming war. Franklin in particular had presumed that regaining Canada would be a part of France's price for helping America. And the ideas that France wished the colonists well and that French ports would be open to American vessels? Jay or any other American lawyer would have been stunned by these notions, for they signaled a sharp departure from the strict neutrality toward America and resigned deference to British wishes that France had displayed since 1763. Open ports would mean, for example, that Tidewater tobacco farmers would have a market for their goods other than in London—say Martinique or Saint-Domingue.

Bonvouloir embellished these points by flattering language specifically suggested by Vergennes: "We admire . . . the grandeur and nobleness of their efforts," he said, and "having no interest in injuring them, should we see with pleasure such a happy conjunction of circumstances as would set them at liberty to frequent our port facilities . . . their commerce would soon prove to them all that we feel for them."

Asked whether he had the authority to convey these messages concerning what the government of Louis XVI would do, Bonvouloir drew his hand across his throat and said, "Gentlemen, I shall take care of my head."

Franklin judged the Bonvouloir messages to be of such great importance that he scheduled two additional evening sessions to hash over every facet of the chevalier's information, and to impart some of his own in regard to American battlefield strengths, the predicted outcomes of current campaigns, and the colonists' needs for guns, ammunition, and trained engineers. To those meetings Franklin likely brought fellow Committee of Secret Correspondence members, one or two at a time, so that all would gain a sense of Bonvouloir and his messages.

From prior meetings with Washington, Franklin knew of the commander's often-repeated plea for professionally trained French engineers. Washington had been disappointed in American ones, whose craft had been learned in the field from British engineers whose own knowledge was based on translated French texts. Since the seventeenth-century heyday of Vauban, whose name was synonymous with effective field cannons and sieges, France had been at the forefront of military engineering. Washington craved people with that expertise.

As Franklin began a final session with Bonvouloir, he set up a chessboard and invited the chevalier to play. But before Bonvouloir could advance a pawn, Franklin removed both kings from the board and announced, "In America we have no need of kings." A startling coup de théâtre, this was a clear warning that while the colonists were eager for French aid they would not accept substituting Louis XVI for their current ruler, George III. The relationship they sought was not a subservient one.

After the last session, Bonvouloir repaired to his room to write to Guines, summing up the discussions like a man breathlessly recounting a courtship's opening moves and shared intimacies. He was so excited that instead of writing in milk to veil the contents, he inscribed the letter in ink. And he folded within it a note that he had received from the committee, containing three sets of questions:

Monsieur de Bonvouloir is begged to examine the following proposition, under the understanding that we are speaking as private individuals to each other:

1. Can he tell us what the views of the Court of France are in regard to the North American colonies? Are they favorable, and if so, how can we obtain official confirmation of this?

2. Could we find in France two competent engineer officers, well recommended and reliable? What steps should we take to obtain them?

3. May we obtain from France arms and other necessary munitions of war in exchange for the products of our country? And may we have free entry into the French ports?

Bonvouloir reported that he had given qualified affirmative responses to all the questions save for official recognition, which request he had rebuffed as "premature, even dangerous," volunteering that the presence of an American plenipotentiary at Versailles would be taken by London as a "tugging of the British beard," a deliberate provocation that could trigger dire consequences.

The Americans believed, Bonvouloir wrote, "that they won't be able to hold [the colonies] without a nation that protects them by sea," and understood that France was in the best position to provide that help. Afraid to carry this message to Guines personally, "for the matters are so delicate that with all the good will possible, I tremble as I walk," he sent the missive in care of a trusted messenger.

Information providers such as Bonvouloir often neglect at their peril the fact that information can flow in two directions. Bonvouloir did not know that his message from America to France contained a highly inaccurate rebel assessment of the Continental forces—as about to seize Boston, Montreal, and Quebec, and as consisting of fifty thousand well-dressed paid soldiers and an even larger number of unpaid volunteers. The reality was far more pallid: Washington's army numbered at most twenty thousand; Montreal's small British force had voluntarily vacated the town, but the Americans could not hold it; and the Continental army was on the verge of being definitively repulsed at Quebec. Moreover, Bonvouloir asserted, the Americans were potent and highly motivated. "They are more powerful than we could have thought, beyond imagination powerful; you will be astonished by it. Nothing shocks or frightens them, you can count on that. Independency is a certainty for 1776; there will be no drawing back."

Despite American and French efforts to maintain the secrecy of the assignations with Bonvouloir, the British government—whose spies were indeed everywhere—knew of the chevalier's mission before he landed in Philadelphia, including details of his ship and its captain's political stripe. In London this news heightened officials' concerns regarding a potential alliance between France and the American colonies. For the Americans to be meeting with Bonvouloir meant to the British that what they had feared, a mutual courtship of France and America, had begun.

PART ONE

A Mutual Courtship
1755–1776

1

"The true science of a sovereign"
—Louis XVI

In Philadelphia, even before the close of 1775 the Committee of Secret Correspondence received verification of Bonvouloir's contention that supplies could readily be obtained from France. Two French export-import traders showed up on Congress's doorstep wanting to provide those supplies and bearing introductions from merchants in Rhode Island and from Washington, to whom after meeting they had sent "two bottles of the Ratifia of Grenoble, three of fruit preserved in Brandy, one dozen of oranges and fifty Small Loaves of Sugar."

Such gifts the traders may have deemed necessary because they were aware that Americans didn't like the French. A dozen years after the close of the French and Indian War, Americans retained a strong residual fear of and distaste for all things Gallic. Washington and some of his current top commanders had served with the British against the French in that war, and none had been able to forget how the French had repeatedly urged their Native American allies to commit savage acts on American settlers, and engendered a fear of their forcibly converting all of New England's Protestants to Catholicism.

Even as Catholicism's grip on the governance of France loosened,

Americans continued to demonize the religion and its adherents. In 1773 a friend and correspondent of Franklin's, the Congregationalist reverend Samuel Cooper, gave the annual endowed lecture at the Brattle Street Church in Boston on the "tyranny, usurpation, fatal errors, abominable superstitions, and other crying wickedness" of the Catholic Church. In June 1774 many Americans railed against Britain's recently passed Quebec Act, which struck down the requirement that Canada's Catholics pledge allegiance to Protestantism and restored French civil law throughout a territory extending a thousand miles along the upper Midwest, a measure seen as enabling the spread of Catholicism to the detriment of Protestantism. A scholar of religion in that period, Michael S. Carter, writes that to New England Protestants in 1775, Catholicism was less a religion than "a form of spiritual and intellectual 'slavery' and that was the antithesis of their free, rational, and pure religion." Another scholar, Glenn Moots, suggests that "anti-Catholic rhetoric was more about politics than it was about theology," since Catholicism was equated with encouraging tyrannical rule.

Contributing to Americans' unease about the French were the works of French intellectuals regarding the New World. While Jean-Jacques Rousseau's essays celebrated enlightened Quakers and imagined "noble savages," most of his fellow *philosophes* literally dismissed Americans as lower forms of human life. The world's preeminent naturalist, Georges-Louis Leclerc, Comte de Buffon, a man so exalted by contemporaries that painters depicted him in one-on-one conversations with Mother Nature, fulminated about the "degeneracy" of the flora, fauna, and geographic features of the New World, even though he, like Rousseau and virtually all others who wrote on America prior to the Revolution, had never visited the place. Buffon opined that the sexual apparatus of Native American males was "enfeebled" to the point of their being incapable of true love for females, and therefore unable to generate family feeling, civilization, or culture. In a popular European book a follower of Buffon derided all that had occurred upon the North American continent since the flood in Noah's time, titling one section of his work, "The Americans' Moronic Spirit." Another influential book, on the "two Indies," East and West, by the Abbé Guillaume Thomas François Raynal, published in 1770 and in many subsequent editions and translations, contained the ultimate put-down of Americans:

> It is amazing that America has not yet produced a good poet, a capable mathematician, or a man of genius in a single art or a single science. Almost all have some facility in everything, but none has a marked talent for anything. Precocious and mature before us, they are far behind when we have reached our full mental development.

But Raynal hoped the Americans would soon catch up. Having meticulously identified all tyrannies, slavery, and exploitations of people around the globe, the elderly scholar had become enthusiastic about America's promise, as had Buffon, who underwrote the first French translation of Franklin's *Experiments and Observations Touching on Electricity.* The *philosophes* marveled over Franklin, who visited France in the 1760s, and over such translated works as Dickinson's *Letters from a Farmer in Pennsylvania,* and increasingly believed that America would be where Enlightenment ideals of toleration and personal fulfillment could brighten the lives of the vast majority of citizens. These thinkers agreed with the semiofficial *Gazette de France,* which proclaimed that in America "an innate taste for liberty is inseparable from the soil, the sky, the forests and the lakes which keep this vast and still new country from resembling other parts of the globe," and warned that Europeans transported there soon developed the same taste.

As America's Revolutionary War began, what appealed to the literate elite of France, and through their works to the nine-tenths of all French who were oppressed by their own ruler, were the rising American principles of "no taxation without representation," equality of citizens rich and poor before the law, the nurturing of an educated citizenry, and the sense of citizens no longer willing to be treated as second-class human beings. François-Jean de Chastellux, a literary lion who was also a senior military officer thrilled to the idea of the vast American continent being peopled "under the auspices of liberty and reason, by men who make equality the principle of their conduct and agriculture the principle of their economy." And Anne-Robert-Jacques Turgot, a *philosophe-économiste*, on becoming comptroller general of France wrote to Louis XVI in terms that echoed the Americans' resistance to unfairness: "It is necessary, Sire . . . to consider whence comes to you the money which you are able to distribute among your courtiers, and to compare the misery of those from whom it has to be extracted . . . with the situation of the class of persons who push their claims on your liberality."

The *philosophes'* growing excitement about America coincided with a rapid decline in their estimation of Great Britain, whose steps toward democracy they had once applauded but that no longer seemed to have the welfare of the people at heart. The American colonists' resistance to Great Britain seemed principled and heroic. So did the feats of their Continental army, composed, as the French believed the ancient Roman army to have been, of citizen-soldiers distinguished by enthusiasm and patriotism.

For more than a decade French reconnaissance reports had fueled the notion of the mutual interests of France and the potentially rebellious British colonies. In a memorandum written before the ink was dry on the 1763 Treaty of Paris, a semiofficial French visitor to America noted Virginians becoming weary of Great Britain's tobacco monopoly, which had shrunk their incomes, and Quakers in Philadelphia and Puritans in New England being increasingly restive about trade constraints. The next year a naval lieutenant visitor filed a similar report. A third report, in 1765, cited dinner-table chatter in Baltimore at which "there was something said about taking up arms, that if the Americans took it in hand, they were able to cope with Britain in America." The report continued:

This country [the British colonies of North America] can not be
long subject to Great Britain nor indeed to any distant power, its
extent is so great, the daily increase of its inhabitants so considerable, and having everything necessary within themselves for (more
than) their own defence, that no nation whatsoever seemed better
calculated for independency, and the inhabitants are already entirely disposed thereto and talk of nothing more than it.

In the three-year interim between that visit and the one by the last
of the French semiofficial pre-Revolutionary observers in 1768, rapid
changes occurred in America. In the wake of the Seven Years' War, the
American colonies had flourished beyond the expectations of their British masters, becoming so widely profitable as to enable a considerable pay-
down of their share of the debt from that war. Such colonial productivity
had spurred the British to greed, as codified in the 1765 Stamp Act and
the 1767 Townshend Acts. These added to the Americans' debt repayment burden and introduced the obligation to cover the expenses of
quartering of British troops on American soil and the salaries of British
colonial governors and judges whose main task was to enforce the new
taxes. All this had considerably angered Americans by the time of the
arrival of the French army veteran Baron de Kalb.

De Kalb, the Baron de Kalb, forty-seven, was an ideal choice
for this reconnaissance. He had a keen eye for military strengths and
vulnerabilities, but also could readily pass as a German officer, having
grown up in Bavaria. He had served for decades with the French army
and had close ties to the soldier and diplomat Charles-François de Broglie. De Kalb was such a large and robust man that colleagues referred
to him as a giant. Choiseul, then the foreign minister, had given him
precise instructions for his American visit, such as to "acquaint himself
with the greater or lesser strength of the [colonists'] purpose to withdraw
from the British government," as well as their resources to do so and
willingness to accept French assistance.

De Kalb's reports to Choiseul in 1768 rejected myths about the

Americans then circulating in Paris, such as that the British had soothed their unrest by repeal of the Stamp Act. The truth was just the opposite, he reported; the repeal had demonstrated to the colonies that their "value to the mother country is their best safeguard against any violation of their real or imagined privileges." De Kalb's conclusion: "The present condition of the colonies is not such as to enable them to repel force by force, [and an alliance with a foreign power] would appear to them to be fraught with danger to their liberties."

That was not the message Choiseul had sought, having told Louis XV that an uprising by the British colonies was imminent, and he did not respond to this or other de Kalb letters. The baron continued to ply him with hundreds of clippings from American and British papers, but to no avail.

After Choiseul was dismissed in 1770, his replacement proved to be much less of an Anglophobe, as evident from a March 1774 note to George III from Louis XV, saying that Louis approved of the "more vigorous policies . . . to bring the [American] colonies back to obedience. . . . His Britannic Majesty . . . has for too long a time been needlessly wearing himself out by seeking to use means of sweetness and reconciliation." Louis XV's death two months later, and the ascension to the throne of his grandson, Louis-Auguste, transformed the French political, economic, and social landscape in many ways— among them, France's willingness to become involved in the increasingly contentious affairs of Britain's American colonies.

Born in 1754, the second son of the Dauphin, Louis-Auguste upon the death of his older brother in 1761 became second in line for the eventual throne; then, in 1765, upon the death of his father, he became the heir apparent. Two years later his mother died, which left the thirteen-year-old an orphan whose main influence was his grandfather, a sybarite, reprobate, spendthrift, an arbitrary and secretive ruler, and the loser of a costly and humiliating war. The teenager was bright enough and hale, but fleshy, unappealing, and shy especially around women, and not in the least martial-spirited as were his younger brothers. A studious boy, he developed a liking for maps, including astronomical ones, and also learned English well enough to get through David Hume's six-volume *History of England*. "Never let people read your mind," his French confessor taught, and Louis-Auguste agreed, becoming habitually so reserved that his silence in response to questions was taken for stupidity, although it was often a refusal to commit until he had a firm grasp on the proper answer. At fifteen Louis-Auguste was married to Marie Antoinette, the fourteen-year-old daughter of the most powerful woman in Europe, the Hapsburg empress Maria Theresa. The underage newlyweds were initially kept from cohabiting by chaperones and later by their own sexual ineptness and apparent disinclination, which prevented consummation of the marriage.

All of that had occurred when, in the spring of 1774, Louis XV, who at sixty-four had appeared relatively healthy, fell violently ill with smallpox and died within ten days. In his youth he had been called *"Louis le bien aimé"* (Louis the Beloved), but by the time of his death he was hated. Many years later, Count Louis-Philippe de Ségur would recall that the closing phase of the reign had been "obscured by inglorious idleness, "adding that the king's "indolence and weakness allowed all the springs of the state to unwind. Power was still arbitrary, and yet authority lost its influence. . . . We did not possess liberty but license."

The new king vowed in private to become *"Louis le sévère."* His strictness, a reflection of his morality, surfaced in his refusal to plunge into the frivolity, luxury, and decadence of the court, choosing instead to devote himself to public affairs. He wished to understand popular opinion and, insofar as possible, to go along with it. A month after he took the throne, Parisians worried whether he was up to the job and contributed a new graffito to the base of the statue of the long-dead king Henri IV, on Paris's Pont Neuf: "Resurrexit." But if Louis brought to the throne a reluctance to quick action, he also brought the sort of staunch moral ethic that he felt had been absent from foreign affairs for decades.

To select his ministers Louis had two lists of prospects, one from the queen and one left by his late father. Marie Antoinette's roster consisted mainly of experienced, practical men such as Choiseul who were partial to the cause of her Austrian family. The Dauphin's, although compiled nine years earlier, consisted of the meritorious but out of favor, as evidenced by its recommendation for first minister, Jéan-Fréderic Phélypeaux, Comte de Maurepas, seventy-three.

The acerbic Maurepas had served competently in various ministries until in 1749 Louis XV abruptly banished him to internal exile for a naughty epigram penned against the royal mistress. In 1774 the elderly Maurepas agreed to become, in effect, the first minister but took only the title of "special adviser." He oversaw the immediate dismissal of most of the sitting senior ministers, and won permission to revive the Parlement, a move that was hailed as liberal but was not since new rules further hamstrung the representatives. Banishing Louis XV's last mistress—Madame du Barry would have a large pension but to receive it she would have to reside in a convent—Maurepas and his wife moved into the apartment at Versailles that du Barry had occupied, connected to the king's quarters by a secret stairway. From there, as a biographer of Louis XVI writes, Maurepas was consistently able to sway the new king "by a long-drawn-out process of subtle blackmail, playing on his master's inexperience and dread of unpopularity."

The Dauphin's list prevented Maurepas from unilaterally choosing the remaining ministers, which allowed the elevation of several men whom Maurepas did not like but were of proven competence. The first was the Comte du Muy, a close friend of the Dauphin who took the minister of war portfolio that he had refused under Louis XV. A second was Turgot, who for thirteen years had been the public administrator at Limoges. The third was described on the Dauphin's list as "sagacious and capable," with "a sense of order." He was a relatively obscure diplomat, the ambassador to Sweden, Charles Gravier, Comte de Vergennes, fifty-five. Maurepas was not eager to have Vergennes in the critical post of minister of foreign affairs, but Louis's aunts were, even though Vergennes was of the lesser nobility.

Such distinctions had guided France's destinies for too many generations. Cabinet ministers had routinely come from the upper nobility, the hereditary *noblesse d'épée* (nobility of the sword)—the families of princes, marquises, dukes, and some counts relatively close in blood to the royal line. The lesser nobility, the *noblesse de robe* (nobility of the gown), were those who had accumulated enough money and property to hold civil offices.

For young men of the lesser nobility, obtaining places in the armed forces and the diplomatic corps required substantial payments to the royal treasury. It was through such a payment that Vergennes, born into such a family—his father was the president of the Parlement of Dijon—entered the diplomatic service at age twenty as apprentice to his uncle, the ambassador to Lisbon. By 1749, after a decade of service, Vergennes was rewarded with a solo assignment, cutting his diplomatic teeth as chief of legation in a small German electorate, where his main task was to counter British influence. He performed well. Hoping next to become ambassador to Bavaria, Vergennes was instead sent to a more distant and much more chaotic post—the Porte, seat of what remained of the Ottoman Empire—where he served for more than a decade, also fending off British sallies, these to control the Black Sea. If at the Porte Vergennes amply demonstrated his diplomatic abilities, he also harmed his further rise in the service there by falling in love with a widowed commoner, Anne Testa. He pledged to support the two children they had conceived out of wedlock, but knew that if he asked the king's permission to marry her, it would have been denied because she was a commoner. In 1767 Vergennes married her anyway, which gave Choiseul an excuse to recall an emissary who regularly disagreed with his policies even while carrying them out. After Choiseul was replaced in 1770, Vergennes was rehired and dispatched to one of the most difficult assignments ever, in Poland, to stop the carving up of what had been a French protectorate by the

European powers that divided its territory among them. He was unable to prevent the inevitable. He was next sent to Sweden to keep its king in power despite a coup d'état backed by Russia and Great Britain. Vergennes's work in Poland and Sweden convinced the new king's aunts of his estimable merit. Still, he never expected the summons to lead the ministry.

Deferential, knowledgeable, hardworking, a man who had proved his devotion to the country, yet was untainted by court intrigues, Vergennes quickly became close to Louis XVI. Contributing to that closeness was that both were extremely devout and agreed on a few basic policy principles. Aiming to restore France's power after its humiliation by Great Britain in the Peace of Paris, in which it was forced to cede many of its colonies and to accept British control of Dunkerque and of the fisheries off Newfoundland, Louis and Vergennes decided on three linked initiatives. First, that France would seek no additional colonies; this was congruent with Louis's view of himself as pacific rather than martial. Second, that France would work to diminish Great Britain's influence in order to build up its own. Third, that France would rearm, as there could be no better guarantor of increased influence than adequately prepared and equipped armed forces.

Louis when younger had been deeply moved by the works of the seventeenth-century writer François Fénelon, in particular his *Maximes morales et politiques tirées de Télémaque* (Moral and political maxims drawn from Telemachus). He had written an introduction for a new edition; Louis XV had read it and ordered the plates destroyed and banned publication of all of Fénelon. One of Louis XVI's first acts, upon becoming king, was to lift that ban and republish the volume, with his own pacific commentary intact:

> The true science of a sovereign . . . consists in earning the confidence of his neighbors and becoming their arbiter. Good faith and moderation are the only paths by which he may reach that end. . . . Not to have the air of peace by fear and baseness, but never to

dream of war except to defend liberty. . . . War is the greatest of evils with which God afflicts men . . . even those who undertake it justly . . . and end it with advantage.

His foreign minister agreed with these sentiments. In Vergennes's first *tour d'horizon* for the young king, in the early summer of 1774, his principal concerns were tinderbox situations on the European continent and France's complicated relations with Spain, its Bourbon family ally. As for the growing possibility of a conflict in Britain's North American colonies, Vergennes mentioned the matter only in passing. In late June 1775, receiving the news of the events at Lexington and Concord, he wrote to one of his ambassadors, "The spirit of revolt . . . is always a dangerous example. . . . That is why we must prevent the spirit of independence from making an explosion so terrible in the British American colonies that its strength is communicated to our own points of interest in that hemisphere."

Six weeks later, on August 7, he authorized Bonvouloir's mission, which sent a message that the colonists could not fail to understand as encouraging them to reject Great Britain and accept the overtures of a possible suitor. On the same day King Louis XVI, using words likely written by Vergennes, wrote to his uncle, King Carlos III of Spain: "Perhaps there has never been an occasion when the likelihood of a war with England seemed less probable." There was no contradiction in those two messages, for Vergennes believed that the many prior wars between France and Great Britain made inevitable a next one, and that France should take the current interlude of peace to prepare for it, in part by opening a courtship to interest the Americans in joining forces against the common enemy.

2

"Arrogance and insults against which my heart revolted." — Comte de Vergennes

France's ability to potentially ally with Britain's rebelling American colonies, as well as to boost its military readiness and flexibility to engage with the rest of the world, was deeply affected by its burgeoning debt. That troubled Louis XVI.

Contrary to public opinion, the young king was more involved than his predecessor had been in the granular details of governance, and had diligent work habits. Eight hours a day he took notes from books and advice from tutors on how to govern—organizing the notes under such topic headings as "the persona of the prince" and "the character and execution of the monarchy"—read state papers, and took part in council sessions. Of principal concern to the council of ministers was the ruinous debt run up during the Seven Years' War. More than a decade after the war's conclusion, interest on the debt continued to hurt France, as did the absence of income from colonies taken away during the war. To discount some obligations in 1770 Louis XV had declared a bankruptcy, but in 1774, when Louis XVI began his reign, debt service still accounted for 30 percent of the annual budget. That was why, after only five weeks on the throne, Louis fired the holdover finance minister, who had suspended payouts on government bonds and had regularly obtained high-interest loans to cover current expenses, and elevated Turgot, whose zeal, competence, and ingenuity had already impressed everyone.

Turgot made his acceptance of the post of finance minister conditional on the king's allowing him to enact the program laid out in his letter of August 24, 1774. What he proposed to do was summed up in a slogan of what he would not countenance: "No Bankruptcy. No Increase of Taxes. No Loans." His program was also to vigorously attack some costly long-standing arrangements. When appointed he eliminated the *pots-de-vin,* the bribes that tax collectors and major trading houses paid government functionaries to obtain monopolies to sell to the army at inflated prices such essentials as ammunition, and he slashed the number of sinecures at court and the subsidies for nobles in attendance.

In the spring of 1775, when at Lexington and Concord there was fired the "shot heard round the world," Turgot and the king were too busy to hear it. They were focused on an internal problem in France, the so-called Flour War in which prices rose overly high during barren harvests. Turgot persuaded Louis to use both tough and magnanimous tactics to resolve the crisis, and these not only ended the crisis but boosted the public's opinion of Louis XVI's abilities. But while the king seemingly backed Turgot's other efforts to stabilize France's finances and thereby make it easier to restore the nation's position of power, he proved unable to fend off the importuning of his family and his courtiers as much as would have been necessary to adequately reform the government's lax and luxe policies. He permitted Marie Antoinette to obtain money from the treasury to pay the Gobelin silks manufactory to create a new silk for her dresses that exactly matched the color of her hair, and for Maurepas to spend 176,000 *livres* on artworks for the palaces.

As Turgot's replacement as minister of the marine, a key post in re-arming the country, the king chose the long-serving police chief of Paris, Antoine-Raymond-Gualbert-Gabriel de Sartine, forty-six. Sartine's senses of organization, of the importance of ports, and of the need to maintain the flow of supplies and repair the dockyards quickly produced results.

And in October, upon the death in office of the elderly minister for war, Louis appointed Claude-Louis, Comte de Saint-Germain, sixty-eight, to that position. A former field marshal, Saint-Germain in his salad days had repeatedly clashed with de Broglie, "the most mortal enemy I have ever had." Resigning rather than serve under him, Saint-Germain then rose steadily in the Austrian, Bavarian, and Danish militaries, becoming defense minister of Denmark before retiring. Entering Louis XVI's cabinet, Saint-Germain attacked his bureaucratic brief with a youngster's energy and the savvy of a veteran of the efficient military of Frederick the Great. The Prussian king opined to Voltaire that hiring Saint-Germain was the smartest move Louis XVI could make.

Saint-Germain had a large target for reform, France's army, top-heavy with officers—some sixty thousand for 217,000 troops—and hampered by a blue-vs.-red divide. The distance in French society between the wealthy nobility and the vast majority of the population, which was low-born and poor, was reflected in the gulf between the blue-uniformed nobility of the sword and the middle-rank officers, who were not from that nobility and whose uniforms were edged with red. As Saint-Germain understood, the two-tier system calcified the upper ranks with excess officers, some of them quite incompetent, while preventing plebeian-born officers from rising to levels of command commensurate with their talents:

> The first class instantly obtains the highest grades [in the army] as if by right, while the second class, by the sole misfortune of its birth or poverty, is condemned to waste its life in the subaltern grades. The custom is doubly pernicious. The first class does not need to work to succeed; it obtains as if by right. And the second does not work because its efforts would be useless. Thus, all striving is destroyed.

Discovering that more than 2,500 men were guarding the king at court, he cut that figure to 1,500, abolishing the storied Musketeers and other elite units that had not seen battle in decades. He also retired 865 super-fluous colonels, halted the practice of purchasing commissions, and began to eliminate the right of officers to raise and pay their own units and then seek reimbursement. Far better in terms of the troops' loyalty to France, Saint-Germain argued, was to have the government pay them directly.

A host of new regulations that Saint-Germain issued in December 1775 cast many officers out of work and augured badly for the futures of others, particularly those in the aristocratic units, from which there came howls of outrage. "The choice of horses, the magnificence of the uniforms, and everything about the [military units at court] announced to all who could see that they were guarding the premier European potentate," one writer argued, charging that the diminution of such pomp debased Louis in the eyes of his fellow monarchs. The king dismissed such concerns and encouraged Sartine and Saint-Germain's efforts to reform the army and navy. In doing so these ministers became Vergennes's allies in reforming foreign policy, for all of their changes had a common objective, countering the pervasive power of Great Britain.

Vergennes had discovered that no matter where he tried to advance his goal of raising France's power in world affairs, "perfidious Albion" blocked the way. When he tried to keep Spain from invading Portugal and pulling France into their war, Britain attempted to goad Spain into that war with the aim of breaking the Bourbon family alliance. When he wanted to make repairs to the port at Dunkerque, Britain refused that as a violation of the 1763 peace treaty, and did the same when France tried to extend its fishing rights off Newfoundland. Such British "arrogance and insults against which my heart revolted made me desire and search for the means to change a situation so little compatible with the elevation of your [majesty's] soul and the grandeur of your power," Vergennes later wrote.

Also pushing Vergennes toward actions against Great Britain was public pressure, as reflected in a French street song:

Vergennes, gobe-mouches,
Ministre sans talents,
Laissez l'Anglais farouche
Battre les insurgents.
Valet bas et soumis,
De toute l'Angleterre.
A Georges III a promis,
Qu-on serait toujours de ses amis
Pendant une ministère.

(Vergennes, who believes all he hears,
Minister without talents,
Who allows the savage English
To batter the [American] insurgents.
Valet base and docile
To all of England,
To George III he's promised
That we will always be friends
During his ministry.)

In December 1775, as Washington's forces faced the British at Boston, as Franklin's committee in Philadelphia dealt with Bonvouloir, and as Saint-Germain's newly issued regulations roiled the French military, in London Arthur Lee learned that he had been appointed by the Committee of Secret Correspondence as its agent to seek aid from France. He had expected the appointment but was of two minds about it: On the one he refused to correspond with the committee while it included Franklin and Jay and did not include any of his friends and relatives, but on the other he was delighted with the appointment because during the previous year he had been privately agitating for a Franco-American alliance and could now do so officially.

Lee had been born in Virginia as the youngest of eight children.

Educated at Eton, he then took a medical degree at Edinburgh. He briefly practiced medicine in Williamsburg, Virginia, but soon returned to London to study law at the Middle Temple and set up shop as a business-man, with a sideline as an essayist under a pen name. At thirty-five he was an habitual outsider with a weakness for intrigue and conspiracy theories that edged into paranoia. His patriotic zeal mirrored that of his congressional-delegate brothers, Richard Henry and Francis Lightfoot Lee, who were among the more radical members of that body. Purists often disdain those who doubt even when the doubters are the more re-alistic: The Lees and their congressional allies, Samuel and John Adams, all early advocates of independence, distrusted Franklin and Jay for what they misperceived as a lingering affinity for Britain. In the spring the Massachusetts-Virginia alliance had put Arthur in line to succeed Frank-lin as agent for the Massachusetts Bay colony, thus making him, in the fall, the logical choice as the Committee of Secret Correspondence's man in London, a decision that Franklin ratified despite being aware of Lee's deep antipathy to him.

Lee knew just where to find help for America: from the Opposition circle around London's mayor, John Wilkes, who had often spoken out against the current British government's American colonial policies. At a Wilkes dinner Lee met Pierre-Augustin Caron de Beaumarchais. Author of the current hit comedy *The Barber of Seville*, the forty-three-year-old Beaumarchais was also an agent of the French court, which now and then called upon him to foil royal blackmailers and scurrilous pamphle-teers, something Beaumarchais knew a lot about since he had written similar pamphlets himself.

Known for his romantic dramas, he had had a romantic rise from mod-est beginnings, initially following his father's watchmaking trade, then eclipsing it by adding Beaumarchais to his name through an early mar-riage to an older woman who died within two years. He also benefited from business training by a mentor who made a fortune selling arma-ments to France during the Seven Years' War. Charming, daring, and endlessly articulate, Beaumarchais was well regarded at Versailles, having been music master to the king's aunts. He was on a quest to induce the French crown to restore his rights as a citizen, which he had lost as a result of a court case and imprisonment. His interlocutor at Versailles was Sartine, whom he had come to know when the minister had been chief of police.

Beaumarchais was in London on Sartine's behalf to conclude a deal with the blackmailer known as the Chevalier d'Éon. The chevalier threatened to expose two dark matters, the existence of the previous king's back-channel communications and espionage network, the *Secret du Roi,* and of a scandalous and as yet unpublished biography of Madame du Barry. In a letter to Beaumarchais, d'Éon said he had been, in turn, "girl, man, woman, soldier, politician, secretary, minister, author." Now he wanted to be properly pensioned off, to have his debts forgiven, and to be permitted to return to France as a woman. Their negotiations were taking a while, which kept Beaumarchais returning to London, where he met Lee.

Lee wanted Beaumarchais to help him buy French arms for the rebels. Beaumarchais took this request to the king but asked Louis for more than Lee had sought—a serious French embrace of the American cause. Beaumarchais argued to the king that France must succor the American "army of infuriates whose vengeance and rage animate every effort" and whose numbers were large enough to trouble the British. He put himself forth as just the man to take charge of supplying the rebels, and promised to turn a profit on that enterprise, assuring Louis that if France put up one million livres, by astute trading in a few years he would return nine million. Beaumarchais sent this letter to the king unsealed, so that Vergennes could first read it; the minister did, and forwarded it to Louis with the caveat that he was unable to verify Beaumarchais's high numerical estimate of American forces. But Vergennes simultaneously adopted that estimate in his dealings with the Spanish ambassador to Versailles, the Comte d'Aranda, volunteering that the American colonists' surprisingly great strength of numbers, and the inability of the British to break the American siege of Boston, had convinced him that Great Britain's war with its colonies would not end soon, and would exhaust that nation.

Those who most desire to have others fight have the least stake in which side wins or in ending the fight quickly. Vergennes, a royalist in favor of neither democratic aspirations nor rebellions against an auto-crat, was a believer in the balance of power. He did not seek the utter destruction of Great Britain's might; rather, he desired to have a di-minished Great Britain and an enhanced France someday jointly keep the peace in Europe. Toward that end he was quite willing to help the Americans prolong the Revolutionary War, since every month that passed while Great Britain was distracted gave space and time to France to rearm.

Beaumarchais helped. He wrote more unsealed letters to Louis XVI. Playing on the not-so-secret fear of the king and council that if the American colonies and Great Britain, rather than continuing to kill each other, patched up their differences they could then make a joint assault on the French Caribbean colonies, Beaumarchais pointed out that the "sugar islands" brought into the French treasury some three hundred million livres per annum—and that helping the Americans, a move that would protect those islands, would cost only three million a year.

Just then, Ambassador Guines also helped along the cause of aid to America by demonstrating anew the perfidy of the British—and his own. The vice that most frequently topples ambassadors is a tilting toward the positions of the country in which they are serving. The Portuguese am-bassador in London sent home a message that Guines had sought to guar-antee to the British that if they ceased backing Portugal in its dispute with Spain over Brazil, France would withdraw support from Spain. France intercepted this message, and Vergennes read it aloud to the king's council, producing the desired effect—outrage from Maurepas and Tur-got, who convinced Louis that by this false promise Guines had not only compromised the Bourbon family compact between France and Spain but had also usurped the king's authority, and therefore must be recalled.

Marie Antoinette tried to save Guines and have Vergennes fired. Vergennes threatened to resign. That, Louis would not permit. Guines was retired and awarded a dukedom. Thereafter Marie Antoinette's influence on foreign policy receded, but in retaliation she withdrew support at court for Mme. Vergennes, distressing the minister.

Vergennes' reputation for farsightedness grew in February 1776 as news ratified his judgment that France should stay out of the Spain-Portugal conflict. Portugal successfully invaded Spain's holdings in South America, spurring Spain to send a fleet and troops to the rescue, a move that effectively shelved Spain's scheme to take over Portugal's portion of the Iberian Peninsula with French assistance.

Into this charged atmosphere at Versailles came Bonvouloir's letter of December 28, 1775, which Guines had forwarded—but not before the now-former ambassador, who had expected the letter to be written in milk, had partially charred it in a misguided attempt to render the supposedly invisible message visible.

Two days after the arrival of the Bonvouloir letter, another Beaumarchais screed reached the king. "Sire," it began, "the famous quarrel between America and England, soon to divide the world and effect a change in the European system, imposes on each power the necessity of carefully examining how the event of their separation will . . . serve its ends or thwart them." Also supporting these letters' inflated estimates of American strength were Vergennes's sources in London and at The Hague. The French press was all for an embrace of the Americans: The *Gazette de France* helpfully dubbed them *"les Insurgents,"* a term, the paper explained, underscoring the notion that the colonists were neither rebels nor traitors but something much more heroic and admirable.

On March 12, 1776, Vergennes submitted a *mémoire* for the king, Maurepas, Turgot, Sartine, and Saint-Germain. It was a dramatic volte-face from his one-year-earlier judgment of the American Revolution as a dangerous example whose spread must be feared. Now Vergennes was in favor of limited intervention in the American uprising to disrupt Great Britain's trade with the colonies, on which it depended so heavily, a loss that he predicted would weaken Great Britain for years to come. While rejecting the idea of a "pact with the insurgents," Vergennes set out four reasons why France could not now avoid taking some action:

> While . . . the continuation of the war [in the American colonies] can be regarded as infinitely advantageous to the [Bourbon] Crowns . . . it can also be feared: 1st That the English Ministry . . . may extend its hands in reconciliation; 2nd that the King of England, by conquering English America, may make [of his armed forces] an instrument for also subjugating Europe . . . ; 3rd that the English Ministry, beaten on the continent of America, may seek compensation at the expense of France and Spain . . . 4th that the Colonies, having become independent . . . may become conquerors by necessity [of] the Sugar Islands and in Spanish America.

All four scenarios, Vergennes insisted, would lead to war between France and the English-speakers.

If Beaumarchais in his letters had written a three-act play leading Louis to the inescapable conclusion that France must intervene in America, Vergennes offered in his memorandum a dystopian novel of a future from which there was no escape but intervention. The present moment was the most opportune for France and Spain to attack Great Britain, he asserted; however, since the Bourbon kingdoms were not at full military strength, any attack must wait a year until that peak of preparation had been reached. But France could not simply do nothing until then, since the absence of a response from France to American overtures would arouse British suspicion. Therefore France and Spain must actively delude the British into thinking that the Bourbons wanted peace between Great Britain and its insurgents and use the next year to aid the Americans clandestinely and to rebuild French and Spanish forces.

The vehicle for aid to the Americans would be a new private company that France and Spain would covertly fund. The memorandum concealed from the ministers the name of the man who would form and lead that company: Beaumarchais.

Louis XVI postponed a decision until all the ministers could submit position papers on it and until Carlos III had an opportunity to weigh in, for such a dangerous and expensive course of action ought not to be precipitously begun.

3

"The want of experience to move upon a larger scale." — George Washington

In March 1776, Fort Ticonderoga's cannons suddenly appeared on the heights above Boston, having been hauled three hundred miles overland in secret. Seeing the cannon, the British fled the city with their troops and a thousand Tories, aboard seventy-eight ships.

Evicting the British from Boston was an important victory for Washington, the Continental army, and the rebelling British colonies. Yet the general understood that such a victory also reflected the army's dearth of artillery, mortars, and other war matériel; he wrote to his brother that it was astonishing for his army to have taken Boston with less than thirty rounds per soldier. Fortunately the British left behind one hundred artillery pieces, and arms and ammunition were continuing to trickle in for the Continental forces, as was enough gunpowder—1.5 million pounds amassed from various sources—to provide for the next several years.

Washington had an equally important and still unrequited need: for engineers. "I can hardly express the Disappointment I have experienced on this Subject," he had told Congress upon taking command the previous July. "The Skill of those [engineers] we have, being very imperfect & confined to the mere manual Exercise of Cannon. Whereas—the War in which we are engaged requires a Knowledge comprehending the Duties of the Field and Fortification."

During the long siege of Boston, no such engineers had been sent to him. And so after chasing out the British Washington renewed his plea for better-trained engineers to properly design and construct works to prevent Boston from being retaken from the sea. Months later, when the overage chief engineer, foisted on Washington by the Massachusetts delegation to Congress, had failed to complete works designed for Boston, Washington let his temper show:

> Who am I to blame for this shamefull neglect, but you Sir, who was to have them executed. it is not an agreable task to be under the necessity of putting any Gentleman in mind of his duty, but it is what I owe to the public, I expect and desire Sir that you will exert yourself in Completing the works, with all possible dispatch, & do not lay me under the disagreable necessity of writing to you again upon this Subject.

Washington had a third, more amorphous deficit to fill, and it required a carefully phrased plea to Congress from him lest his request be deemed a confession of unpreparedness for top command: He needed strategic counsel. For as he observed to Congress in regard to a top subordinate: "His wants are common to us all: the want of experience to move upon a larger scale; for the limited and contracted knowledge which any of us has in Military Matters stands in very little stead." Washington included in that "limited" group his two most experienced generals, Charles Lee and Horatio Gates, both Virginia planters and British army veterans whom he had recommended for their posts. Of the two, Lee had been tested on the most battlefields—far more than Washington—but neither Gates nor Lee had ever commanded more than a few thousand men nor had the fate of a country at stake in his battlefield decisions.

Waiting for strategic counsel to appear, Washington filled the gap by readings, regularly perusing books that he brought from his home library, notably tracts on the campaigns of Alexander the Great and Julius Caesar, along with Frederick the Great's *Military Instructions*. He also recommended these works to his military protégés, Henry Knox and Nathanael Greene; discussing these books strengthened the trio's bonds.

They assumed, as did Gates, Lee, and America's civilian leaders, that after regrouping the British would try to take New York. En route from Great Britain were eight additional regiments of regulars, others from Ireland and Scotland, and the first contingent of what would eventually total seventeen thousand German mercenaries, along with more British warships. London's willingness to incur the added expense of these forces signaled a firmer resolve. In 1775 the British general John Burgoyne had declared that America "must be subdued or relinquished," and nothing that had happened since, even the loss of Boston, gave the British any reason to alter that calculus.

Often a presumption that an affair is taking place, even when it is not, provides impetus to its onset. In early 1776, while Boston was still in British hands, King George's government presumed that Paris and Madrid were already aiding the Americans and were preparing for outright war. Signs of ramping up of the French military were apparent. One was Saint-Germain's published order of March 25, *Ordonnance du roi, portant règlement sur l'administration de tous les corps* (Ordinance of the king, for regulating the administration of all [of the army's] corps). It instituted a schedule of promotion for the middle ranks—fourteen years of service to earn a colonelcy, even if a candidate was of "the most distinguished birth"—a system to be administered by serving officers newly able to veto fast-track promotions of nobles. The ordinance also required officers to remain with their units at all times, a slap at nobles who absented themselves from their military posts to tend their estates.

One of the new Saint-Germain regulations almost caused the overturning of them all: Punishment for even minor offenses would henceforth be administered by blows with the flat of the sword, rather than, as in the past, with a whip. To the French military this was obnoxious on two counts; first, flat-of-the-sword was the standard only in the Prussian army and was therefore not French; and second, as an outraged song contended, *"L'instrument de leur gloire est celui du supplice"* (the instrument of their glory is that of [their] torture). Whispers against Saint-Germain from his opponents in the military and in the nobility of the sword grew louder.

While Saint-Germain's *Ordonnance* was innovative, his memo in support of Vergennes's March 12 memo on possible aid to America was merely dutiful, as were Maurepas's and Sartine's.

Then there was Turgot's. In a council of ministers, the worth of a member's recommendation depends more on his current political capital than on the brilliance of his ideas. Turgot's memo raised substantive objections to aiding the Americans; however, by the time he offered them his clout had been compromised. In January, at his behest, the king had proposed fundamental changes to the economic heart of the postfeudal way of life, in the form of Six Edicts. These sought to do away with the *corvée*, which obligated the peasantry to repair roads and take on other onerous tasks for fifteen days a year as slaves to the local lord, as well as the *jurandes* and *maîtrises*, arrangements through which hereditary guilds controlled who was permitted to do carpentry, stonemasonry, baking, and other crafts. The opposition to the Six Edicts crystallized in a manifesto by the king's brother Charles-Phillipe, known as Monsieur: *Les machines du gouvernement français* (the mechanisms of the French government). He wrote that the British, "persuaded that the surest way to degrade a people was to alter their societal structures and change their character," had conspired to install Turgot on the council, and that Turgot's proposed reforms were actually a British plot to undermine France's stability. The Parlement rejected the Six Edicts. Then Louis convened a *lit de justice* (literally, bed of justice, a formal review body) that overruled Parlement and enacted the reforms. He wrote to Turgot, "I am grieved that an edict so well founded in reason and in equity has raised up so much opposition. But there are so many private interests opposed to the general interest. The more I think of it, my dear Turgot, the more I repeat to myself that there are only you and myself who really love the people."

By April, when aid to the Americans reached the council of ministers' agenda, Turgot's grip on the position of finance minister had become tenuous. Nonetheless, his memo in reply to Vergennes's was remarkable in its challenges to basic foreign policy assumptions. Citing Vergennes's line that the outcome of the American rebellion was "not within human foresight to prevent or to divert the danger," Turgot charged that since "nothing can hinder the course of events which must certainly lead, sooner or later, to the absolute independence" of those colonies, there was no reason for France to become involved. The gravest danger to France was not from a potential loss of its sugar islands, he charged, but from the inadequacy of its finances. Turgot contended that the expense of administering and defending those Caribbean colonies was so high that the islands were as much a liability as an asset. He would not say that France should refuse to rearm—of course it must do so!—but he painted Vergennes's proposal as a budget buster that would accelerate France's slide into debt. War could bankrupt the state, Turgot asserted, and war on behalf of American independence was also an inherently bad idea, for when American independence inevitably occurred, "I firmly believe that every other mother country will be forced to abandon all empire over her colonies, permit an entire freedom of commerce with all nations, and content herself with sharing this freedom with others, and with preserving the ties of friendship and fraternity with her [former] colonies."

Vergennes did not so much answer Turgot's critique as dismiss it, in a memo, *Réflexions sur la situation actuelle des colonies Anglaises et sur la conduit qu'il convenient à la France de tenir à leur égard* (Reflections on the actual situation in the English Colonies and the conduct that it is appropriate for France to take in regard to them). There was no need to fear a future united American colonies, the memo argued, because upon their achieving independence "there is every reason to believe . . . they will give their new Government a republican form, and . . . republics rarely have the spirit of conquest." Rather, an independent America would be wholly aimed at what Americans best understood, "the pleasures and advantages of commerce." Vergennes argued that the opportunity to aid the Americans presented the king with a once-in-a-lifetime chance to diminish Great Britain's power. And he had an ingenious, low-cost, low-risk solution for that aid: renting French ships of war to business-men to convey war supplies to Saint-Domingue, where they would be exchanged for American tobacco, rice, and indigo; then non-French ships would transport the war matériel to America. No paper trail con-necting the insurgents to the French government would be found even if the ships were captured, as the entire matter would consist of transac-tions between commercial enterprises. In this endeavor, *Réflexions* sug-gested, the Spanish should join.

When Madrid hesitated, Vergennes exhorted Spain to keep France's aid plan secret, because—just nine months after Louis had told Carlos III that war with Britain was less likely than ever—"Our [joint] peace with England is nothing but precarious, it is a smoldering, banked fire that could explode at any moment." Spain agreed to contribute a million livres but was reluctant to do more.

Louis's decision to accept the *Réflexions* plan for France to back the rebels clandestinely was ratified by the news, in May 1776, of the Amer-icans' victory at Boston. Dancing in the streets of Paris and popular joy comforted the king: The Americans were winners and were beating back the British, and were therefore worthy of further assistance and wooing. Also helping this cause were the exits from his cabinet of the naysayers, Turgot and a second *philosophe,* orchestrated by Maurepas. Although Louis liked Turgot and had agreed with him, the king did not possess enough self-confidence to fight on behalf of his favorite against the com-bined weight of the privileged. Shortly the *corvée,* the *jurande,* and the *maîtrises* were restored, and the onerous tax system continued without check.

Louis's commitment to aid the Americans that spring took the form of two definitive steps—one high, moral, and public, and the other concealed and deniable. The first was a May 12 directive to all French ships to actively "defend the principle of liberty of the seas and the right of asylum," which was to be extended to any foreign vessel that sought French protection from Great Britain's navy, or from privateers or any other assailant. The second was to arrange to pay one million livres to Beaumarchais to underwrite the activities of the company he had established and given a false Spanish name, Roderigue Hortalez & Cie., and to send an equivalent amount to a trading house in Nantes that could readily put the money into a credit account there for American use.

That spring New York needed fortifying against a potential British invasion, and Washington gave that task to Charles Lee. While the fortifications erected there at Lee's direction were judged adequate by both leaders, Washington sensed that they were not of the caliber that might have been designed by graduates of France's vaunted engineering school. Similar problems arose with the fortifications built north of New York on the North River (as the Hudson was then known), and along Philadelphia's Delaware River frontage. The latter site drew the attention of the leaders of Pennsylvania's Committee of Safety, Franklin among them. He had in hand a recommendation of a man "well instructed in the Military Art of which our Foibbles hardly know the Name." That engineer, the Chevalier Gilles-Jean Barazer de Kermorvan, recommended by Franklin's Parisian translator and disciple, Dubourg, had crossed to America specifically to help with engineering projects. The committee commissioned Kermorvan to design and supervise the building of Philadelphia's defenses. His designs were reasonable, but his poor supervision of workers and his limited ability to get along with the committee left the defenses unfinished.

The task of completing them fell to a newer arrival, Tadeusz Kościuszko, thirty, a Polish officer who had spent five years in Paris taking private lessons in engineering, since as a foreigner he could not matriculate at the Royal Engineering School at Mèzieres. Kosciuszko impressed Franklin, who had him design the defenses at Billingsport, on the south side of the Delaware, and at the new Fort Mercer, and redo those at the fort on the north side of the Delaware River, which would become known as Fort Mifflin. The Pole also ordered sunk in the river bottom several dozen, iron-tipped *chevaux-de-frise* (literally, "Frisian horses") that would rip the bottoms from large ships, and so effectively prevent warships from completing the journey from the Atlantic into the port of Philadelphia. When General Horatio Gates took over supervision of Philadelphia's defenses, the Pole, more comfortable in French than English, was delighted to converse with Gates in French, and they became friends.

There were then in America about a dozen French officers, none of them graduates of the French Royal Engineering School and most of them similar to Bonvouloir and Kermorvan in having had peripatetic careers. Washington's continued suspicion of the ones who appeared at his headquarters seeking to serve with the army was edging into antagonism. In a letter to a French resident who had recommended several soldiers of fortune, Washington cited an unnamed French officer who, after being given a command by Congress, engaged in "Treachery and Ingratitude . . . in Deserting and in Taking Command of a Party of the Enemy in Canada." The French officers' near universal ignorance of the English language, Washington added, "makes them rather unwilling and Impatient under the command" of those who did not speak French. Still more French officers arrived, unbidden yet able to persuade Congress to give them commissions. "You cannot conceive what a weight these kind of people are upon the Service, and upon me in particular," Washington wrote to Congress's president, John Hancock. "Few of them have any knowledge of the Branches which they profess to understand,

and those that have, are intirely useless as Officers from their ignorance of the English Language."

That spring John Adams had been trying to get Congress to recognize three pending matters as so intertwined as to be incapable of separate consideration: independence, the administration of the thirteen colonies as a single unit, and negotiations with other countries:

> Foreign powers could not be expected to acknowledge Us, till we had acknowledged ourselves and taken our Station, among them as a sovereign Power, and Independent Nation. That now We were distressed for Want of Artillery, Arms, Ammunition, Cloathing and even for Flynts. That the people had no Marketts for their Produce, wanted Cloathing and many other things, which foreign Commerce alone could fully supply, and We could not expect Commerce till We were independent.

Adams was insistent that any treaties signed with foreign nations be restricted to commercial matters. America should pursue perfect neutrality, eschewing military or political alliances that would obligate the country's support for its partners in future European conflicts.

Congress agreed, and in the same time period in which Beaumarchais was establishing Hortalez & Cie to aid the American cause, the Committee of Secret Correspondence sent Silas Deane, thirty-eight, to France to obtain a commercial alliance. A Yale graduate, lawyer, and international trader, Deane had been a Connecticut delegate to Congress until turned out in an election in the fall of 1775. He had won the admiration of Franklin, Jay, and others as a thoughtful partisan; he had helped plan the capture of Fort Ticonderoga and had written the first draft of regulations for the Continental navy. He was also close to the colonies' leading trader, Robert Morris, who joined the Committee of Secret Correspondence in December. Deane and Morris had been the major suppliers of munitions through their contacts in Europe and the Caribbean. Knowing the committee's business, trusted by its members, and having previously traded with Europe, Deane was a logical choice for agent, although his knowledge of French was sketchy.

"It is probable that the court of France may not like it should be known publickly that any agent from the Colonies is in that country," the committee's instructions to Deane began, going on to assure him that Franklin's friend Dubourg would obtain an audience for him with Vergennes. Should Deane find Vergennes to be overly "reserved," he should repair to Paris, give the minister time to come to him, and then convey America's need for "clothing and arms for 25,000 men with a suitable quantity of ammunition and 100 field pieces," along with large amounts of linens, woolens, and other articles, ostensibly "for the Indian trade." Deane was also to have assistance in his endeavors from his former student and another Franklin friend, Dr. Edward Bancroft, as well as from Arthur Lee. Deane also carried a second commission, from a separate congressional committee headed by Morris, to be America's purchasing agent in Europe working for a commission on all goods handled. Such commission contracts were common in Congress. Morris had several of these, as did another Committee of Secret Correspondence member and some of Deane's former fellow Connecticut delegates, for matters that included the building and outfitting of ships and the purchase of provisions for the army.

While Deane was being dispatched to do the work of two congressional committees, two other committees were at work on related matters. One was assigning Thomas Jefferson to write a draft of a declaration of independence, and a second was assigning John Adams to write a draft of a "model treaty" that an independent America could use in dealing with other nations.

Great Britain was aware of these undertakings, and tried to avoid both a declaring of independence and a possible alliance between its rebellious colonies and France by floating a rumor that America's suitor was two-timing the rebels: that France was about to sign a "partition treaty" with Great Britain that would cede part of the American continent to France in exchange for France helping Great Britain to quell the rebellion. The rumor contended that the model for such a carving up had already been used in Europe—Poland, partitioned among several European nations. That reasoning convinced the *Pennsylvania Evening Post,* which fretted, like a protective aunt, "Do not the tyrants of Europe think they have a right to dispose of their subjects in the same manner that a farmer in this country disposes of his livestock?"

Deane left for France carrying a May 15 congressional resolution that was just short of an actual declaration of independence. It stated that because the colonies had had no response from Great Britain to their petitions for redress, and because no effective British government entity then functioned in the colonies, Congress "therefore resolved that it be recommended to the respective Assemblies & Conventions of the United Colonies, (where no Government sufficient to the exigencies of their Affairs has been hitherto established,) to adopt such Government as shall in the Opinion of the Representatives of the People best conduce to the happiness & safety of their Constituents in particular & of America in general."

After Deane sailed the two committees appointed an agent for the Caribbean who would report to Deane as well as to them. William Bingham, twenty-four, was Morris's junior business partner and secretary of the Committee of Secret Correspondence. To replace him as secretary Franklin and Morris chose Tom Paine, whose pamphlet, *Common Sense,* had become required reading by Congress and a bestseller among the American public. Bingham was to go to Martinique, ostensibly as a private trader with his own and Morris's money at risk. But he was also to act as an intelligence agent with a brief to learn whether a French fleet headed to the islands was for their defense or to aid the British against the American insurgents. He was also to act as an agent provocateur, for which purpose he carried blank letters of marque and reprisal, to be given to privateers. His instructions were quite detailed: Purchase 10,000

French muskets with bayonets, then dispatch 2,500 to America on the ship that had brought him to Martinique, and divide the rest into parcels of 1,000, distributed among "swift sailing well escorted vessels" to ensure that they stayed out of British hands.

The Deane and Bingham missions were congruent with the culminating lines of the Declaration of Independence, as adopted by the committee that had assigned Jefferson to write its first draft and that was ratified by the full Congress and published on July 4, 1776. The former colonies resolved that, as "Free and Independent States [we] have the full Power to levy War, conclude Peace, contract Alliances, establish Commerce, and to do all other Acts and Things which Independent States may of right do."

The proclamation of the Declaration of Independence was still unknown in Europe as Beaumarchais and Dubourg ramped up efforts to buy and forward war matériel to America. In London the playwright and Arthur Lee hatched plans; henceforth Lee would sign his letters to Beaumarchais as "Mary Johnston." In one "Mary" hastened to tell "Mr. Hortalez" to skip the niceties and get on with the task—to ship goods to America without first obtaining the promised tobacco, since that commodity was not easy to transport. In France, Dubourg furthered the cause by coming to terms with the French army's chief artillery officer, who was eager to sell cannons to the Americans, viewing the sale as a marvelous opportunity to get rid of outmoded stock and hasten the army's purchase of new cannons—of his design. To make an inventory, the artillery chief dispatched his subordinate, Colonel du Coudray. All that had to be done to conceal the old cannons' point of origin, Dubourg reported to Vergennes, was file off the fleurs-de-lis and the engraved Latin motto, Ultima ratio regis (the last argument of the king). Vergennes thought that concealing three hundred big pieces from British spies was unlikely, and that their transport to America would be construed by London as a casus belli. But he did not stand in the way. On July 5, 1776, Dubourg wrote excitedly to Franklin in Philadelphia that he was happy to report that France was arming more grandly and rapidly than he had previously thought possible, and that he was *"bien content quand ma chère patrie aura cause commune avec la votre"* (very pleased that my dear country will make common cause with yours).

The next day, when Silas Deane finally arrived in Paris, many weeks before the Declaration of Independence became known there, the French had already decided on and funded aid to the American cause, had readied several avenues to providing it, and were rearming so that they could eventually fight a war against Great Britain. Helping the American rebels, now the citizens of the newly declared independent country, the United States of America, was a strategic decision on the part of the government of Louis XVI, and did not reflect any agreement with the American tenets of liberty, equality, and justice for all.

A week later, when William Bingham arrived in Martinique, France's American-friendly martial preparations were even more in evidence than when Deane had arrived in Paris. On July 11, during a battle near that port, the ship in which Bingham had sailed, the *Reprisal*, traded salvos with a British sloop, *Shark,* until the action was ended by the French fort firing shots across the bow of the *Shark*. This forced the British to veer off, permitting the *Reprisal* to reach the inner harbor and moor. This and other evidence of Bingham's welcome in Martinique reflected the extent to which the Versailles directive to accommodate the Americans was being carried out. The French governor of Martinique soon teamed with Bingham and the local French naval forces' commander to encourage American privateers to seize in the nearby waters British ships and cargoes worth hundreds of thousands of pounds. With their permission, these prizes were either brought into port for sale or had French warships escort them through the dangerous parts of the Caribbean to a point where they could most easily make a run for America. During Bingham's first six months in Martinique, 250 British vessels were intercepted and brought to ports for sale.

The commander of the British fleet in the Leeward Islands protested these seizures and sales to his French counterpart there, but received no satisfaction. He glumly wrote home, "Their Lordships will perceive that all kinds of Protection, and Countenance, is given to the American Rebels, at the French Islands."

PART TWO

Approaches and Retreats
1776–1777

4

"Dukes, marqueses, comtes and chevaliers without number" — Silas Deane

Silas Deane's small-town-America honesty, industry, and forthrightness availed him little at Versailles, a court beset by shifting allegiances and favor trading, or with Vergennes, who did not want the British to know that he was dealing with the Americans. Still, Deane kept conjuring for Vergennes, in his beautiful hand, fantastical dual adventures—a Franco-American toppling of a British island in the Caribbean, and of one off Newfoundland, and a hindering of British trade by forcing up ship insurance rates in London. These were beyond naïve. The basic idea that Deane was selling in these letters—that a commercial pact with America would be good for both countries—demonstrated his lack of understanding, for what he so highly esteemed, an increase in trade, was of no importance to a cabinet whose disdain for Great Britain was based on a belief that its government was too in thrall to its merchants.

Aiding Deane's efforts was a better written, much more persuasive argument for the importance of America, the Declaration of Independence, which became known in France in the late summer. While to Americans the Declaration was an unequivocal statement of their right to sovereignty and to control their destiny, to Europeans it was the quintessential expression of a passionate people willing to fight for their inalienable rights, a quest worthy of admiration in a monarchist France undertaking a modest loosening of the strictures binding its people's lives.

As a dedicated royalist Vergennes was no fan of the Declaration. But as an astute foreign minister he recognized it as certifying that no rapprochement of Great Britain and its colonies would take place in the near future, and as evidence of London's ineptitude in having allowed matters to reach such an impasse as to compel America's issuance of the Declaration and to propel the new nation in France's direction.

On August 31, 1776, a year after asserting that preventive war was almost always a mistake and six months since contending that France was not ready for war, Vergennes made a new presentation to king and council, arguing that the propitious moment had now arrived for a preventive war against "the incontestable, hereditary enemy of France, jealous of her grandeur, natural advantages, and situation," on which revenge must be taken for past "injustices, outrages, and perfidies." Maurepas and the other ministers did not bother raising objections to this war cry, because the decision was moot: Spain had no intention of joining in a war against Great Britain, and Louis was unwilling to fight without his Bourbon ally. "If we are forced to make war on England," Louis would shortly write to Vergennes, "it must be for the defense of our possessions and the abasement of her power, not with any idea of territorial aggrandizement on our part, aiming solely to ruin their commerce and sap their strength by supporting the revolt and secession of her colonies."

Vergennes did what he could, short of war, to further that objective. He encouraged French merchants' efforts to ship gunpowder through Caribbean ports. He provided havens for privateers. He directed Deane to work with Dubourg and Beaumarchais to obtain supplies. He fed positive American battlefield reports to the gazettes that his ministry supervised and subsidized; *Les Affairs de l'Angleterre et de l'Amérique* printed translated excerpts of Paine's *Common Sense*, state constitutions, bills of rights, and other legislative acts. Finally Vergennes encouraged French officers to approach Deane to seek commissions in the Continental army.

And they did. Hundreds of them, in the summer and fall of 1776, importuned Deane to serve in the American military. Chief among their reasons for doing so was uncertainty regarding their futures in a French military roiled by Saint-Germain's reforms, which had already retired their elders and was still engaged in cutting back their numbers. In America, they hoped, a French colonel could prove himself in battle, earn a field upgrade to general, and return home in triumph. In America, the officers believed, promotions would be based on merit rather than—as they continued to be in France despite Saint-Germain's efforts—on one's nobility.

Absent from their motivations, however, was any desire to be commanded by George Washington. For decades in France he had been regarded as the "assassin" of Jumonville. In 1754 in Pennsylvania, at the beginning of the French and Indian War, Washington's troops, which included the Native American Tanarcharison, known as Half King, had ambushed those of the commander of Fort Duquesne, Joseph Coulon de Villiers, Sieur de Jumonville, and killed the French diplomat. For the next twenty years Washington's reputation in France was mud. However, once he had forced the British to vacate Boston, French officers began to revise their estimate of him, since any man who bested the British was a hero to Anglophobes.

In evaluating French supplicants for American army positions Deane operated at a double disadvantage: He was deficient in French and unable to discern truth from embellishment in military résumés. He pleaded for congressional guidance, beset every morning, he wrote, by "a levee of officers . . . as numerous, if not as splendid, as a prime minister," featuring "dukes, generals, and marqueses and even bishops, and comtes and chevaliers without number, all of whom are jealous, being out of employ here, or having friends they wish to advance in the cause of liberty."

Some of these men appeared to be spectacularly qualified, among them the authors of respected texts on artillery and cavalry, holders of the Croix de Saint-Louis, veterans whose military service dated back to the 1740s and 1750s, and men with recommendations from literary luminaries.

Perhaps the most relevantly credentialed applicant was Philippe-Jean-Charles Tronson du Coudray, thirty-eight, scion of an old family, second in command of France's artillery, the author of *L'ordre profond et l'ordre mince, considérés par rapport aux effets de l'artillerie*, an expert on the iron chemistry central to forging cannon—and, most critically, the man who had conducted the inventory of France's excess munitions. To Deane it made sense to send to America, along with the cannons, commanders and technicians who knew how to position, operate, and repair them. As he wrote to Congress:

> Considering the importance of having two hundred pieces of brass cannon with every necessary article for twenty-five thousand men provide[d] with an able and experienced general at the head warranted by the Minister of the Court, with a number of fine and spirited young officers in his train and all without advancing one shilling, is too tempting an offer for me to hesitate about.

Suitors make allowances for their beloved's minor faults; Deane sloughed off Coudray's offensive manner and numerous demands—to be accompanied by his brother-in-law and an entire suite of officers and their servants, all to be lodged in the officers' quarters on board, and for him to have the title of major general. Deane demurred only at granting the title, explaining that such designations must be awarded by Congress.

The artillerists were to sail aboard the *Amphitrite*, one of three ships that Deane and Hortalez & Cie had chartered. The *Amphitrite* would carry 52 cannons, 32,840 cannonballs, 6,132 rifles, 255,000 flints, and other supplies. Coudray scoured French ports, collecting men and matériel. Saint-Germain signed an order allowing the munitions to be stowed on board, which was done at night.

Among the other accepted officers eager to sail in the *Amphitrite* were three veterans. One was a scion of an old family, an artillery expert who had seen battle in Corsica, François Louis-Teissèdre de Fleury, twenty-seven. A second was the cavalry master Augustin Mottin de la Balme, forty-three, who had honed his skills in the Seven Years' War and was the author of *Élémens de tactique pour la cavalerie,* a man who had had the signal honor, for a commoner, of presenting the book personally to Louis XVI. The third was Hubert de Preudhomme de Borre, fifty, who had spent his entire life in the military. One junior officer, Pierre Charles L'Enfant, twenty-one, had no military training but was designated an engineer although he was only an architectural student and a protégé of Beaumarchais.

Just a few aspirants could converse easily in English—because it had been their native language. Colonel Thomas Conway, forty-one, had been born in Ireland but had lived in France since the age of six. He and his brother-in-law, Denis-Jean-Florimond Langlois du Bouchet, twenty-four, also an officer, visited Deane. While Deane offered Conway the major-generalship he had denied Coudray, he would not do the same for du Bouchet. The younger man's career in the French army had been inter-rupted twice; first he had to resign over a duel and flee the country, and then, upon his return he found his upward path halted by the exile of the family's patron, the Duc de Choiseul. He readily agreed to serve as a volunteer in America because he considered himself a "Rousseau repub-lican" who embraced the cause of liberty "with heated passion."

Since Deane did not think it proper to be seen at Le Havre, to inspect supplies on the *Amphitrite* and other ships he sent William Carmichael, a young American. Beaumarchais also went to the port, under a false name, but then blew his cover by directing rehearsals of *The Barber of Seville* there. Also undermining secrecy were the officers and sailors scheduled to go aboard, overheard in taverns boasting of their cargoes and intended destination. British agents reported to David Murray, Vis-count Stormont, the British ambassador in Paris, the number of French officers and the contents of the holds of the *Amphitrite* and other ships. Stormont, a forceful and wily diplomat, protested to Vergennes, who, fol-lowing the script set up to assure deniability, told him the ships were headed for Caribbean garrisons.

Of the dozens of French officers at Le Havre, the highest in nobility was Charles-Armand Tuffin, Marquis de la Rouërie, thirty-five, who after being accepted by Deane had prepared by obtaining letters of credit and introductions to Robert Morris, by bringing three servants and quite a bit of baggage, and by deciding that in America he ought to be called simply Armand. His father's death when Armand was young had put him in charge of a fortune. He attended the Royal Military Academy alongside others of the high nobility, and afterward, like many of them, served in a court guards unit. In 1766 he fell in love with an opera singer without realizing that she was his uncle's mistress. His mother's brother, more bemused than annoyed, brushed away the prospect of a duel, but the young hothead managed to find another to fight, with a cousin of Louis XVI, and for that was exiled. A supplicant to enter an abbey, he was asked whether he was in search of God; no, he responded, just trying to get away from men. He attempted suicide but was rescued. American service beckoned.

The Baron de Kalb, now fifty-five, also at Le Havre, was the only aspirant who had spent time in the colonies and was able to converse in English. He had written to one of the Americans he had met on his earlier trip "that if the war between England and her colonies . . . should continue, I could with pleasure devote the rest of my days in the service of your liberty." He and his commander at Metz, Marshal Victor François de Broglie, fifty-eight, brother of the diplomat, had recently hosted evenings in Paris in honor of Deane, to encourage French officers to apply for commissions.

De Kalb dutifully reported to Deane from Le Havre on the antics of Coudray and Beaumarchais. Deane's distress would have deepened had he realized what de Kalb's own game was: He had secretly pledged to de Broglie to lay the groundwork in America for him to replace Washington as head of the Continental army. De Kalb had explained to Deane that there was a need in America for a man of proven battlefield merit: "A military and political leader is wanted, a man fitted to carry the weight of authority in the colony, to unite its parties, to assign to each his place, to attract a large number of persons of all classes, and carry them along with him, not courtiers, but brave, efficient, and well-educated officers, who confide in their superior, and repose implicit faith in him." De Broglie and de Kalb believed that the announcement of such a man going to America would have a tremendous positive effect on Europeans, dispelling all their doubts about the Americans' ability to win the war. Deane did not disagree, but could not pledge what the marshal desired, substantial advance payment for such services. He did sign an employment contract for the baron and fifteen junior officers. They resigned their army positions and went to the docks to await transit to America. De Broglie remained at home to prepare for the summons to supreme command.

Two years earlier, Marshal de Broglie had been host and superior officer to an even younger marquis, a seventeen-year-old who, after deliberately insulting the king's brother at court, had been sent to serve at Metz under the marshal, to whom he was distantly related and emotionally indebted. He was Gilbert du Motier, Marquis de Lafayette, and his father had died in battle in de Broglie's arms. In 1774 de Broglie included Lafayette in a dinner at Metz for Prince William Henry, Duke of Gloucester and Edinburgh, a younger brother of King George III. No urging for a cause is better done than by a person who has obvious reasons to be against the cause but is not—thus the éclat of the exiled Gloucester when he revealed his sympathy with the American rebels and urged Lafayette and de Broglie to go to America to assist them. Upon Lafayette's return to Paris and becoming a lieutenant with the Noailles dragoons, he conveyed his excitement at the prospect to two of his best friends, his brother-in-law, Louis-Marie, Vicomte de Noailles, and Philippe-Henri, Marquis de Ségur. All three were close to King Louis XVI in bloodlines, age, and familiarity, having served in court-based regiments and been fellow military academy cadets with the king's brothers. Secretly the three pledged to one another to join Washington's army.

Their enthusiasm and ardor for the American cause had several bases. First, they were more-or-less unemployed: Saint-Germain's spring 1776 ordinance had ended Lafayette's active service. But more important, all three young noblemen had thrilled to the championing of individual liberties by Rousseau, Voltaire, and Montesquieu. Furthering that ideal fused in their minds with the pursuit of *gloire* (glory), a concept that had become central to the French understanding of the obligations of the *noblesse d'épée*. *Gloire* could best be achieved through a combination of proper birth, correct conduct, and battlefield heroics. It required winning the sort of undying combat fame that assured a place in the history books and merited the respect of discerning, noble-born colleagues. "An extreme ardor for *gloire* devoured my young heart," du Bouchet would recall. Lafayette, Noailles, and Ségur—as well as du Bouchet, Fleury, and de la Rouërie—believed that achieving *gloire* was what they owed the rest of humanity for their lives of luxury. As Ségur would explain, "It became impossible not to indulge the hope, however illusory, held out to us by men of genius [the *philosophes*], that a period was approaching in which reason, humanity, toleration and freedom would rise above the ruin of popular errors and prejudices, which had so long enslaved the world and deluged it with blood." But the nobles "only enrolled ourselves under the banners of philosophy in the hope of distinguishing ourselves in the field, and of reaping honors and preferments; in short, it was in the character of heroes of chivalry that we displayed our philosophy."

Deane was impressed as much by Lafayette's marvelous decorum and expansive and optimistic nature as by his wealth and position; although Lafayette was still a teenager, he seemed to have a preternatural ability to lead and was cognizant of the responsibility incurred in leadership. Deane happily granted him, too, a major generalship, and in a recommendation letter to Congress that Lafayette cosigned, referred to "his high Birth, his Alliances, the great Dignities which his Family holds at this Court, his considerable Estates in this Realm, his personal merit, his Reputation, his Disinterestedness, and above all his Zeal for the Liberty of our Provinces."

Lafayette, Noailles, and Ségur had no idea that Louis XVI might bar the door. The king had already permitted the resignations of dozens of other army officers so they could go to America. But the council could not permit the abandonment of France by men so close in blood to the king while the government was trying mightily to avoid involving France in a direct war with the enemy of the new country that the young nobles wished to serve. Yet the absence of royal permission was not ultimately what kept Ségur and Noailles from crossing the Atlantic just then—it was money. Their incomes remained in the control of their families, who were opposed to their going. Only Lafayette, steward of one of France's largest fortunes, could use part of that fortune to charter the *Victoire* to take him to seek *gloire*.

The supplies that Washington hoped for from France were most desperately needed. Since his victory in Boston in the spring of 1776, the Continental army's fortunes had gone rapidly downhill, with severe losses to the British on Long Island, and in New York, Westchester, and New Jersey during the summer and fall. Only Washington's ingenuity in avoiding wholesale captures of his men kept the American cause alive. When the rebels were occasionally able to employ three or four cannons, as at Pell's Point (in the present-day Bronx) on October 18, 1776, they could hold off the British; but more often that fall, the Continentals remained significantly undersupplied and were forced to abandon large caches of matériel, thereby making it impossible for Washington even to contemplate sizable counterattacks.

In mid-December, the fortunes of the Continental army had sunk so low that Washington wrote to his cousin and estate manager, Lund Washington:

> I think the game will be pretty well up, as from disaffection, and want of spirit and fortitude. . . . Matters to my view, but this I say in confidence to you, as a friend, wears so unfavourable an aspect (not that I apprehend half so much danger from Howes Army, as from the disaffection of the three States of New York, Jersey & Pensylvania) that I would look forward to unfavorable Events, & prepare Accordingly . . .

Then he read Paine's brutally honest letter to the cause, "The American Crisis," in the *Philadelphia Journal*, and decided that it could rekindle the flame of liberty in his soldiers. He ordered it read to them. "These are the times that try men's souls," it began. "The summer soldier and the sunshine patriot will, in this crisis, shrink from the service of his country; but he that stands it Now, deserves the love and thanks of man and woman. Tyranny, like hell, is not easily conquered; yet we have this consolation with us, that the harder the conflict, the more glorious the triumph."

To reverse sagging troop morale and Congress's view of him as too cautious, Washington knew that he needed to take dramatic action, and soon, before the end of the current enlistment period. This propelled him to his most daring military venture: In a raid on Christmas Eve, he and a small band of men crossed the ice-choked Delaware River and surprised and overwhelmed Hessian and British troops to take Trenton. The victory revivified the American cause and his own éclat.

As Washington had been preparing that Delaware crossing, Benjamin Franklin was crossing another Rubicon of sorts, the river Seine, near another capital, Paris. America's most senior and experienced diplomat, he was being sent to the court of Louis XVI for two linked purposes: to secure French aid for the American cause, and to prevent the British from convincing Louis XVI and his ministers that the American Revolution was near an end and that the colonies would soon be reunited with the mother country. For the aid being sought now by America was far beyond munitions and uniforms. As the Committee of Secret Correspondence was writing to Franklin, Deane, and Lee just then:

> If France desires to preclude the Possibility of North America's being ever reunited with Great Britain, now is the favourable Moment for establishing the Glory, Strength, and Commercial Greatness of the former Kingdom by the Ruin of her ancient Rival.

A decided Part now taken by the Court of Versailles, and a vigorous Engagement in the War in Union with North America, would with Ease sacrifice the Fleet and Army of Great Britain. . . . The inevitable Consequence would be the quick Reduction of the British Islands in the West Indies, already bared of Defence by the Removal of their Troops to this Continent. For Reasons herein assigned, Gentlemen, you will readily discern, how all important it is to the Security of American Independence, that France should enter the War as soon as may be, and how necessary it is . . . to procure from her the Line of Battle Ships, you were desired in your Instructions to obtain.

Franklin's prior visits to France had been love fests celebrating his scientific achievements, which culminated in his 1772 election as a fellow of the French Academy of Sciences. In 1776 he was still well-enough known in France that he was feted at each stop along the route to the capital. Seventy-one, and accompanied by two young grandsons, he had decided to hype interest in his mission by adding a bit of mystery. He let the public imagine that he might have come to France to retire or to escape debts. "I have not yet taken any publick Character," he wrote to Hancock, judging it not prudent to do so until he knew "whether the [French] court is ready and willing to receive ministers publicly from the Congress." Lord Stormont in a report to London dismissed all such mystery: "As [Franklin] is a subtle artful Man, and void of all Truth, He will . . . use every means to deceive . . . and will hold out every Lure to the Ministers, to draw them into an open support of [the American] cause."

Actually, Franklin had decided on a "publick character." When last in France he had worn a fine suit and a powdered wig, to fit in at court. This time he would appear in plain clothing and a fur cap, to emphasize that he was a symbol of American virtues and values.

Franklin's arrival in Paris was just in time. Deane was writing to John Jay that he was feeling very alone in France, "without Intelligence, without Orders, and without remittances, yet boldly plunging into Contracts,

Engagements, &. Negotiations, hourly hoping that someone would arrive from America."

Franklin's presence did more than elate Deane. It began a seminal change in how America related to France. No longer would there be any need for pretense, such as Deane's cover of appearing to acquire goods for the Indian trade—that had been an appropriate disguise for a purchasing agent of rebelling colonies, but now Franklin, Deane, and Lee were duly authorized commissioners of an independent sovereign state. Their determination to be very direct in their courtship of France shone through the first note that the trio sent to Vergennes, dated December 23, 1776, the day after Franklin reached Paris: "We beg leave to acquaint your Excellency that we are appointed and fully empowered by the Congress of the United States of America to propose and negotiate a Treaty of Amity and Commerce between France and the said States."

5

"The arrival of these great succours raised the spirit of the Rebels." — Lord Stormont

In early 1777, after the *Amphitrite* had been several days at sea, Coudray had a temper tantrum over food supplies inadequate to a transatlantic voyage and insisted on returning to France, among other reasons to meet Franklin, whose arrival had been rumored on their day of departure. The captain put in at Lorient.

Deane and Franklin were aghast. The ship's return to Brittany caused it to fall under the ban on ships departing for America, put in place only days after its first departure, and which had already resulted in the unloading of two other Deane-Beaumarchais ships. While the *Amphitrite*'s cargo remained on board, Deane pleaded with Vergennes to release the ship and the supplies vital to the American cause. Franklin and Coudray asked Captain Lambert Wickes, forty-one, to inspect it. In the nascent American naval service Wickes was already a star, having successfully delivered Bingham to Martinique in the *Reprisal*, taking prizes en route, and then having ferried Franklin to France, seizing additional prizes on that journey. Examining the *Amphitrite*, Wickes "found her So Much Lumbered and Short of Provision that I think they Did well to put in." He also recommended lightening its load by leaving behind

Coudray's "most useless officers" and redistributing the weight aboard by having army officers' servants bunk with the crew. Coudray agreed to remove the sixty-year-old Borre and others, but he also tried to excuse himself from travel in the *Amphitrite*, a notion that Deane labeled "absurd," since he was the expert who was traveling with the precious cargo of cannon.

Beyond pleading for the release of the *Amphitrite*, the commissioners proffered to Vergennes and to the Spanish ambassador, Aranda, the model treaty sent by Congress. A trade treaty and specifically not a military one, as written by John Adams it insisted on American neutrality toward all nations other than Great Britain, and freedom of the seas and of trade. Many of its paragraphs had been adopted from clauses in European treaties already ratified by long usage, to help position the United States of America as a sovereign nation able to make commercial arrangements with other sovereign nations.

A chief task of a diplomat is conveying news to his superiors immediately upon acquiring it and without embellishment. On January 4, 1777, Franklin reported to Congress the initial reactions to the model treaty: The Spanish ambassador was "well-dispos'd towards us," but as for France, although "the Cry of this Nation is for us . . . the Court it is thought views an approaching war [with England in consequence of an alliance with the United States] with Reluctance." Franklin told the South Carolina lawyer John Laurens, twenty-two, who visited him after leaving behind a wife and infant daughter in London, and while on the way home to join the army, that he did not yet know whether France would help the United States in a meaningful way.

The commissioners, going a bit beyond their instructions, promised Vergennes and Aranda that if France and Spain provided a higher level of military aid, the United States would guarantee the integrity of all French and Spanish West Indian possessions and any new ones conquered during a war. They coupled this promise with a threat: Should the Bourbons not quickly come to their aid, "We may possibly, unless some powerful Aid is given us . . . be so harass'd and put to such

immense Expence, as that finally our People will find themselves reduc'd
to the Necessity of Ending the War by an Accommodation."

Vergennes swatted away the overblown American promise and threat,
responding to the commissioners, over the signature of Louis XVI:
"France and Spain, in allowing the Americans to enjoy all the facilities
which they accord to friendly nations in their ports, indicate sufficiently
their manner of thinking regarding the united provinces. What more
could be required of them?" He accompanied this mild rebuke with a
modest reward—the final release of the *Amphitrite* and another munitions ship, the *Mercure,* to sail, although only with permission to go to
the Caribbean.

"Let Old England see how they like to have an active enemy at their own
door; they have sent fire and sword to ours," Congress's Marine Committee had written in its orders to Wickes, whose *Reprisal* also left a French
port on the day that the *Amphitrite* and *Mercure* sailed. Wickes was to
"proceed on a cruise against our enemies . . . directly on the coast of
England, up the channel." The capture of merchantmen and of a British
naval vessel were the desired outcomes; even more so was sowing alarm
among the British populace. The *Reprisal* quickly seized four merchantmen, and in hand-to-hand combat the crew overcame the crew of the
British packet *Swallow.* The British had expected American vessels to now
and then capture merchant ships, but Wickes's seizure of an official British vessel and his bringing it into a French port was a larger outrage. Stormont wrote to the Admiralty: "Nothing certainly can be more Contrary
to the friendship France professes for us, than suffering the Rebels to
make this use of Her Ports."

The ambassador's strong and detailed protest to Vergennes was based
on information stolen for him by a network of spies, among them the
American-born Edward Bancroft, thirty-two, who while working for
the commissioners copied their correspondence for Great Britain. Since
July 1776, Bancroft had been passing information to Stormont and to

William Eden, the British intelligence chief in London, enabling them to truthfully boast of knowing the thoughts of the American commissioners before Congress did. Bancroft never considered himself a traitor to America. He initially began turning over materials as a British patriot eager to have the colonies remain British. Blackmailed into continuing, he adopted the methods, manners, and zeal of a professional spy. He sometimes put stolen information in a sealed bottle in a dead drop, a tree in the Tuileries Garden.

Stormont's purloined information exerted pressure on the commissioners and on Vergennes in the three-handed chess game being played by France, Great Britain, and the United States. Among the pawns were Wickes, his prizes, and his sailors, who included many Frenchmen. But pawns have some freedom of movement, and when the French demanded, in response to British protests, that the *Reprisal* put to sea and leave French territory, Wickes pumped water into its hold so that it was too leaky to sail, thereby gaining extra time in a French port. The British, having blocked the advance of that pawn, next sent into play a more powerful piece—akin to a chess knight or bishop—dispatching warships to the Bay of Biscay to intercept any American vessels attempting to bring prizes into French ports. The French countered by directing into that bay a similar-strength piece, a squadron of their own, to patrol those waters with instructions to avoid hostilities but not to allow British behavior disrespectful of the French crown.

Franklin, an inveterate chess player who had written a treatise on the game, now recognized that France needed more time to refurbish and renew its military and to persuade Spain to cooperate. He did not push for an immediate alliance. But he did what Deane had not dared do— fueled the French public outcry for alliance with America. He also sought to demonstrate to Vergennes that if France did not make such an alliance an American shift toward Great Britain was still possible, by meeting openly with British emissaries and conspicuously dining with Turgot, Choiseul, and others out of favor with the French court. And while doing all this, he had the time of his life.

Previously Franklin's favorite period of close friendships and intellectual stimulation had been his time in Edinburgh, to which he traveled several times from London. It was in Scotland that he had received his first honorary doctorate, enabling him thereafter to be referred to as Doctor Franklin, and to converse as equals with philosopher David Hume, economist Adam Smith, geologist James Hutton, and others of the Scottish Enlightenment. In 1777 in Paris, Franklin found the equivalent of those friendships among the *philosophes*, and something more—attention paid to him by the cultured women who invited him to their salons. Ségur, Lafayette's perceptive young noble friend, could not help but notice what Franklin and his American colleagues were introducing into upper French society:

> Nothing could be more striking than the contrast between the . . . polished and superb dignity of our nobility, on the one hand, and on the other hand, the almost rustic apparel, the plain but firm demeanor, the free and direct language of the envoys, whose antique simplicity . . . seemed to have introduced within our walls, in the midst of the effeminate and servile refinement of the eighteenth century, some sages contemporary with Plato, or republicans of the age of Cato.

Franklin's cachet in social circles increased after he moved to Valentinois, the Passy estate of Jacques-Donatien Le Ray de Chaumont, fifty, a wealthy trader, investor, and advisor to Vergennes and Louis XVI. Chaumont's home was also near those of some of Franklin scientist friends as well as of his banker, Ferdinand Grand. Franklin's and Chaumont's broadening body types, thinning hair, and omnipresent spectacles made them seem brothers, and they became close friends. Chaumont had had a chance meeting with Stormont in Sartine's office, in which the always-aggressive ambassador accused the trader of aiding the Americans, and when Chaumont denied it, Stormont showed him intercepted communications documenting that aid. Chaumont then made a confession: As his father lay dying, the son had pledged an "immortal hatred" of the British for having seized and sunk four of the father's ships in 1755, and had sworn to take revenge.

Franklin and Deane turned away the great majority of the French officers who continued to besiege them, including one whom Franklin already knew: Achard de Bonvouloir. Since his Philadelphia rendezvous with Franklin, Bonvouloir had been to Canada, been captured and paroled, and now wanted to work for France and America. Bonvouloir later said that Franklin gave him letters of recommendation, but none were ever found. He took ship for Haiti and thence to St. Augustine, where there were many other French army veterans; but since the city was under British rule he was unable to reach the American colonies and eventually returned to Haiti.

The one group of French officers that Franklin did pursue, as had Deane, were the engineers desired by Congress and Washington. Saint-Germain chose and vetted for the insurgents a quartet of graduates of the Royal Engineering School in Mézières, a foursome led by Louis Le Bègue de Presle Duportail, thirty-three. The ninth child of ten, he was born near Orléans into the family of a lawyer-politician named du Portail. After some shenanigans at the engineering school, a stint in a brig, and much good work in classes, Louis graduated just after the close of the Seven Years' War, and thereafter made steady progress, although hampered by not being of the upper nobility. By 1776 he had changed his name to Duportail. Testament to his prowess was that the engineering school recommended him to Saint-Germain to write a new set of rules for the engineering corps. Duportail's new regulations were designed, as he put it, to give the engineers "the military consistence that they ought to have" while reducing the number of fortifications and the amount of officers needed to maintain them, and mandating that future promotions be awarded only on the basis of merit. But he was also an apostate to the Mézières doctrine that engineers must master and stick to the craft of

drawing plans for fortifications. For Duportail "construction of fortifications proper was a distinctly subsidiary function of the art of fortification, and military engineers should not waste their time paying too much
attention to it," as a historian of engineering in the period puts it. Duportail's heresy was advocating that all engineers should aim to provide strategic counsel to the top command.

Duportail suggested to Franklin that for secrecy they communicate
in Latin, since "it is certain that if my going to America is noised abroad,
neither I nor any officer of the Corps will be permitted to leave France."
Franklin, self-taught in Latin, was not comfortable in the language, so
they stuck to French. Duportail, with the express backing of Saint-
Germain, asked to be designated as head of America's engineering corps
and sought a guarantee that in America he would be advanced in rank
beyond the one he held in France, and to be free to return home when
winter shut down the year's campaign. Negotiations continued until Duportail announced that he had just been honored with appointment as a
lieutenant colonel in the Royal Corps of Engineers, a group that previously had consisted only of the upper nobility. His three subordinates,
all fellow Mézières graduates, had also been taken into the corps, although at lower ranks, in the expectation of their being of great service
to America.

Once at sea, the *Amphitrite*'s captain needed to wiggle out of what he
had pledged to the crown: Under pain of imprisonment for disobedience,
to sail only for Saint-Domingue. Coudray had the military passengers
aboard write the captain an exculpatory letter insisting that it was necessary to head for Boston. In March 1777 the captain informed the crew
of this change in plans, cushioning it by announcing that they would
receive extra pay for entering a war zone.

Lafayette was having more trouble than the *Amphitrite* had in arranging his rendezvous in America. He had predicted to Franklin and Deane
that his departure for America would cause a ruckus, but neither he nor

they were prepared for its magnitude. The opera-worthy tale of his transit to America involved midnight departures, permissions sought and denied, Lafayette's dizzily hectic weeks in London at the request of the new French ambassador there (a Noailles, his wife's uncle) that included being introduced to George III, narrow escapes, an initial sailing, an attack of conscience while at sea, a costly return, an order for the young man to be prevented from leaving the country—not quite a *lettre de cachet*, which enabled a government minister to imprison a man for a potential crime, but close enough—and an eventual escape, incognito and in defiance of Louis XVI's explicit orders, culminating in a grand sailing from a port in Spain with de Kalb and others, all in the eyes of a French populace that approved of Lafayette's passion and heedlessness. An irked Vergennes told a friend—who told Stormont, who put it in writing to London—that Lafayette's embarking was "unaccountable folly," and if the young man were to be caught at sea by the British and roughly treated that would be an appropriate response to his folly. "On the whole," Lafayette wrote to Carmichael, "this affair has produced the *éclat* I desired, and now that everyone's eyes are on us, I shall try to be worthy of that celebrity."

All three of the initial cluster of Beaumarchais-Deane ships—there would eventually be ten altogether—managed to cross the Atlantic. One was stopped by the British near the American coast and had its cargo confiscated. The *Mercure* made Portsmouth, New Hampshire, in mid-March, but its hold was not full. So when the heavily loaded *Amphitrite* reached Portsmouth at the end of April 1777, there were huzzahs. It brought over more cannon than the Continental army had ever previously had available for battle, as well as pickaxes, tents, and other war matériel so broadly needed that the cache was divided and sections of it dispatched to many of the far-flung Continental armies and depots. Major General William Heath, who spoke French, soon wrote Washington that Portsmouth was "swarming" with French officers, two of whom, de la Balme and Coudray, were "much superior to any that I have as yet seen." Heath also reported exasperation at having to advance money to them, as well as to Conway and Fleury, for journeys to Philadelphia; but on the whole he expressed exultation and relief, for he knew, as did Washington, that with these munitions America's forces would be well-enough stocked for the 1777 campaign season.

And that was only part of it. Beaumarchais would later boast that he had leveraged the French and Spanish 2 million livres into 5.6 million, and with it rented ships carrying 300,000 barrels of gunpowder, 30,000 muskets, 3,000 tents, 200 cannons, 100,000 musket balls, clothing for 30,000 troops—and used the remainder to pay the expenses of transporting and victualing thirty officers during their three months in transit.

"The arrival [in America] of these great succours," Stormont wrote home from Paris upon learning of the Portsmouth welcome of the *Amphitrite*, "greater I believe than ever were furnished by a nation pretending to be at Peace, has raised the spirits of the Rebels and of their numerous Well-Wishers here."

The Marquis Charles-Armand Tuffin de la Rouërie had embarked on the *Morris* with his baggage, servants, and a full load of munitions. The ship made a relatively swift crossing but within sight of the Delaware River was captured by the British. The marquis managed to escape, although not with his baggage. He was soon interacting with Congress, where he proved to be as diplomatic and ingratiating as his encomiums said that he was brave and resourceful. He offered to serve without pay, and to be called Colonel Armand. His initial meeting with Washington had the commander praising his good sense and modesty. Placed in a unit of non-English speakers, most of them German-born, after an initial skirmish he was given command. In Armand's first major encounter with the enemy his unit lost thirty of eighty men; nonetheless the senior Continental army officers were pleased with his leadership. There was a palpable need for his sort of experienced, battle-tested midlevel commander able to guide the actions of regulars and militia who had had little or no combat experience.

De la Balme, the cavalry expert, in Boston presented copies of his books to John Adams, who was as impressed as Heath had been. But Washington believed the American terrain unsuited to cavalry, and he already had a small detail of dragoons serving as his personal guard and as occasional scouts. Placing that unit under de la Balme's command would cause problems. Congress believed they found the ideal niche for de la Balme: inspector general of cavalry.

In an uprising in which democratization is an integral aspect of the proposed solution to political governance, any assertion of privilege will meet resistance. Coudray, Conway, and Borre (who had managed to cross aboard the *Mercure*) asserted such privilege upon arriving in Philadelphia, demanding that Congress honor their agreements, which would rank them as high in the American army as Nathanael Greene, Henry Knox, and John Sullivan, the field leaders during the past two years. Those generals warned Congress that if they were to be passed over and the French given high commands, they would resign and go home. Washington supported their protests. "Altho no one will dispute the right of Congress to make appointments," he wrote to his fellow Virginian Richard Henry Lee, "every person will assume the previledge of judging of the propriety of them; & good policy, in my opinion, forbids the disgusting a whole Corps to gratifie the pride of an Individual; for it is by the zeal & activity of our own People that the cause must be supported, and not by a few hungry adventurers. . . . I am haunted and teazed to death by the importunity of some [of the French] & dissatisfaction of others." Lee understood Washington's distress but told him, "The strongest obligations rest upon us (tho' the inconvenience is great) to make good engagements," even though Lee believed that earlier French arrivals had tricked the delegates by displaying "sagacity enough quickly to discern our wants, and professing competency," and so "were too quickly believed."

To help Washington deal with the situation, Congress passed an edict that allowed him to determine whether foreign officers commissioned by Congress were useful, and to dismiss those he deemed unworthy. Washington accordingly refused to award field commands to French officers that were commensurate with the elevated positions given to them by Congress, unless and until the officers had proved themselves in battle in America. Thus Borre and Conway, nominally brigadier generals, Washington assigned to the tasks of colonels. The wisdom of doing so was soon borne out. In camp the junior officers accused Conway of conduct unbecoming an officer and of abusing the troops. Conway's superior, Major General William Alexander, Lord Stirling, wanted him punished. Washington declined to censure Conway or to break him in rank, attributing Conway's transgressions to his unfamiliarity with American military rules and expectations. Washington excused Conway's bad behavior because he knew that he would need every experienced field leader he could muster in what he anticipated would be a large and perhaps even a decisive battle against the considerable forces of General Sir William Howe.

6

"France has done too much, unless she intends to do more." —Benjamin Franklin

The American commissioners had succeeded in the preliminaries, obtaining some war matériel from France, but not in the main event of garnering direct and substantial military support. In the spring of 1777, new instructions from Philadelphia enabled the commissioners to offer, in exchange for such military support, half of Newfoundland and a share of the fisheries. Thinking it a generous offer, the commissioners were startled to have it rebuffed.

Their dismay revealed that they had not believed Vergennes's repeated protestations that France was not looking for conquest. That spring Vergennes emphasized the message to Louis XVI, noting, "The glory of conquering kings is the scourge of humanity; that of beneficent kings, its benediction." The line was a restatement of a maxim in Fénélon's *Telemachus*, and specifically chosen to resonate with Louis, who had written an introduction to that book. Maurepas was not the only master manipulator of the king.

In Franklin's next note to Vergennes he took another tack, warning that since Great Britain was pouring resources into the 1777 campaign against America, should France not act now it might irrevocably loose the most favourable opportunity ever afforded to any Nation of Humbling a Powerfull, arrogant + Hereditary Enemy. . . . *The King + Ministry of Britain already know that France has encouraged and assisted the Colonys in their Present resistance; and they are already as much incensed against her, as they would be, were she openly to declare war. In truth, France has done too much*, unless she intends to do more.

When this rationale, too, failed to move Versailles more in the Americans' direction, the commissioners next looked for alternative European partners.

Arthur Lee traveled to Spain, on his own initiative and without first being invited by the court. His presumption was not rewarded; no Spaniard in a high position would see him, and his attempts to secure assistance for America reaped only a small loan and modest amounts of free munitions, blankets, and clothing, to be deposited at Havana and New Orleans. In Amsterdam, Deane, while enjoying a better reception than Lee had in Spain, found the Dutch resistant to furnishing direct loans. In Vienna and Berlin, to which Lee next traveled, he was rebuffed and had his important papers stolen by the British. When Lee asked Frederick the Great to expel the British emissary who confessed to the pilferage, the Prussian monarch demurred.

The next American proffer in hopes of an alliance, made by Franklin on April 7, was to the Spanish ambassador in Paris, Aranda: If Spain would join America in the Revolution, the United States would declare war on Portugal, "and continue said war for the total Conquest of that Kingdom," and also fight alongside France and Spain to recapture their former possessions in the Caribbean. This astonishing offer, too, was rejected—it was made at precisely the wrong moment, just after Portugal's king had died and his daughter was using her ascension to the throne as opportunity to end Portugal's war with Spain over South America.

Refusals by Madrid, Berlin, Vienna, Amsterdam, and Lisbon caused

Franklin to write home, in May 1777: "Feeling ourselves assisted [by France] in other Respects cordially and essentially, we are the more readily induced to let them take their own Time, and to avoid making ourselves troublesome."

But the commissioners were determined to trouble Great Britain, and had at hand the means to do so—blank commissions for privateers sent by Congress, a ship they had bought for privateering, renamed the *Surprise*, and an able captain, the Irish-born Gustavus Conyngham. On a previous commercial run, after being captured by the British, Conyngham, thirty-three, had retaken his ship and sailed it into Amsterdam. Soon after leaving port in the *Surprise* on May 1, 1777, he captured a British mail packet, demanding and receiving its "surrender to the Congress of America." Spotting the official seal on the mailbags, Conyngham returned to Dunkerque and dispatched them to Franklin in Paris. The British were apoplectic. At Vergennes's request, the American commissioners returned the mailbags and did not raise too much of a fuss when the French seized Conyngham's prizes and put him in jail. According to the *London Public Advertiser,* Conyngham had done considerable damage, and not just to property: "The Capture [of the mail packet] is a complete Refutation of what we have been told so often concerning the reduced state of the Americans. . . . [The First Lord of the Admiralty] may blush *for once* at having suffered such an Insult so near our very Doors, after such *repeated* but *Impudent Boasts.*"

While Conyngham was out of circulation, the commissioners dispatched Wickes with the *Revenge* and two other ships. Flying a false flag—the Union Jack—he soon captured and scuttled a British brig, and then in the Irish Sea took eighteen merchantmen, sinking seven of them. "It is extremely mortifying to proud Britain that all her boasted Naval Power cannot prevent her being insulted on her own Coasts," Franklin gloated. The *London Chronicle* reported that residents of the Jersey and Guernsey coasts were fearful about Americans cruising in plain sight, and the *St. James Chronicle* wrote that even British shipping lanes from Plymouth to London were no longer safe. Some British ships of the line, scheduled to be sent to the European Atlantic or American coasts, were reassigned to the Irish Sea.

Supposedly to assist Vergennes in assuaging British ambassador Stormont, the commissioners ordered Conyngham to return to America. But once away from shore he yielded to the importuning of officers and crew to again raid the British coasts. In July and August he took prizes, forced ship owners to pay ransom, and in other ways made a shambles of British protection of shipping until, his ship battered and chased, he took refuge in a Spanish port. Chaumont, Franklin's host at Passy, handled the disposal of these and many other prizes brought by American privateers into French, Dutch, and Spanish ports, while successfully obscuring insurgent hands in the transactions.

In the Caribbean, the Martinique-based William Bingham made similar efforts to harm Great Britain and added another twist, using what he described to Congress as the "Self Love" of the "trading people of France." American privateers took British merchantmen in Caribbean waters—easy pickings—and brought their prizes into French-controlled ports to be sold, a sequence of events that in Bingham's view provoked the French and British "to mutual Depredations on each other, by Sowing the Seeds of Jealousy and Discord betwixt them, & by affording them matter for present Resentment, & renewing in their Minds the objects of their antient Animosity."

As a result of American raiders taking hundreds of British merchantmen in 1776–77, four British West Indies trading companies went bankrupt. Also, insurance rates for vessels traveling to and from the Caribbean or India soared by 15 percent for escorted-convoy vessels and 30 percent for those not in convoys. Rates rose even for ships that never left British waters.

Bingham reported one inadvertent tricking of the British. Among his tasks was to oversee the transfer of supplies from Beaumarchais-Deane ships to smaller ones headed for the United States. After removing the *Seine*'s munitions for reshipment, he reembarked it as a French-owned vessel, ostensibly bound for the Newfoundland fisheries but with secret orders to dock in Boston. The British stopped it, found those secret orders, and condemned both ship and cargo. France protested that the ship was theirs, the British accused the French of duplicity, and an international incident resulted. Bingham reported:

> That part of [the *Seine's*] cargo which was taken out was consequently saved to the United States, & the capture of the remainder was so happily disposed to occasion a subject of reciprocal complaint & altercation between the [British and French] courts, that everyone believed I had fixed the matter accordingly, & gave me credit for my plan, as a deep scheme of Machiavellian policy.

The shipping losses so incensed the British that Stormont informed Vergennes that Great Britain would shortly issue an ultimatum to France to stop providing help to American privateers or risk open war. That spurred Vergennes, on July 23, to ask Louis XVI "either to abandon America to herself or to help her effectively and courageously" by an outright alliance. The rest of Europe would not likely take sides against France if it did so, Vergennes asserted. France's queen was an Austrian princess, so Austria would not retaliate; Prussia disliked Great Britain; and Sweden knew that its internal problems would only be worsened by a foreign war. The most likely disturbers of Eurasian stability, Russia and Turkey, had just signed a peace accord, calming fears of a Balkan war that could tie down French forces and prevent their use in a war against Great Britain.

Maurepas opposed what he deemed Vergennes's rush toward war. His prime ministerial ally was Jacques Necker, a banker who had finally been permitted to fully replace Turgot as finance minister. A Swiss and a Protestant, Necker had refused to become a French citizen or a Catholic, so in the council he could not vote, but his opinions bore weight with the new minister of war, the Prince de Montbarrey. Vergennes's chief backer in the council continued to be Sartine, and he had important extramural allies, the most potent being public opinion, for the king wanted very much to be in tune with public opinion. Louis was also influenced toward a closer embrace of America by the professional military's desire for a war in which to advance their careers, and by businessmen who saw America's vast commercial potential. But he yielded once more to caution, and again pinned his decision on Spain. Carlos III's new, hardnosed first minister, José Moñino, Conde de Floridablanca, fifty-nine, categorically refused Spanish participation in the war.

Louis did authorize a few French actions to prepare his country should war with Britain break out anyway, and to prevent undue French zeal from provoking such a war: He recalled the Newfoundland fishing fleet, halted naval patrols in the Bay of Biscay, and banned Conyngham, Wickes, and other raiders from French ports. Vergennes wrote to the council that for France to pass an edict compelling the surrender of American prizes "will have the effect of declaring [the American ship commanders] and their countrymen to be pirates and sea-robbers," but the council passed it anyway. He grumbled to Noailles in London that banishing the American privateers was "carrying consideration [for Great Britain's wishes] as far as it is possible to do, and if our proceedings do not give satisfaction, we must forever give up trying to satisfy a nation so hard to please." But Great Britain prevailed for the moment, as American naval activity from French bases ceased. Conyngham had already transferred to Spain. Wickes stopped taking prizes and set sail for America; in sight of the American coast his ship foundered, killing him and almost all of its 130 hands. The other American raiders operating off the French coast either returned home or remained in port.

Arthur Lee, the third commissioner, had concluded that the American pursuit of France was corrupt, that Beaumarchais was a charlatan and a thief, that Deane had unlawfully mixed private business with public and defrauded the United States, and that Franklin had become a French dupe. Lee's letter campaign to Congress to block payment to Beau-marchais, recall Deane, and compromise Franklin fed the growing divide in Philadelphia between the radicals who had early on pushed independence, mainly the Adamses and the Lees, and the moderates, once led by Franklin and now by Morris.

Deane had no idea that his integrity was being questioned back home. Communications from America were so sparse that he remained in ignorance that his wife had died until, six months after the fact, he learned of her death from a newspaper account. Deane further had no clue that his standing with Congress was also being undermined by the bad behavior of some French officers whom he had commissioned, among them Conway and Coudray. Conway's flagrant classism was both-ering more than his superiors; it caused his brother-in-law, du Bouchet, to decide, after Conway had objected to his proposed promotion, that he must distance himself. Obtaining a transfer to the Northern Depart-ment, du Bouchet told Conway, "You have compromised my reputation," and he also accused Conway of something far worse: depriving du Bouchet of an opportunity for *gloire*.

Coudray's designation by Deane as in charge of the army's artillery and engineers was a larger problem. Knox already oversaw the artillery. While Congress tried to fashion a different slot for Coudray, Washington sent the artillerist to Philadelphia's safety committee to design defen-sive works for the Schuylkill and Delaware Rivers. There Coudray's abrasive personality and his incessant seeking of extraordinary privilege immediately compromised his welcome. He also deprecated the earlier work done by Kościuszko and others, declaring in his first report: "As to the Situation [at Billingsport], it is well-chosen; it commands the River in the narrowest Part. . . . As to the Plan or Projection, it is very bad." He labeled Fort Mifflin "badly situated," its battery "improperly directed," and the installation categorically unable to "prevent the Pas-sage of the Enemy." When Philadelphia did not respond instantly he complained that to prevent his men from being rendered "useless,"

Congress must "accelerate the slowness of the Civil and Military administration . . . to procure the means of execution." He wanted one thousand workmen every day, including Sundays, to ready the defenses within a month.

When, in mid-July, Duportail and his colleagues arrived in Philadelphia, Congress quickly realized that they were the trained military-fortifications engineers who had been sought. The two French groups claiming the title of engineer clashed. Egotism, an excess of amour propre and a willingness to take umbrage at minor slights—the characteristics of all such clashes—were much in evidence. Duels were narrowly avoided. One of Lafayette's companions wrote home that when Duportail's group spoke to Congress, Coudray "was unmasked, and it was proven that he had deceived Congress about everything, even his status, because he [had been] head of an artillery brigade, and not a brigadier-general, and the son of a wine merchant from Rennes [and not noble-born]."

Washington asked Duportail and his group to construct works on the western side of the Schuylkill, where Coudray's group was not engaged, since, as Washington advised the area commander, "I would not wish Monsr. Portail to interfere in their quarter, and setting [him and Coudray] to work together would only create confusion and widen the Breach." Adding to Duportail's distress was that Congress commissioned him as colonel, a rank he protested as too low to assure obedience to his commands by the enlisted men who must dig, hew, haul, and carpenter. In August, when Congress elevated Coudray to a newly minted post, inspector general of ordnance and military manufactories, Duportail and his fellow Mézières graduates made plans to return to France the following January, at the end of their term of employment, but until then to do whatever Washington wanted.

By the time Lafayette presented himself to Congress in July 1777, he was just another in a long run of French officers, many of whom were causing trouble. After a harrowing trip overland from Charleston,

Lafayette handed his letters of introduction to Morris and was referred to Congressman James Lovell of Massachusetts. Lovell surprised Lafayette and his entourage by his articulate and colloquial command of their language, and by the vehemence of his pique at Deane. He also went on a tirade against Borre for his incompetence in the field, Conway for terrorizing his men with endless drills, and Coudray for his insufferable manner. Such deplorable activity by French officers, Lovell implied, demonstrated that there was no reason to honor Lafayette's commission. The marquis and his men were stunned.

Lovell was soon mollified in regard to Lafayette, although not to Deane, whose recall he began to advocate. Congress offered Lafayette a high rank on the condition that he serve as a volunteer with no expectation of a field command. Lafayette, insulted, wanted to sail for home, but de Kalb persuaded him that in light of the brouhaha attendant on his leaving France he would look ridiculous should he return without having served in America. The country's newest major general then accepted assignment as a Washington aide-de-camp.

De Kalb had an even more difficult time with Congress, which first refused to honor his commission and then asked him too to serve without pay. As he told his wife, "Though I ardently desired to serve America, I did not mean to do so in spending part of my own and my children's fortune—for what is deemed generosity in the Marquis de Lafayette would be downright madness in me, who does not possess one of the first-rate fortunes." Only after de Kalb threatened to expose Deane's doings to the American press and to sue Congress for bringing him to North America on false premises did he win permission to stay and to be paid for his service, a course of action urged on Congress by Lafayette.

Lafayette's non-English-speaking companions were sent home without much of a murmur from him, but he interceded for de Kalb because they had become good friends. The middle-aged, non-noble-born veteran and the young, noble would-be soldier had bonded during the marquis's period in hiding, prior to their departure from France, when he had lived at de Kalb's home south of Versailles. And as the pair had crossed the Atlantic, de Kalb helped the marquis learn English. De Kalb would shortly write to the secretary of the French War Department:

> The friendship with which [Lafayette] has honored me since I made his acquaintance, and that which I have vowed to him because of his personal qualities, oblige me to have that deference for him. No one is more deserving than he of the consideration he enjoys [in America]. He is a prodigy for his age; he is the model of valor, intelligence, judgment, good conduct, generosity, and zeal for the cause of liberty for this continent.

By August 24, 1777, when Washington astride a white horse marched his twelve thousand troops through Philadelphia on their way to fight the British approaching the city, Lafayette rode at his flank. He had charmed Washington as he had de Kalb, by his willingness to learn, intelligence, optimism, and courteous behavior. Washington asked two aides, John Laurens and Alexander Hamilton, both of whom spoke French—Hamilton from having been raised in the French-speaking Caribbean and Laurens because of his French Huguenot background and education in Geneva—to assist Lafayette in learning English. The three became inseparable, and known for their conjoint drinking and carousing.

Conway, however, was becoming more difficult. In August, Washington received another agitated letter from Major General Stirling, contending that Conway

> has endeavoured to throw Contempt on every order I have Issued. . . . On [the brigade major's] Informing him, that I had sent for a Guard . . . his Answer was, "Tell my Lord I do refuse him the Guard". . . . Nothing would at present have prevailed on me, to have [complained again], but the InJustice I should do myself in Risqueing my reputation in the hands of a man Capable of disobey-

ing my Orders, and that perhaps at a time when it may be attended with the most Serious Consequences to the public as well as myself.

Washington again made allowances for Conway, needing every experienced officer he could muster for what was expected to be a large and potentially decisive battle against the British for control of Philadelphia.

In the midst of the American army's crossing of the Schuylkill to go to that fight against the British, Coudray decided not to dismount while he was being ferried across. His mount reared, and horse and rider fell into the river and drowned. Although Congress posthumously promoted Coudray to major general and gave him proper obsequies, the artillerist was not widely mourned. Many of those he had brought with him made plans to return to France. Congress then appointed Duportail as inspector general of the engineers.

On September 11, 1777, Washington's twelve thousand men fought eighteen thousand British and Hessians at Brandywine Creek in the largest set battle of the war. For the first time the Americans had reasonable amounts of gunpowder, ammunition, and field artillery. However, over the course of a very long day the Continental forces were defeated, mainly due to poor decisions by Washington, attributable to some bad information coming to him but also to his being outmaneuvered by Sir William Howe. Even so, the British were impressed by the ferocity of the Americans in the fight and by their resistance to panic. Not long after the battle Howe entered Philadelphia from the land, bypassing the riverine defenses that were to have shielded the capital.

Brandywine Creek was a calamity for the Continentals but not a total disaster because the bulk of Washington's army was able to avoid capture. In significant measure their escapes were due to the officers managing orderly retreats. Among those specifically praised for such actions at Brandywine were Armand, Fleury, Conway, and Lafayette. And the day had been very difficult; Conway later said that he "never saw so close and severe a fire" as at Brandywine at the head of the Ninth Pennsylvania regiment; his incessant parade-ground training of his troops paid off in their discipline under fire. The only outright failure, among the French officers, was Borre's; his leadership of a Maryland division was so bad, and his post-battle explanations were so unsatisfactory, that upon being threatened with a court-martial he resigned.

Lafayette distinguished himself while stemming an unruly retreat. Turning his troops around, he rallied them and directed their fire at the British until the enemy came within twenty yards, and only then led them to safety. Blood from the marquis's left calf was seen brimming into his boot. He was still in the saddle twelve miles later when, in obvious pain, he used his horse to block troops from making a second poor retreat. Later Stirling's French-speaking aide, Captain James Monroe, helped the marquis off his horse, and then Washington—according to Lafayette's later recollection—instructed the surgeons, "Take care of him as if he were my son."

The commander and the marquis were adopting each other. Lafayette, fatherless since the age of two, courted Washington's paternal favor. Washington, also fatherless at an early age and without children of his own, was already acting as a substitute father to Hamilton and other aides. Washington's usual pattern was only to become close to an officer after that officer had demonstrated his capability and bravery in battle. The commander judged Lafayette's wounds and battlefield feats as evidence that the marquis was worthy of his trust. Their personal relationship, composed of equal parts paternal tutelage, filial devotion, mutual admiration, and friendship, helped their nations toward acceptance of a partnership alliance.

Among the other foreign fighters who fought well at Brandywine was a Pole, Kazimierz Pulaski. Washington had given him command of his personal cavalry guard, and some accounts have Pulaski saving Washington's life by heading off an attack on the general's position. In France, Pulaski and de la Balme had been rivals for the regard of the elderly philosopher Jean-Jacques Rousseau, and in America they vied for the position of cavalry expert. Congress had previously appointed de la Balme as a colonel and inspector general of cavalry, but after Brandywine they brevetted Pulaski as a brigadier general of cavalry. De la Balme's appeal to Congress at this indignity was fruitless—a friendly biographer characterized his protests as containing "soupçons [of] presumption, vanity, and egoism"—and so he decided to return home. But he did not do so, instead concocting a scheme to invade Canada with a mounted regiment that he would underwrite and lead.

Recuperating at Bethlehem, Lafayette realized that lack of information in France about the tides of battle in America, along with the carping of returned French officers, would cause Louis XVI, Vergennes, and the council of ministers to worry—not about the Americans winning but about them losing. The question would arise: If the Americans were on the verge of collapse, should France augment its aid to prop them up, or diminish that assistance to prevent Great Britain from redirecting its ire across the Channel? Lafayette felt that proper publicity in France would help the cause, and asked his wife to circulate his letters. In one he instructed her how to respond should people in France assert that the war in America was going badly. In another he provided ammunition to counter expected expressions of sour grapes from fellow officers who had been sent home from America prematurely.

Those sour grapes were also the target of a French artillerist who had been in America during 1777 and returned to write a highly sympathetic analysis of the Continental army's strengths, interlaced with a critique of certain French officers in America. While French officers who were "self-disciplined, intelligent, fair to their inferiors, and sympathetic to the principle of equality" assimilated well in America, others who lacked those qualities did not. In words that could be applied to the conduct of Conway, Coudray, and Borre, the artillerist derided those "who do not understand how an officer should act, who dress up in elaborate uniforms, who cause a lot of trouble—officers who are a plague to others and no good to their friends [and who] are particularly enraged by the fact that they find themselves completely ignored in a country where no consideration is given to birth, name, rank, wealth, or letters of recommendation." He recognized that some French officers looked askance at the American army because of what they viewed as its lax discipline, but:

> The fact that the [American] soldiers do not show a sense of discipline and respect for their officers when they are not on guard duty or in ranks can be explained by the national character and by the spirit of liberty, independence, and equality that these people possess. Yet whenever insubordination becomes too flagrant it is punished, though . . . the punishments inflicted take into account the fact that except for the difference in military rank the offender is the equal of the man he has offended.

De Kalb had reached similar conclusions. He liked America and its army, and regretted only that he had not obtained his commission in time to fight at Brandywine. He had, however, seen enough of Washington to advise de Broglie that the American commander was "the most amiable, kind-hearted, and upright of men [even though] as a General he is too slow, too indolent, and far too weak; besides, he has a tinge of vanity in his composition, and overestimates himself." And so, despite Washington's shortcomings as demonstrated at Brandywine, de Kalb in the same letter began to break the news to de Broglie that making him the leader of the American forces was "totally impractical [because] it would be regarded no less an act of crying injustice against Washington, than as an outrage on the honor of the country."

De Kalb was not yet on Washington's staff on October 3 when the commander decided to make a surprise attack on the British at Germantown, a suburb of Philadelphia, where Howe had stationed some forces. But the British had set up well there for defensive purposes, and so the attack did not surprise them. Conway's Ninth Pennsylvania was again assigned a leading position, but this time, according to Laurens, who observed Conway that day, he had no stomach for the fighting. Later Laurens and a second officer wanted to accuse Conway of cowardice and provide evidence at a court-martial, but Washington dissuaded them. During the battle other French officers acquitted themselves well, Fleury, for instance, having his horse shot out from under him and taking several balls through his hat. Artillery captain Thomas Antoine Maudit du Plessis and Laurens attacked in tandem, Laurens throwing himself into the battle with enough fervor that afterward he could inform his father that he'd been promoted and was no longer a "supernumerary."

Amid dense fog and the confusion produced by several American units wearing clothing that was mistaken for British and that drew friendly fire, during the Germantown battle 152 Continentals were killed, 521 wounded, and 438 captured. Washington contributed to the defeat by directing too many troops to assault one relatively small target. Nonetheless, Germantown demonstrated the Americans' grit and willingness to attack even when the odds were against them. Reporting the Battle of Germantown to Congress, Washington tried to have it judged not by the fact that twice as many American as British had died but by his contention that had there been no fog the Continental army would have won.

Congress was not convinced, and an effort to curb Washington's power gathered momentum. It was fueled in part by the French officers' demonstrations of battlefield expertise, and particularly by the self-reports of Conway, with whom the representatives could converse in English and who unfailingly touted his own prowess. Congress contemplated reestablishing the Board of War to oversee Washington's actions, and to commission an inspector general with the power to examine any army unit or installation and report to Congress, frankly and outside the military chain of command, regarding the troops, their discipline, their morale, and their battle readiness. The name of a certain Irish-born French militarist of vast experience was mentioned as the leading candidate for the position.

7

"If ever destruction was complete, it was here." —Joseph Plumb Martin

In the summer of 1777 the French army held a series of war games in which the forces of General Jean-Baptiste-Donatien de Vimeur, Comte de Rochambeau, fifty-two, opposed those of Marshal de Broglie. The games were intended in part to test the relative efficacy of Rochambeau's *"ordre mince"* (thin lines) versus de Broglie's *"ordre profond"* (deep lines), but the true differential turned out to be the protocols recently codified by Saint-Germain—even as the minister was being replaced in office. When Rochambeau's men prevailed in the first set of games, de Broglie protested that the maneuver his opponent had used was improper since it was not sanctioned in the Saint-Germain ordinance. Rochambeau demurred, pointing out the page and section in which the maneuver was detailed. During a second round, de Broglie's forces triumphed, and afterward he sent a gracious note to Saint-Germain, asserting that Rochambeau's inadequate attention to Saint-Germain's rules had allowed de Broglie to best the younger general.

. . .

Military appointments made for political reasons are more subject to change than those made on merit. Thus Saint-Germain was cashiered by Maurepas on grounds other than competence; and in America, Congress three times in a few months changed the general in charge of the Northern Department. In the spring Congress replaced General Philip Schuyler with Horatio Gates, mostly to separate Gates from Washington, of whom he had been openly critical.

Gates readied a headquarters in Albany while he fended off the political machinations of Schuyler to retake the command. He sent Kościuszko to Fort Ticonderoga to review its defenses. "We are very fond here of making Block houses, and they are all erected in the wrong places," Kościuszko reported. He found defenses being built too close to the fort. He later contended that he was distressed that no fortifications were being considered for the highest point near the fort, Sugar Loaf Hill, later called Mount Defiance, and that on this and other matters he clashed with Ticonderoga's resident American engineer, Jeduthan Baldwin. However, his contemporary correspondence, and that of Gates, does not mention the Mount Defiance idea, perhaps because they considered its sides too steep to permit dragging cannons and building supplies to its crest. Fort Ticonderoga's vulnerability had not been rectified by the time Congress fired Gates and reappointed Schuyler to head the Northern Department.

On the night of July 4, 1777, John Burgoyne's forces, sweeping down from Canada, occupied that strategic high point near Ticonderoga and started dragging cannons to the top. Burgoyne later commented that the Americans' "manner of taking up the ground at Ticonderoga convinces me that they have no men of military science." After the Americans realized that the enemy's forces and cannons were on the heights, General Arthur St. Clair and his council unanimously agreed that the fort had to be abandoned, an operation that would take place in the middle of the next night. St. Clair later stated that his reasons for leaving Ticonderoga owed more to the greater size of Burgoyne's forces than to his presence on the heights. Matthias-Alexis Roche de Fermoy, a French participant in the American war councils, almost ruined that escape when in a drunken stupor at two in the morning he accidentally set fire to his camp, illuminating the preparations. A floating bridge over the lake, begun by Baldwin and finished by Kościuszko, enabled the escape. Washington called the loss of Fort Ticonderoga "not within the Compass of my reasoning," but was relieved that the army avoided capture and hoped that "the Confidence derived from [Burgoyne's] Success will bring him into Measures, that will in their consequences be favorable to us."

Washington believed that the British plan to end the American Revolution was for Burgoyne's forces, marching south and conquering as they went, to join Howe's, which were marching north with the same objective, and to have their conjoint, end-to-end control of the North River fatally separate the radical New England colonies from the others. Burgoyne had indeed suggested such a plan, and since landing in Canada in May had been attempting to complete his part. But Howe had not agreed to the plan, and he was the senior commander. As summer ripened, he advised Burgoyne that his activities near Philadelphia precluded joining his army to Burgoyne's. "One can only speculate about Howe's motives," writes the historian Don Higginbotham, and suggests that Howe was known to dislike "interior campaigning," preferring operations in which his troops could be transported and supplied by sea, as they had been to the Philadelphia area.

Henry Clinton, in charge of the British forces in New York, also was hesitant to send his men north to aid Burgoyne, but Burgoyne pushed ahead anyway. However, after recapturing Ticonderoga his pursuit of the Continentals ran into trouble, due to the ingenuity of Kościuszko and Baldwin. With three hundred troops Kościuszko felled trees to block roads as soon as American troops had passed them, destroyed bridges, and dammed and diverted streams to frustrate Burgoyne's advance. Baldwin made similar efforts. The British were forced to build forty bridges and causeways, and to take twenty days to traverse twenty-two miles, a rate of progress that quickly ate up their supplies just as their supply lines from Canada were also being compromised. Burgoyne exacerbated his difficult travel by his insistence on bringing along fifty-two cannon, some too heavy for the roads and bridges.

Congress had reacted to the loss of Ticonderoga by once again removing Schuyler from command and giving the Northern Department to Gates. These abrupt changes of command reflected the desperation afflicting everyone on the Rebel side, from the civilian overlords to the frontline troops and militia. Washington, almost alone, refused to give in to hopelessness, engage in finger-pointing, or foster failure. Even though he knew that Gates wanted to oust him as supreme commander, Washington provided Gates with the best resources and the most battle-tested frontline commander and troops, Daniel Morgan and his five hundred sharpshooters, plus units from Massachusetts. He also persuaded Gates to make more use of a man he knew Gates did not like, Major General Benedict Arnold, whose resignation Washington had refused to accept once he learned of the loss of Fort Ticonderoga. He pressed Gates to accept Arnold on account of Arnold's extensive knowledge of the North River valley and fighting abilities. Should Gates's forces be unable to fend off Burgoyne's, Washington knew, more would be lost than an army. The Revolution itself would be in peril.

The American tactics first paid off at battles near Bennington, Vermont in late August. Burgoyne's forces suffered, losing 10 percent of their soldiers. He told London that while Bennington had "little effect upon the strength or spirits of the army," those spirits were deeply affected by the local populace's unwillingness to assist the British, by the rebel militias' mysterious ability to show up at just the right spots to harass his troops and to regularly catch and hang messengers to and from Howe.

The Gates forces dug in at Bemis Heights, a high bluff ten miles south of Saratoga, New York, behind a Kościuszko-built breastworks of three-quarters of a mile. A Baldwin-built nine-hundred-foot-long, sixteen-foot-wide floating bridge across the North River brought in the Rebels' Massachusetts brethren along with cattle and sheep, and cannons and other supplies originally from *Amphitrite* and *Mercure*. These influxes, and the quality of the defensive works, made the Americans better prepared for this British attack than they had been for any engagement during the entire course of the war. Gates did have to ration ammunition on the first day, until more arrived from Albany, but he did not have to fret about only having cannons with too-limited ranges, or too few of them, or a less than adequate number of troops.

On September 19 the weather was near the freezing mark, with hoarfrost on the fields. This helped the defenders, among whom was Florimond du Bouchet. For several weeks in camp, Gates had treated the young French officer cavalierly, refusing to allow him into a tent; du Bouchet in response made a covering of pine branches and lived "like Robinson Crusoe on his island." He also found in the camp an old acquaintance, Kermorvan, now a Morgan sharpshooter.

At Bemis Heights while under fire du Bouchet seized control of a battalion whose leader had been killed, and with it captured two British cannons. Morgan's sharpshooters, directed from Gates's headquarters by Arnold, did the most damage to the British, killing nearly every British officer on one field. Arnold then wanted to throw reserves into the battle to achieve a big victory, but Gates would not permit it. The fighting at Bemis Heights on September 19 thus ended with neither the attackers nor the defenders able to claim complete victory. In the aftermath of the battle, Gates granted du Bouchet admission to the officers' sleeping tent and gave him permanent command of the troops he had led on the field.

On September 21, with the forces only a mile or so apart, Burgoyne was about to renew his attack on Gates when he received a coded letter from Clinton: "You know my poverty [in soldiers]; but if with 2,000 men, which is all I can spare from this important post, I can do anything to facilitate your operations, I will make an attack upon Fort Montgomery, if you will let me know your wishes." That fort, well south of the Bemis Heights area, was a key rebel outpost. Burgoyne agreed that a Clinton attack there would siphon defenders from Bemis Heights, and decided to wait for it to take place before again assailing Gates. He waited and waited. From the American camp his men heard the unmistakable sound of a *feu de joie*, a rifle-firing ceremony. A few days later he learned the reason for it: other American troops under General Benjamin Lincoln had retaken Ticonderoga and now controlled Lake George, completely cutting Burgoyne's supply line. Lincoln had then marched some of his men to Gates's camp. In the fortnight since the first battle of Bemis Heights, Gates had been further reinforced with cannon, nearly all of which had come from France, as had over 90 percent of the ammunition and the rifles. Also, he now had more than twice as many troops as the British.

Burgoyne, with no relief known to be on the way from New York, and his men on short rations, needed to act soon. On October 6 he distributed twelve barrels of rum to his men, and the next morning they once more attacked Bemis Heights.

In the middle of the fighting Arnold, with permission from Gates, made his way out of headquarters into the field, where he fought with such fervor that to some colleagues he seemed quite mad. Gates remained mostly behind the lines and conducted the overall battle, although he occasionally conferred with Arnold in the field. Arnold's inspiration, leadership, and bravery helped the American forces triumph. The British and Hessian troops were routed so completely that the attackers abandoned their guns, were pursued to their own lines, overwhelmed in a redoubt, and continued to flee. Burgoyne was almost killed as bullets tore into his horse, hat, and waistcoat; and his most experienced and favorite subordinate was fatally wounded. Arnold was shot through his already wounded leg by a barrage that also killed his horse, toppling it over on him and pinning the leg underneath. Lincoln was shot through the ankle.

For a day Burgoyne marched the remainder of his men north, toward Saratoga. There, ten days later, still without reinforcements from New York, and with his army almost completely bereft of supplies and surrounded by American forces, Burgoyne surrendered six thousand men and forty-two cannons. It was the largest and most significant American victory of the war—and French armaments, munitions, and expertise had been essential in making it possible.

News of the victory at Saratoga reached Washington indirectly, for it seemed as though Gates had arrogantly chosen to report the victory to Congress before informing his superior officer. The real culprit was the messenger, Gates's aide Captain James Wilkinson, who was attempting to aggrandize his own role in the battle so he could get a promotion. Gates's victory fed into the growing congressional discontent regarding Washington's leadership, and it led to the reestablishing of the Board of War by men who had long been opposed to Washington, such as General Thomas Mifflin, and to a plan to promote Conway to major general. Washington, learning of the possibility of a Conway promotion, wrote Congress that if there was any truth to the rumor, "It will be as unfortunate a measure as ever was adopted," adding, "General Conways' merit then, as an officer, and his importance in this Army, exists more in his own imagination than in reallity; for it is a maxim with him to leave no service of his own untold nor to want any thing which is to be obtained by importunity." Such an elevation, Washington asserted, would end the cooperation of Knox, Greene, and Sullivan, who would refuse to serve under Conway, and it would render his own command untenable: "To Sum up the whole, I have been a Slave to the service: I have undergone more than most Men are aware of, to harmonize so many discordant parts, but it will be impossible for me to be of any further service, if such insuperable difficulties are thrown in my way."

Congress went ahead with the promotion, but then there was a hitch. On November 3 Stirling received word via Wilkinson (who had overheard a discussion in Gates's camp) that Conway in a letter to Gates after Saratoga had written, "Heaven has been determind to save your Country; or a weak General and bad Councellors would have ruind it." Stirling, who several times had had to report Conway for bad conduct, forwarded this morsel to Washington, who took Conway's remark as an unequivocal insult to his leadership. He wrote a short note to Conway repeating the attributed sentence but not its provenance. Conway responded:

> I Believe i can attest that the expression *Weak General* has not slipped from my penn, however if it has, this Weakness by my Very Letter can not be explain'd otherwise even by the most Malicious people than an excess of Modesty on your side and a confidence in Men who are Much inferior to you in point of judgment and Knowledge. i Defy the most Keen and inveterate Detractors to make it appear that i levell'd at your Bravery honesty, honour, patriotism or judgment of which I have the highest sense.

Conway also denied having written the offending sentence; however, he admitted that he had such negative sentiments and asserted that such grumbling was the norm among officers in armies; threatened to trash the conduct of the war in America to his friends in France in terms that might lessen future aid to the United States; and said he would permit Gates to send Washington a copy of the original letter.

"The perplexity of his style, and evident insincerity of his compliments, betray his real sentiments, and expose his guilt," John Laurens wrote to his father of the Conway letter, which Washington had shared with him. The French had a word for it, the young aide continued: "Persiflage, or humouring a man."

Conway offered to resign and return to France, citing the likelihood of an impending war between France and Great Britain, Washington's coldness to him, and the promotion of Baron de Kalb, who, Conway pointed out, had been of inferior rank to him in France. Washington informed Conway that if Congress allowed Conway to resign, he, Washington, would not stand in the way. Congress's response was to appoint Conway to the new post of inspector general of the army, with power to inspect, investigate, and report directly to Congress.

Washington made no move to confront Conway, for he had a more pressing matter to deal with—preventing British resupply of Philadelphia from the Atlantic. He had finally been able to welcome de Kalb to the army and to command of a new division of two brigades, and now sent him, along with other senior-level commanders, to reconnoiter the forts near Philadelphia to determine whether they were defensible. At stake was control of the Delaware and Schuylkill Rivers that flanked Philadelphia and provided that city's access to the Atlantic.

In many histories of the Revolutionary War the Battle of Saratoga looms so large that Washington's near-simultaneous actions to hold the Delaware and Schuylkill Rivers against General Howe receive short shrift, perhaps because they were not as clear-cut a victory as the capturing of an army. But in war, preventing a terrible loss is often as important as achieving a success. Washington knew the importance of holding Fort Mercer on the New Jersey side of the Delaware River and Fort Mifflin on the Pennsylvania side for as long as possible. Should the forts be lost, Washington reasoned, Howe could be readily reinforced by sea with added men and supplies, and emboldened to more actively pursue the tattered Continentals. Such a sequence of events, he summed up to Congress, would "have thrown the Army into such a situation, that we must inevitably have drawn on a general Engagement before our Reinforcements arrived, which, considering our disparity of Numbers, would probably have ended with the most disagreeable Consequences." He emphasized that "Nothing, in the Course of this Campaign, has taken up so much of the attention and consideration of myself and all the General Officers, as the possibility of giving a further releif to Fort Mifflin, than what we had already afforded."

To each fort, along with substantial reinforcements, Washington sent a French officer with artillery and entrenchment experience, Captain du Plessis to Mercer, and Major Fleury to Mifflin. Both men had already proved themselves in battle under Washington's appreciative eye, and were among the best-qualified men on the continent for these vital tasks at the two forts.

As experienced soldier-engineers, du Plessis and Fleury were aware, as was Washington, that the forts would eventually have to be given up to numerically superior forces, but that it was imperative to hold them until ice closed the rivers to navigation. Both men also understood that such hold-the-fort assignments, common during European wars, had long provided prime opportunities to achieve *gloire*.

Du Plessis prepared for an attack by intentionally abandoning part of the outer defenses in order to create a "re-entrant salient angle" through which the enemy would have to enter but at which he could aim four cannons with langrage shot—scrap metal, an anti-personnel measure. On October 22, when a large contingent of Hessians under a well-respected leader attacked Fort Mercer, they entered a killing zone in which more than five hundred of them were killed or wounded. Fort Mercer remained untaken. Washington would shortly recommend to Congress a promotion for du Plessis, asserting that beyond his valor and service to the country, "he possesses a degree of Modesty not always found in men who have performed brilliant actions."

Fleury found Fort Mifflin's defenses in deplorable shape, which ratified the prior assessment of the much-maligned Coudray. Fleury set out to improve them and did so before the British started daily bombardment. He also, each evening after the bombardment had ceased for the day, sent out crews to repair the damage. He wrote to Hamilton, Washington's aide, that he was no longer worried about the adequacy of the defensive preparations, contending that the garrison "wants no Retreat—its Refuge is in its Pallisades and its Courage. Let it be reinforced . . . and the Enemy will not be so soon Masters of the River—but we must have men." "Our batteries were nothing more than old spars and timber laid up in parallel lines and filled between with mud and dirt," recalled Joseph Plumb Martin, an American soldier-diarist at Fort Mifflin; however, Fleury, "a very austere man . . . kept us constantly employed day and night; there was no chance of escaping his vigilance." Washington sent an additional four hundred men to Fort Mifflin, and when Fleury complained to Hamilton, about the colonel in charge there, that his "obstinacy is equal to [his] insufficiency," Washington instructed that colonel to yield to Fleury's expertise, and when he did not, recalled him and sent in a new commander. Fleury, wounded several times, remained at his Mifflin post.

After a month of bombardment had not dislodged the Americans from Fort Mifflin, on November 9 the British began a much heavier assault with cannons, mortars, grenade throwers, and sharpshooters. By November 15 high tides and rain had raised the level of the Delaware River enough to allow the British to float in large ships with their big cannons. The British positioned three in one river channel and three in another, and together with the British shore batteries this made for more than two hundred cannons aimed at Fort Mifflin. One estimate from the fort was that they were being fired upon at a rate of a thousand cannonballs per hour. Even so, it took the British six more days to reduce Fort Mifflin and kill or wound 250 of the Americans within. "If ever destruction was complete, it was here," Martin wrote. On the sixth night the Americans evacuated the fort and the wounded in vessels propelled by muffled oars; Fleury was among the last to leave, setting fire to the fort as the final boatload departed.

Washington was resigned to the loss, but angered because Gates had not sent men from Saratoga fast enough. "Had the reinforcements . . . arrived but ten days sooner," he wrote to his brother, "it would, I think, have put it in my power to have saved Fort Mifflin . . . and consequently have rendered Phila. a very ineligible Situation for [the British] this Winter."

Fort Mercer also had to be abandoned as no longer defensible. Du Plessis remained there until the very last and blew up the powder magazine, even though he lacked the long fuse kept in reserve for such situations and thus was in great danger of perishing with the blast. He survived.

Once Mifflin and Mercer fell, British supply ships pulled up to Philadelphia, crews began clearing the chevaux-de-frise, and Howe received reinforcements. But it was already too deep into winter for the British to launch a new offensive against Washington's troops. According to a contemporary British veteran of many sieges, the resistance put up by the American forts on the Delaware "cost us two of the most precious months of the year," during which the British were unable to pursue the Americans. The delays to Howe's forces inflicted by du Plessis and Fleury at Forts Mercer and Mifflin were as important to the survival of the American cause as the delays to Burgoyne's forces caused by Kościuszko and Baldwin in the run-up to Saratoga. And both sets of delays were due to the ingenuity of French-trained engineers.

Another contribution by the French was made in the wake of the loss of the forts on the Delaware: sage advice. General Anthony Wayne, a Washington favorite, sought to attack Philadelphia and submitted a plan to do so. On November 24, 1777, Washington convened a council of war on this subject with his high-ranking officers, who included Duportail, just appointed a brigadier-general, Lafayette, and de Kalb. It was to address just this sort of critical question that Washington had yearned for experienced strategic counsel. Duportail's memo (translated by Laurens) directly addressed the question's most salient point:

> To attack the Enemy in their Lines appears to me a difficult and dangerous Project. It has especially this very considerable Inconvenience: the exposing [of] our Army in case it does not succeed, to a total Defeat. . . . Now does it become this Army which is the principal one, to run such Risques—*does it become it to stake the fate of America upon a single Action?* I think not.

To reject Wayne's plan Duportail dissected it in detail, showing how each proposed facet courted utter failure—a frontal attack over the ice, risking two thousand men in a chancy maneuver, and no provision for escape if the attack failed. Compared with the other memos that Washington received, including Lafayette's, Duportail's was a cut above—masterful, demonstrating an impressive breadth of strategic vision and an argument based on thorough, very tough analysis.

In going beyond the specifics of Wayne's attack plan Duportail offered the essence of strategic counsel, urging Washington henceforth to openly embrace what few commanders in history had been able to see through to completion: a Fabian strategy. Fabius Maximus, a Roman general and consul, forbade his troops to engage in pitched battles or directly confront Hannibal's in the Second Punic War, choosing to wear down his numerically superior army through small raids and cutting supply lines. Initially vilified, Fabius was later lauded. In Europe, French gazettes had already favorably compared Washington's strategies to Fabius's. Although Washington was reluctant to admit that Fabius was his model, after the signal defeats of Brandywine Creek and Germantown, he was ready for Duportail's encouragement to do so. And during the remainder of the war, Washington almost never made an important strategic decision without first seeking the French engineer's counsel. As he wrote to General Lincoln, "You cannot employ [Duportail] too much on every important occasion."

After the majority of the generals had agreed that attacking the British in Philadelphia was foolhardy, Washington sought more permanent winter quarters for his army, and when Valley Forge was chosen over other sites he had Duportail design its defenses. Even before completion the works convinced Lord Howe's scouts of the fruitlessness of a British assault on Valley Forge.

Would the American cause survive? Duportail asked rhetorically in a letter to Saint-Germain. His answer: "There is a hundred times more enthusiasm for this revolution in a single café in Paris than in all the united colonies," but the surrender of Burgoyne and the demonstrated incompetence of General Howe provided reason for optimism. Had Howe pressed his advantage after Brandywine, the Revolution would have been over, Duportail believed, but Howe "conducted his activities with a sluggishness, a timidity, that astonishes me every day." He feared that Howe would be replaced by a more competent general who might overwhelm the Americans if by spring they were not better trained and equipped.

Should France send twelve to fifteen thousand men to assist the Americans? That, he wrote, "would ruin everything. People here, though at war with the English, hate the French more than they do the English . . . and in spite of all that France has done and will do for them, they would prefer to become reconciled with their former brothers."

Lafayette, whose leg wound was mostly healed, asked Washington, in his improving English, to "Consider, if you please, that Europe and particularly France is looking upon me—that I want to do some thing by myself, and justify that love of glory which I let be known to the world in making those sacrifices which have appeared so surprising, some say so foolish." Washington sent Lafayette to Greene, who permitted him to take four hundred men and raid the picket lines at Gloucester, Pennsylvania.

Lafayette's raid was a French-led affair, with Armand, du Plessis, and other companions heading units. Ignoring the potential damage to America and France should he be captured, Lafayette led a surprise charge against the Hessian positions and, despite the arrival of British reinforcements, his group managed to kill twenty of the enemy and take fourteen prisoners. Greene lauded Lafayette's actions in the field; Washington attached that Greene encomium to his request to Congress to now award Lafayette the command of a division. They did; and on the same day that Lafayette learned he was to lead a Virginia division he received a letter informing him of the birth of his second child.

De Kalb, the most experienced French soldier, chafing because he had yet to see action, in December importuned Washington for permission to attack the enemy's rear guard, and was asked to content himself with observation. His small band "hung on the rear of the enemy for five miles," he reported to de Broglie, "and it appeared that nothing could have been easier than, with four field pieces, to have utterly defeated and indeed cut off and captured a part of the rear guard." Using this incident as example, he added, "I am convinced that [Washington] would accomplish substantial results if he would only set more upon his own responsibility; but it is a pity that he is so weak, and has the worst of

advisors in the men who enjoy his confidence." There were rumors floating about that Congress would replace Washington with Gates. That
possibility spurred de Kalb to write to Henry Laurens from Valley Forge.
Regarding the American commander whom he had once thought of
supplanting with de Broglie, de Kalb expressed a feeling shared by many
of the experienced French officers:

> I cannot but observe, in justice to General Washington, that he
> must be a very modest man . . . for forbearing public complaints
> on that account, that the enemy may not be apprised of our situ-
> ation and take advantage of it. He will rather suffer in the opinion
> of the world than hurt his country. . . . He did and does more every
> day than could be expected from any general in the world in the
> same circumstances. . . . I think him the only proper person . . .
> by his natural and acquired capacity, his bravery, good sense, up-
> rightness and honesty, to keep up the spirits of the army and the
> people, and I look upon him as the sole defender of his country's
> cause.

PART THREE

Making the Connection
1777–1778

8

"France and Spain should strike before England can secure the advantage." —Victor-François de Broglie

Conclusions that appear inevitable often require the most time and effort to make happen. Both Franklin and Vergennes believed that a Franco-American connection was the desirable, the logical, even the inescapable solution to problems besetting both countries. Yet on September 8, 1777, the American commissioners in Paris wrote home, as though complaining to an intimate diary, that "the Ministers of France still continue to act with their former duplicity," both assuring the commissioners "of their most friendly wishes and intentions and verif[ying] those intentions by Substantial Proofs and favors," and also continuing to placate the British, so "there must necessarily be much insincerity to one or another in this contradictory conduct."

Applying to Vergennes for more credit to purchase war matériel, they were flabbergasted to learn that he already knew their intimate secrets; Stormont had presented a summary of their requests the previous day. This revelation confirmed Lee's belief that there were spies in their midst, and Deane's belief that efforts toward a Franco-American alliance would be in vain. To Franklin, who had presumed that the commissioners were under British as well as French surveillance, the more upsetting aspect

of the stolen information was Vergennes's use of it to justify French unwillingness to meet further American monetary needs.

France's resolve seemed to shift with every rumor from the American
battlefield. The commissioners definitely felt a cold wind after the arrival
of news of Burgoyne's summer capture of Ticonderoga and of Howe's
defeat of Washington at Brandywine. If America was not going to continue to keep Great Britain's forces occupied, how could France justify
more aid? In October and November 1777 the London newspapers
suddenly went silent regarding the war in America, as did those in
Amsterdam, the city to which sailing ships often brought less filtered war
results. In this news vacuum, too much attention was paid at Versailles
to Ambassador Noailles's report that in a speech King George III had
for the first time used the term "peace" and omitted the word "submis-
sion," heretofore the only permissible outcome of the rebellion.

On the morning of December 4, 1777, Beaumarchais was visiting
Valentinois. The playwright needed urgently to plead with Franklin, who
had confiscated for the commissioners the cargo of the returning *Amphitrite*, which Beaumarchais considered to be his vessel. "I have lost the
fruits of my most noble and incredible work," he would write to Vergennes regarding this confiscation. Thus he was present when an American messenger rode into the courtyard and Franklin emerged from the
house to brace him, asking, even before the young man dismounted, "Sir,
is Philadelphia taken?"

"Yes, sir," the messenger replied.

Franklin turned away, hands clasped behind his back at the disheart-
ening answer, and started to return inside.

"But sir," the young man called after him, "I have greater news than
that. *General Burgoyne and his whole army are prisoners of war!*"

The commissioners rejoiced. Franklin wrote two celebratory notices,
a broadsheet heralding the victory, immediately distributed, free, in tens
of thousands of copies, and a letter to Vergennes announcing the "total
reduction of the forces under General Burgoyne, himself and his whole
army having surrendered themselves prisoners." Howe had taken Phila-

delphia, Franklin conceded, but "having no Communication with his Fleet, it was hoped he would soon be reduced to submit to the same terms as Burgoyne, whose capitulation we enclose."

One benefit of a crisis to its participants is that even as it heightens the need for decision it reduces the number of possible responses to the problem. Saratoga did not make France choose to forge an American alliance—it had long since embarked toward one—but Saratoga did persuade him who most needed persuasion, Louis XVI. In council Vergennes painted the American victory as good news but problematic because now the Americans might believe they were in good enough shape to no longer need French aid, or they might use it as a lever in obtaining a reconciliation with Great Britain on favorable terms. The king and Maurepas now agreed with Vergennes that there was as much if not more danger in refusing a closer connection with the Americans as in making one. Another element in Louis's assent was his awareness that France was now adequately prepared for the war with Great Britain that would ensue from an American alliance. In the Caribbean, France's augmented forces and ships could defeat a British run at its vulnerable colonies. At home Sartine's shipbuilding program had brought the navy to parity with the British, and the recalled Newfoundland fishing fleet could provide seasoned hands for those warships while the British would have to impress men to fill theirs. "An offensive on the part of France is absolutely necessary in 1778 since it would act as a preventive war," wrote the diplomat Victor-François de Broglie, who in 1765 had submitted to Louis XIV a plan for a Franco-Spanish invasion of the British Isles that he now updated and offered to the new king. "The English, an extirpating and avaricious race, seeking to establish an universal monarchy, would soon aggrandize at the expense of French and Spanish possessions in the Americas, in the Antilles, and in Asia. Before England can secure the advantage, France and Spain should strike."

Vergennes congratulated the American commissioners, informed them that the next installment of their subsidy, three million livres, was on its way, and requested that they resubmit the proposals for an alliance that had languished for a year. On December 12 he invited them to his home to convey that the king's council had resolved that America and France should fashion a treaty, not on the basis of temporary advantage but of mutual interest, so as "to make it last as long as human institutions would endure."

"Fifty thousand troops, have not, in three years, been able to obtain secure possession of fifty miles of ground in America," the *Public Ledger* wrote at the news of the capture of Burgoyne's army. An Opposition Member of Parliament commented that "The amazement of the whole [British] nation was equaled only by the consternation they felt" at the event. And the historian and MP Edward Gibbon, previously a staunch advocate of suppressing the rebellion, wrote that he would no longer consent "to the prosecution of a war from whence no reasonable man entertains any hope of success."

But George III refused to accept the loss of an army as the end of the war. He insisted that hostilities against the rebels continue. He did assent to a broad strategic review, however, which recommended decreasing the emphasis on land battles and increasing maritime pressure. He also agreed that if France became more involved, British focus should shift to the Caribbean. Finally he allowed the dispatch of a peace commission to offer his American subjects almost all that they had ever wanted except independence, conditional on their return to the Empire. Parliament was in recess but would take up the peace commission idea upon its return.

William Eden, the head of British intelligence, had already sent Paul Wentworth to Paris to tip those generous terms to the insurgents. A stockbroker who had once lived in America, Wentworth knew Franklin and Deane and had a convenient cover story for being in Paris—to visit a mistress. He sent Deane an anonymous mash note: "A gentleman who has a slender acquaintance with Mr. Deane wishes to improve it; but fearing objections to an Unexpected visit, asks the favor of a private interview," and suggested a clandestine rendezvous. Deane responded drily that the next day at his rooms on the Rue Royale he would welcome any and all callers. On December 13, they spoke about the battle tactics of Roman emperors, Maurepas's gout, and what treasures could be obtained in Parisian pawnshops, and made a date for a more serious tête-à-tête the next day at a café. Showing up for it, Wentworth found Deane seated with Franklin and Lee; at his approach the two pointedly walked away.

Undeterred, he offered "General Ideas for the Preliminaries of an Accommodation and Perpetual Union between Great Britain and the Colonies." These included a "cessation of hostilities" on land and sea; the British vacating Philadelphia but not New York; "the king's authority to be restored to the level of 1763" (before the Stamp Act); a general amnesty; and Congress to metamorphose into committees able to affect the deliberations of Parliament. Wentworth also verbally promised high honors to Deane and political offices for all the commissioners if they agreed to the proposal.

Franklin forwarded a copy of the document to Vergennes. The minister's annoyance was exacerbated by the report of a friend of Wentworth's, who at Vergennes's insistence queried him about his contact with Deane: Wentworth said that he'd simply popped over to Paris to ask Deane to forward funds to his relatives in America. The patent falsity of this story forced Vergennes's hand. On December 16 he sent his deputy Conrad Alexandre Gérard to assure the commissioners that Louis XVI would sign a treaty because "it was manifestly in the Interest of France that the Power of England should be diminished by our Separation from it," as the commissioners reported.

"The destruction of the army of Burgoyne, and the very confined state in which Howe finds himself have totally changed the face of things," the king would shortly explain to Carlos III. "America is triumphant and England abashed." A Bourbon-American connection must be consummated soon or it might never be, he warned the Spanish king, given that Lord North's government would shortly dispatch a peace-negotiating team to America authorized to do what Wentworth proposed.

While Louis's uncle in Spain contemplated whether or not to join the proposed alliance, to help Congress reject the British peace initiative Vergennes agreed to dispatch a frigate to America with word of an imminent Franco-American pact. The information was deemed so secret that Simeon Deane, Silas's brother, who was carrying the document, was instructed to sneak into the port and hide until embarked on the *Belle Poule,* whose destination was in sealed instructions to the captain, only to be opened at sea. Of course the British learned of it; Wentworth wrote Eden: "These dispatches contain the resolution to declare + support the Independency of the United Colonies." Due to bad weather, during the holidays the *Belle Poule* remained in port.

On Christmas Day—Deane's fortieth birthday—the American commissioners dined at their neighbor's. Charles Hector Théodat, Comte d'Estaing, forty-eight, had recently been promoted to admiral after having spent decades in the army and then as a governor in the Caribbean, a position combining naval and army responsibilities, before switching into the navy. His rapid rise in the navy, it was said, was due to his being a favorite of Louis XVI and Marie Antoinette. Much talk of the day was about the royal couple: in the wake of a summer visit by the king's brother-in-law, who expressed surprise and annoyance that Louis's and Marie Antoinette's marriage had yet to be consummated; the young couple had then agreed to intimacy coaching, and rumor had it that the king and queen had since entered upon conjugal relations, producing the excited hope that their union would soon result in a new Dauphin. At the dinner Franklin proposed a toast: "To a perpetual and everlasting understanding between the house of Bourbon and the American Congress." No objection arose from d'Estaing, whose animosity toward the British derived from an embittering year as a British prisoner of war.

On New Year's Eve a friend of Franklin's made an unexpected visit. James Hutton was a Scottish physician whose research into rock formations was earning him the title of father of the science of geology. Hutton had ostensibly come to ask Franklin's help in protecting his religious Moravian sect brothers in Pennsylvania—but almost surely to discuss reunification. Chaumont advised Vergennes, *"Je vois bien de l'Empressement à Ecouter les propositions et j'ai peur"* (I observe much Eagerness [on the part of Franklin] to Hear the propositions and I am afraid).

Vergennes was also upset because Franklin did not report his meetings with Hutton, and because he met with Wentworth on January 6—when Wentworth read to Franklin, twice, a proposal for a peace treaty, and then remained for dinner with him, Chaumont, and other guests. That very evening Vergennes convened an emergency king-and-council meeting in Maurepas's chambers, the first minister being abed with a bad attack of gout. Also affecting deliberations on the American problem was a new crisis brewing in central Europe. On December 30 the Bavarian ruler had died, leaving no direct heirs. His brother-in-law, the Holy Roman Emperor of Austria, Joseph II, coveted parts of Bavaria and quickly marched in to occupy them. This rapidly deteriorating situation might soon entangle France. That was certainly the expectation in London; North hoped for a war, "provided it would completely occupy the French." In Paris that same possibility caused Louis and the council to determine that even as they hastened an American alliance they would not publicize it, to prevent emboldening the contenders in the Bavarian succession from using France's involvement in the New World as an excuse to rearrange the borders of the Old.

On January 7 the *Belle Poule* sailed. Not far offshore it was stopped by two British warships demanding its identity and to perform an inspection, which would disastrously have revealed the announcement of a forthcoming Franco-American alliance. Its captain, although outgunned, responded, "I am the *Belle Poule*, frigate of the King of France; I sail from sea and I sail to sea. Vessels of the King, my master, never allow inspections." The British ships accepted this explanation and let it proceed. When the *Belle Poule* was well out to sea, its captain opened his sealed orders. Discovering that his destination was America, he realized that he did not have enough victuals for such a long voyage and returned to port.

The message of a forthcoming Franco-American connection remained undelivered.

On the evening following the late-night Maurepas bedside council session, in Deane's apartments Gérard opened the first formal treaty-making meeting with a surprise demand that each commissioner must pledge, aloud, to keep the proceedings absolutely secret. Met by silence, he explained that this demand had been made necessary by Franklin's reticence in informing Vergennes about Hutton. That poke in the side evoked a reluctant assent. "Given the distrust in which the Doctor's dispositions are held," Gérard reported to Vergennes, "I think I have won an interesting point." Deane and Lee also agreed to secrecy. Gérard then announced that he was authorized to convey that Louis XVI was fully committed to American independence and would do "what was necessary to achieve this goal."

Gérard revealed more than he should have about France's fears, however, when he pleaded that the commissioners consider "the necessity of immediately preventing the effect of all the snares and all the maneuvers which England is employing to seduce the Deputies." The way to do so was through a military alliance in addition to the commercial one. Franklin, Deane, and Lee had no congressional guidance for responding to the prospect of a military alliance. And it was by no means certain that Washington would accept French troops serving alongside Americans. Franklin asked whether Louis XVI was ready to declare war on Great Britain. He was informed that such a declaration was not in the plan, since France wanted either to force Great Britain to begin the war or to achieve American independence without it.

Gérard then demanded that the deputies ratify the king's promises as good enough to forswear further attempts at reunification, and left for an hour so they could formulate their answer. He returned to find Franklin writing: "The immediate conclusion of a treaty of commerce and alliance would induce the Deputies to close their ears to any proposition that did not have as its basis entire liberty and independence in both politics and commerce." This satisfied Gérard. Franklin then asked for a draft of a treaty. He would have it within a few days, Gérard pledged. France desired no new territory, and he felt that it would be "good policy" for France and the United States to agree "not to halt the war until the English are expelled from the continent of North America." The complete-expulsion component was based on what Deane confided— that Franklin still lusted after Canada. This strategy did the trick: These notions were "applauded . . . with a sort of rapture," and Franklin "confessed that he saw nothing therein that was not noble and just." A late-session problem arose when Gérard cautioned that France could not guarantee Spain's participation. Franklin's frown gave Gérard the opening to lay on the table an ace held for this purpose: that any Franco-American accord would contain a secret protocol enabling Spain to join the alliance when it felt able to do so. Smiles replaced the frowns, and the two sides parted, Gérard reported, satisfied at the outcome and its future promise.

For ten days after the initial Gérard session, Franklin, thinking that Vergennes was in a hurry, slowed down. He was too busy to look at documents. He was temporarily indisposed. But Vergennes was not in a hurry; on the contrary, he needed time to work out provisions to which the Americans could most readily agree. He had in hand the Adams-crafted model treaty; that document contained some passages that he did not like, but insofar as possible he adopted its language. The commercial treaty's guiding principle, "the most perfect Equality and Reciprocity" between the partners, was stated in its preamble. Each granted the other the status of most favored nation. The military one permitted the United States to keep Canada, other portions of North America, and Bermuda, should they be captured during the war, and permitted France to retain any Caribbean isles won in combat—Adams's draft said nothing of such matters. In the most important clause, France agreed not to end any war with Great Britain until American independence had been assured.

That Vergennes had guessed right about the acceptability of the provisions became clear when negotiations resumed on January 18. They thereafter went smoothly, more so for Franklin and Deane than for Lee, who remained unable to quell his suspicion of everything French. Lee contributed to the treaty in regard to its legal implications, and when he would not sign particular provisions, Franklin, desirous of a united front, requested that Vergennes drop them, which he did.

Stormont, looking for clues as to what was going on between the French and the Americans, concluded that all the signals were bad. He found Vergennes uncharacteristically hurrying him out of the office, and Maurepas claiming illness as a reason not to see him. He tried another way of pressuring Maurepas, through Nathaniel Parker Forth. A year earlier Forth, a stockbroker and longtime Paris resident, had met and intrigued Maurepas, to the point of Maurepas asking Stormont to have Forth named a special envoy. Forth soon produced a coup, persuading Maurepas to countersign a memo promising that neither France nor Great Britain would build more battleships. Vergennes blocked it by telling Stormont that such an agreement was invalid as it lacked the royal signature. Forth was accepted at Louis's summer residence at Fontainebleau, and during a hunt killed a boar with his leaded riding crop, for which he was much celebrated.

Early in January 1778 Forth, in a contentious meeting, taunted Maurepas, saying that if he sincerely wanted peace between Great Britain and France he would push Louis to expel Franklin and Deane. Maurepas asked in return what George III would give France if they did so. When Forth was evasive, Maurepas exploded that "if France were mad enough, I say *assez folle*, to make any agreement with [the Americans], that England would not *à aucun prix* [at any price] make it up [with them] and they both fall upon us. . . . Time will shew, and prove that we had more reason to fear you than you to fear us." Maurepas challenged Forth to go to England and learn what George III would do for France should France break off with the Americans, and he pledged to sound out Louis on the matter. Forth went to London but was unable to obtain a price for French cooperation. By the time he returned to Paris, Maurepas would no longer see him.

Hutton sent Franklin a thank-you note and a query as to whether anything could now be done to forestall a Franco-American pact. Franklin had not received the query when he wrote to Hutton, charging that Great Britain had "lost the esteem, respect, friendship and affection of all the great and growing people, who consider [the British] at present, and whose posterity will consider you, as the worst and wickedest nation upon earth." When Hutton's note arrived, Franklin went further:

I abominate with you all Murder, and I may add the slaughter of men in an unjust cause is nothing less than Murder; I therefore, never think of your present Ministers and Abettors, but with the Image, strongly painted in my View of their Hands red, wet, and dripping with the Blood of my Countrymen, Friends, and Relations. No peace can be signed by those hands.

On February 4 Vergennes received definitive word from Montmorin, ambassador to Carlos III, that Spain would not sign at present but wanted to reserve the right to do so later, and pledged to continue clandestine funding for America. Receiving this news, Louis XVI had no further excuse for delay.

The signing ceremony took place on February 6, 1778, in the Foreign Ministry's office in Paris, with Gérard doing the honors for France. Lee and Deane wore their finest suits. Franklin had on an old brown velvet Manchester. When Deane asked why he had worn that particular garment Franklin responded, "To give it a little revenge," explaining that he had worn it on January 29, 1774, when at a British Privy Council meeting he had been verbally attacked and abused in front of King George III. Lee wanted to sign each document twice, claiming that Congress had appointed him a commissioner both for Spain and France. Franklin, Deane, and Gérard limited Lee to a single signature, although he added to it, "Deputy Plenipotentiary for France and Spain."

Franklin and Deane wrote Congress a note to accompany the documents. The first pact, based on the model treaty, was one of "Amity and Commerce." The second, to be kept secret for the time being, was even more important:

> a Treaty of Alliance, in which it is stipulated that in Case England declares war against France or occasions a War by Attempts to hinder her Commerce with us, we should then make common Cause of it. . . . The great aim of the [second] Treaty is declared to be, to "establish the Liberty, Sovereignty, and Independency absolute and unlimited of the United States as well as in Matters of Government as Commerce." And this is guaranteed to us by France together with all the Countries we possess, or shall possess at the Conclusion of the War.

9

"When an Enemy think a design against them improbable they can always be Surprised." —John Paul Jones

As 1777 yielded to 1778, General Howe's British force continued to occupy Philadelphia, while the main body of the Continental army wintered at Valley Forge in considerably less comfort, and with no assurance of any progress being made in Paris toward a Franco-American alliance. Nothing furthers the growth of conspiratorial thinking more than a stalemate; and these spurred the congressional anti-Washington forces to intensify efforts to supplant him as America's military leader. The plotters tried two ploys. One was to offer to Lafayette, through the Board of War, and without consulting Washington, command of an expedition to conquer Canada with Conway as its military leader. The second was to send to Henry Laurens, the president of Congress, an anonymous compilation of anti-Washington charges, "Thoughts of a Freeman," which congressional rules would force him to read aloud to the members and solicit comments, thereby providing them with a way to express their dissatisfaction with the commander in chief.

Instead of craftiness, the plotters by these moves displayed their ineptness, for they misjudged the willingness of Lafayette and Laurens to become dupes.

Lafayette was indeed intrigued by the prospect of using his influence on the French-speaking Canadians and his military prowess on the British army in Canada, and he had been an admirer of Conway. But his fondness for Conway had already faded as a result of having naively praised him to Washington prior to learning of the chief's anger over Conway's "weak leader" letter. The marquis had since apologized to Washington and been forgiven for the lapse, but it made him adamantly opposed to any expedition that did not have Washington's express approval. Moreover, as he wrote to Washington, "They will laugh in France when they'l hear that [Conway] is choosen upon such a commission out of the same army where I am principally as he is an Irishman, and when the project should be to show to the Frenchmen of [Canada] a man of theyr nation, who by his rank in France could inspire them with some confidence."

Lafayette sensed that the government of France was paying attention to the reported activities of its officers currently serving in America; and even as his letter crossed the Atlantic, lists of those officers and their billets in America were being compiled by the French for their military and diplomatic archives.

The Board of War, led by Horatio Gates and Thomas Mifflin, reacted to Lafayette's objection to the expedition by offering to have him lead it with Conway as the second—Conway had already been sent to Albany to prepare. Lafayette again demurred. He proposed, as an alternate second, de Kalb, a "wise . . . good officer . . . not over-powered by the clamours of an unbounded ambition." Conway would be his third. Further, should Washington not consent to the expedition or should Lafayette's conditions not be met, he would resign and return home, and he was certain the other French officers in America would do the same "within two days." The Board of War then fully agreed to Lafayette's terms.

On opening the "Thoughts of a Freeman" letter, Laurens saw that it was unsigned, which gave him a way around the congressional rule; since the letter was anonymous, he refused to read it to the members and said he planned to throw it into the fire. Instead he forwarded the letter to Washington inside a note to his son John. Washington, thus alerted as to the precise shortcomings with which his detractors sought to tar him, was able to prepare thoroughly for the visit of a congressional delegation to Valley Forge. At his request Hamilton compiled, from reports by officers and copies of Washington's missives, fifteen thousand words on the inadequacies of the supply system, lack of cooperation from state governments, and congressional inaction on troop pay.

The visiting committee consisted of Washington doubters, including its chairman, the Massachusetts delegate Francis Dana, a lawyer who had been a Sons of Liberty leader in the 1760s. None of the visitors to Valley Forge had had any idea of the appalling hardships that the troops were enduring. After Washington awed Dana by acquainting him with those conditions, he flattered him with an invitation to dine and spend the night at the commander's lodgings, and then in a late-night meeting frightened him, saying, "Mr. Dana—Congress does not trust me. I cannot continue thus." Dana sputtered that most delegates considered Washington indispensable. Upon returning to Congress, Dana became a vocal Washington supporter and converted enough other delegates to that position to assure the commander in chief's continued control of the army.

Meanwhile Lafayette was en route to Albany with a French posse—Duportail, du Plessis, de Kalb, and more than a dozen other French officers. After arriving, dismayed by the lack of supplies and men and by the fierceness of a winter that prevented travel into Canada, Lafayette realized what the Gates-Mifflin plan was: for Washington's protégé to fail on this expedition and slink back to France, providing the plotters with an additional impugning of Washington's leadership. Lafayette immediately petitioned Congress and the Board of War to abort the Canada mission.

The impasse took time to resolve, and in the interim he interested himself in Native American matters. He commissioned Jean-Baptiste Gouvion, one of Duportail's engineers, to design and erect a fort for the Oneida and Tuscarora.

During one of Lafayette's absences, Conway tried to assume command, and de Kalb, whose promotion Conway had tried to block, beat back the attempt. De Kalb described the incident to de Broglie, asserting that in the confrontation with Conway he had maintained his position "with more warmth and obstinacy than I should have done against any other on another occasion."

The Canada invasion was called off, and Lafayette and de Kalb were directed to return to Valley Forge. As Lafayette wrote to Washington while en route, just as Congress had deemed his and de Kalb's presence at Valley Forge absolutely necessary, "I believe that of General Conway is absolutely necessary to Albany, and he has receiv'd orders to stay there, what I have no objection to as nothing perhaps will be done in this quarter but some disputes of indians and torys."

While Conway's fortunes had rapidly risen and fallen, so had those of his brother-in-law. Du Bouchet, a hero of the Saratoga campaign, was afterward taken ill and given permission to return to France. In January 1778 he embarked from Baltimore, bound for Haiti. Not far off the coast the British intercepted his ship; upon their discovery that he was a French officer he was arrested and transported to one of the worst prisons in America, the *Judith*, a ship afloat in New York Harbor. He and the other prisoners were considered traitors and treated accordingly. Aboard a crowded hellhole, they were frequently deprived of water and food, and du Bouchet thought he would surely die. Between 1776 and 1783 some eleven thousand prisoners did die on those ships, which were run by the vengeful Irish-born Tory William Cunningham. After three weeks aboard the *Judith*, du Bouchet and two compatriots feigned having so severe a communicable illness as to require their being segregated from the rest of the prison population for fear of contagion. In the middle of the night, from that more isolated area they made their way off the ship and into a tied-up rowboat. Setting out on the East River they almost miraculously happened upon a French cargo ship bound for Saint-Domingue that agreed to take them aboard. From Haiti they were able to obtain berths on a ship heading to France.

In late February of 1778, the *Belle Poule* was forced back to port again by bad weather. Silas Deane, upon being apprised of the news, hurried with it to Versailles, where he applied to Vergennes to provide a different, speedy French ship to now take the actual treaties to America before North's peace commission could arrive there. Vergennes agreed. He was still worried about the actions of the British, principally because of an apparent news item from London that George Washington had signed a peace treaty. Franklin assured him that this was fake news, among other reasons because "No Treaty would be entered into with Howe by Washington, when Congress was at hand."

Arthur Lee objected to Deane's hasty transaction with the foreign minister; but then Lee had been fulminating over nearly everything that Deane and Franklin did or failed to do, even after the treaties were signed. His unrelenting nastiness occasioned a tough letter from Franklin:

> It was near nine at Night when the News [of the *Belle Poule*] arriv'd; and Mr. Deane set out immediately. If we could have imagin'd it necessary to have a Consultation with you on so plain a Case, it would necessarily have occasion'd a Delay of that important Business till the next Day. . . . We think Mr. Deane deserves your Thanks, and that neither of us deserve your Censure.

In the wake of the treaty signing, France canceled all leave for naval personnel and stepped up repairs and shipbuilding. Contingents of soldiers were marched to camps in Brittany, Normandy, and Picardy, the camps deliberately visible to stoke British fears of an invasion and to spur the reserving in British home waters of a portion of their navy to guard against that possibility. The American commissioners also made aggressive plans: for Captain John Paul Jones, thirty, to raid the British coast in his sloop, *Ranger*. One objective was for Jones to seize British combatants so they could be exchanged for Americans sailors being held in terrible conditions in British home islands jails—for just as in America du Bouchet and others were being treated abominably on the *Judith* and other prisons because they were presumed to be traitors, so American sailors in British jails were being miserably treated because they were considered pirates.

Born in Scotland, a son of the Paul family, John Paul had added the Jones name and come to America only after killing a mutinous sailor during an attempted takeover of a ship. Among the earliest officers to join the Continental navy, he complained of non-advancement until, in mid-1777, his big opportunity arrived: command of the twenty-gun *Ranger*, with orders to sail into European waters. Finding it ungainly, he reduced its cannon to eighteen, added tons of lead to the ballast to shift its center of gravity, and reconfigured its masts and sails. At Passy he may have begun an affair with Mme. Chaumont as well as made business arrangements with her husband for the sale of expected prizes. The supposed affair with Mme. Chaumont burnished his reputation among Parisians as dashing and reckless.

Jones learned from Franklin that the ship he had next expected to command, *L'Indien*, a forty-gun frigate being built by the commissioners in Holland, would not be his because the commissioners had postponed its completion during the delicate treaty negotiations with France. But they were eager to use the *Ranger* for raids on Jones's terms. He had written to them, "When an Enemy think a design against them improbable they can always be Surprised and Attacked with Advantage." Whereas in regard to Wickes and Conyngham the commissioners had been cautious, needing to prevent actions that would unduly provoke France to protect its fragile peace with Great Britain, now that the Franco-American alliance had been sealed they gave considerable latitude to Jones: "Proceed with [the *Ranger*] in the manner you shall judge best, for distressing the Enemies of the United States."

Anchored at Quiberon Bay, near a French squadron commanded by Admiral Toussaint Guillaume La Motte-Picquet, Jones sent a message that the *Ranger* was prepared to render a thirteen-gun salute if he would reciprocate. The Frenchman was willing to answer only with nine; Jones objected until informed that nine was the number used to salute high-ranked dignitaries of republics. The resultant salute was the first officially given in Europe to the flag of the United States of America. While continuing to prepare, Jones struck up a friendship with an even more senior admiral, Louis Gouillette, Comte d'Orvilliers, sixty-nine, who on learning of Jones's raiding plans offered the support and experienced military guidance that Jones had been unable to obtain in America. Jones also discussed with him a grandiose pipe dream: for French and American vessels to cross to New York, destroy Lord Howe's squadron, and then do the same with Britain's Newfoundland fisheries fleet.

The only men not happy with Jones's plans for raiding Britain were his officers and sailors. One American officer tried to decline to sail by contending that regulations forbade an officer of his rank from serving in a ship with fewer than twenty guns. Such excuses were a cover for the men wanting the *Ranger* to function more as a privateer, taking prizes in whose sale they could share, than as a warship of the Continental navy on a mission to wreak havoc.

On March 4, as Deane was preparing for the signal honor of being presented at court to Louis XVI, he was stunned to receive a letter from Congress recalling him. The missive gave no reason for this recall other than so that Deane could personally brief Congress on European affairs. Franklin, also puzzled by the recall, tried to assure Deane that Congress would return him to Paris by the fall to continue working out the treaty's commercial details, since Deane was America's most experienced commercial negotiator. Franklin, Deane, Carmichael, Bancroft, and Beaumarchais all presumed that Lee's complaints had spurred the recall. Vergennes and Gérard worried that it might portend a rejection of the Franco-American pacts by a recalcitrant Congress unduly influenced by Francophobes.

On March 8, British cabinet officer Lord Germain wrote to General Clinton, quoting the "king's secret instructions" for the following summer in America: "If you shall find it impracticable to bring Gen Washington to a general + decisive Action early in the Campaign, you will relinquish the Idea of carrying on offensive operations within land." The Franco-American pact had not yet become known in London but Great Britain, assuming that there would be such an agreement, instructed Clinton to disperse some of the troops then in New York to territories more at risk from France, namely Canada, Nova Scotia, and the Floridas. On March 10 the Admiralty also ordered its ships to seize any vessels thought to be heading to American shores even if they were escorted by foreign warships, including those of France.

On March 13, some five weeks after the Franco-American alliance treaties had been signed in Paris, Ambassador Noailles in London presented a copy of the commercial alliance to the Court of St James's. That evening the British summoned Stormont from Paris. Shortly thereafter Noailles was ordered home. News of the Franco-American pact produced a huge shift in British public opinion regarding the American Revolution, encapsulated in a newspaper headline of what was now desired: WAR WITH FRANCE AND PEACE WITH AMERICA. On March 17 Great Britain declared war on France, and in London on March 20, during the most martial parts of an extra performance of Handel's oratorio *Judas Maccabaeus,* ordered by King George III, the audience clapped heartily, "filled with a true spirit of indignation and resentment against our natural, and insidious enemy."

That same day at Versailles the American commissioners were formally presented to Louis XVI. Lee and Deane wore rented ceremonial swords to go with their powdered wigs and finery. Franklin, having deemed his wig ill fitting, did not wear one, would not put on a sword, and refused to purchase a new suit for the occasion. He did, however, forgo his usual fur cap and carried a modest white cloth one under his arm. For Deane the event was bittersweet; after having strived for nearly two years and successfully achieved the breakthrough that this ceremony recognized, he was being recalled home as though he had failed at the task.

Once Deane's recall notice had arrived, and more so after the ceremony at Versailles, Arthur Lee brazenly accused Deane and Franklin of playing fast and loose with public and private accounts, failing to consult him on every matter, and allowing Vergennes to choose Gérard as France's ambassador without Lee's knowledge or permission. These spurred Franklin to write a series of notes:

> There is a Stile in some of your Letters . . . whereby superior Merit is assumed to yourself in point of Care, and Attention to Business, and Blame on your Colleagues is insinuated. . . . I hate Disputes. I am old, cannot have long to live, have much to do and no time for Altercation. If I have . . . borne your Magisterial Snubbings and Rebukes without Reply, ascribe it to the right Causes, my Concern for the Honour and Success of our Mission, which would be hurt by our Quarrelling . . . and my Pity of your Sick Mind, which is forever Tormenting itself, with its Jealousies, Suspicions and Fancies.

Franklin did not send these missives. Instead he crafted a less irate though no less forthright response to Lee, after which he ceased writing to him for several months.

The success or failure of any message often depends on its timing. In mid-April 1778, nearly a month after Simeon Deane had left for America with the Franco-American pacts, the North government finally dispatched in the same direction its own team of three, under Frederick Howard, the Earl of Carlisle, twenty-nine, and including Eden and a former governor of West Florida. The Carlisle commission's proposals, which would grant virtually everything that the rebelling colonists had demanded before the onset of hostilities, refuted many of Great Britain's war aims—in particular, the right to tax Americans with or without their consent. All that Great Britain would retain was the right to tax non-British imports to America. One critic grumbled that should the Americans accept these proposals, they would be better off than Britons, as they would have all the advantages of being British citizens and few of the burdens.

At nearly the same moment of the Carlisle commission's sailing, Silas Deane also embarked, with Gérard. They first traveled aboard a small ship in an attempt to conceal that once they were offshore in the Mediterranean they would transfer to join d'Estaing, whose fleet was so large that it had drawn many observers: Eleven ships of the line and fourteen other vessels with a total of 1,394 cannon, all of it underwritten by sizable loans from Chaumont.

D'Estaing aimed to reach America in time for a late spring campaign. But his progress on the thousand nautical miles between Toulon and Gibraltar was delayed by weather and by problems of command and personnel. Among his captains were Pierre-André de Suffren de Saint-Tropez, forty-nine, considered the best French naval commander; Louis-Antoine de Bougainville, also forty-nine, whose circumnavigations of the world in 1766 and 1769 were highly respected and who, like d'Estaing, had been a soldier before becoming part of the navy; and Jacques-Melchior Saint-Laurent de Barras, fifty-eight, who had first gone to sea at fourteen. These senior men resented d'Estaing's too-rapid promotion to vice admiral—he had been in the navy only a few years and had never commanded a squadron in battle. Their subordinate officers, all noble-born, were annoyed at d'Estaing's willingness to include on each capital ship three "auxiliary" officers from the ranks of ordinary citizens. As Bougainville wrote in a diary, he was unacquainted with any of the petty officers on his ship, and "We are sailing with neither watch muster nor quarter-bill, with a crew three-quarters of whom know nothing about maneuvers, guns or the sea. And nearly all are seasick." The ships also had physical defects, two being markedly slower than the others. What with all these difficulties, d'Estaing's fleet took five weeks to clear Gibraltar.

The British Admiralty was well aware of d'Estaing's dispatch. Lord Germain wanted to intercept the fleet before it reached the Atlantic, but the Earl of Sandwich, First Lord of the Admiralty, contended that too few British ships were available to perform that task, and his view prevailed.

As d'Estaing proceeded westward, his way uncontested by the British, John Paul Jones set out in the *Ranger,* aiming to damage British coastal towns in retaliation for the wanton damage that British raiders repeatedly inflicted on Connecticut coastal towns. In a voyage lasting only twenty-eight days Jones seized two merchantmen, sinking one and sending the other to a French port to be sold; captured the British sloop *Drake,* and took two hundred prisoners after a "warm, close, and obstinate" gun battle; and mounted predawn raids on a coastal town and on Whitehaven, the Scottish port of his birth. Brazenly invading the mansion of a provincial lord, he missed capturing that peer, who was not at home, but won the hearts of a few Britons by setting loose on shore fishermen he had captured before encountering the *Drake,* and later tried to win more by a gallant attempt to return the provincial lord's silver to the lady of the house.

British newspaper accounts demonized Jones, who was five foot six and of fair complexion, as a large, swarthy pirate, which only heightened the impact of his raids. No English seaport had been attacked since 1667; now Jones had done so, forcing the Admiralty to deploy more warships on coastal patrols, a move that prevented them from being sent to America.

Although Floridablanca, Spain's first minister, had refused to have Spain sign the Franco-American alliance, he did commit Spain to a policy of "benevolent neutrality" toward the new country. Bernardo de Gálvez, recently appointed viceroy of New Spain, resident in New Orleans, and Diego Joseph Navarro, the new governor of Cuba, were eager to help the United States and to counter British cavalier actions toward Spain's colonies. When Virginia governor Patrick Henry requested 150,000 rifles from New Orleans, Gálvez worked with an American agent to find and transport these. Spanish funds and matériel found their way up the Mississippi to George Rogers Clark and his American forces, fighting in areas west of the original thirteen states. The citizens of St. Louis extended credit to Clark, who used it to buy munitions to defend the city. Gálvez's benevolence permitted American soldiers to train in New Orleans while outfitting raiding ships to be sent against British targets in the Gulf of Mexico.

Floridablanca also dispatched to America two agents to represent Spain's interests, the brothers-in-law Don Juan de Miralles and Don Juan Elegio de Puentes. Traveling separately, both reached the United States in the spring of 1778. However, a congressional request made through them, to open the port of Havana to American trade, was declined; Governor Navarro sent word that it would be better to keep the trade in New Orleans and not overly provoke the British.

Madrid continued to assure Versailles that Spain would likely act in concert with France on America once the treasure fleet returned from the New World late in the year, but even then might refuse if it saw no benefit. Floridablanca appeared not to care whether the United States achieved independence or if some additional trade would then accrue to France and Spain. "For herself," he confided to Aranda, ambassador in Paris, "Spain has no other objective than to recover the shameful usurpations of Gibraltar and Minorca, and to cast out of the Gulf of Mexico, the Bay of Honduras, and the Coast of Campeche, those [British] settlers which trouble her no end."

10

"To hinder the enemy from rendering himself master." —Louis Duportail

The exception that should prove the rule just as often provides evidence of the rule's inadequacy. At a moment when Franklin and Deane had just been instructed by Congress to send no more European officers to America, another suitor showed up on their doorstep, with such good recommendations—from Saint-Germain and Vergennes, who almost never personally recommended anyone—that he seemed a terrific fit for the Continental army: Friedrich Wilhelm Ludolph Gerhard Augustin, Baron von Steuben, forty-seven, a Prussian who spoke no English but was fluent in French and had spent his entire life as a field officer in various militaries and as an aide to Frederick the Great. Two aspects of his character trailed him: first, that he was a superbly talented quartermaster and disciplinarian; and second, that he was suspected of homosexuality to the point that neither France nor Prussia was now willing to have him in its army. Some rumors said that he had been on the verge of being arrested in Prussia when he fled to France and, for the same reason, was unable to remain very long in Paris.

The Americans had been made aware of the charges of pederasty but seemed unconcerned. However, Deane informed Steuben, recent instructions made it impossible to offer a paid position. Franklin would not even agree to pay Steuben's expenses in crossing to America, issuing his denial, Steuben later recalled, "with an Air & Manner to which I was then little accustomed." A week later Saint-Germain suggested that Steuben serve in America as a volunteer, and Beaumarchais agreed to underwrite his passage.

The playwright then composed a series of letters, ostensibly from the principalities in which Steuben had served, to Washington, Morris, Laurens, and other leaders. The one from Franklin and Deane to Washington the Americans obligingly signed. It asserted that during the Seven Years' War Steuben had been a major general. Actually he had been *maréchal général de logis*, director of logistics or quartermaster general, a much less exalted position. Moreover, as the most recent Steuben biographer writes of the content of these letters, "Nearly every statement was falsified or exaggerated, every detail—about Steuben's rank and experience—deliberately misrepresented."

Steuben embarked from Marseilles along with his greyhound, his military aide-de-camp, and his secretary, Pierre-Étienne du Ponceau, seventeen, rumored to be his sexual partner. Du Ponceau's love for Shakespeare and other English literary giants had driven him at an early age to learn English and to study linguistics. Unwilling to become a monk, he had escaped to Paris with Milton's *Paradise Lost* in one pocket and a spare shirt in the other. There he entered the Beaumarchais literary circle and did occasional translations for members of the court. On board for America, he jotted down ideas for a "universal language and alphabet."

Landing in Portsmouth, Steuben sent the Beaumarchais-composed note to Washington. It stated:

> The Object of my greatest Ambition is to render your Country all the Services in my Power, and to deserve the title of a Citizen of America by fighting for the Cause of your Liberty.
>
> . . . . I could Say moreover (Were it not for the fear of offending your Modesty) that your Excellency is the only Person under

whom (after having Served under the King of Prussia) I could wish
to pursue an Art to which I have Wholly given up my Self.

Steuben requested a reply in the care of John Hancock in Boston, where
he and his group were heading.

Du Ponceau while on board had made a bet that his dashing appearance in uniform would enable him to kiss the first American lady he saw on land; he managed to persuade a lass to help him win this wager. By the time the Steuben retinue reached Boston, du Ponceau was already feeling like an American. They were welcomed and celebrated by Hancock and Samuel Adams, among others. Du Ponceau found Sam Adams amazed at his republicanism.

Washington's reply advised Steuben to deal with Congress in seeking a commission, but added that he would be welcome at Valley Forge. In such exchanges with foreign aspirants Washington was unfailingly courteous, and behind this one was a hope that Steuben might supplant Conway as inspector general. At a stopover in York, Steuben, having heard of the difficulties between Gates and Washington, declined Gates's offer of a domicile. Du Ponceau had similarly learned of Conway's misbehavior and was mortified, having known Conway since his childhood, when "with him I had lisped my imperfect first English accents."

At Valley Forge, after Washington had spent time with Steuben, listened to his evaluation of the condition of the troops, and watched as he began to shape them up, he appointed Steuben "acting" inspector general, to supersede Conway.

Steuben and du Ponceau became friends in camp with the few Americans who spoke French—Laurens, Hamilton, Monroe, and Captain Benjamin Walker, who became Steuben's life companion, as well as Katie Greene, the much-admired wife of General Nathanael Greene. The young American officers were awed by Steuben; de Kalb and Lafayette, who knew much more about European armies, not so much, but they also formed lasting friendships. The juniors responded well to Steuben's stories of cavalry charges and his ability to discuss with them the works of the pillars of Enlightenment literature. The Americans' enthusiasm for sophisticated discourse was mirrored in their letters, such as one that du Ponceau later recalled receiving from Laurens, written in English, French, Latin, Greek, and Spanish. Du Ponceau formed his closest friendship with Monroe; they wrote on each day that they did not spend time together, exchanging books, literary preferences, and mutual encouragement. In the Monroe-du Ponceau exchanges, and in those of the other young French and American officers at Valley Forge, the understanding grew of the higher purpose of the Franco-American connection: More was at stake than helping America sever a prior connection to an overbearing parent; the struggle was for the liberation of all peoples, everywhere, oppressed by tyrannical rulers.

That ideal was reflected in a plan, hatched by Laurens and Fleury, to raise a battalion of three thousand slaves who would be given their freedom in exchange for frontline service in the army. L'Enfant, who had come to Valley Forge and was assisting Steuben, asked to be an officer in that battalion. Washington agreed with Laurens that slaves were a neglected resource and objected only that mustering them into the army would impoverish their owners. Henry Laurens, also a slave owner, offered more significant resistance, and his son John dutifully shelved the plan.

Duportail drew up a far more practical plan for aiding the army, by professionalizing a corps of engineers that he would lead. Washington enthusiastically forwarded and recommended the plan to Congress.

The awful Valley Forge winter birthed many other dreams. The restless Colonel Armand decided that he must soon strike out on his own and, with Washington's permission and Lafayette's encouragement, petitioned Congress to raise and equip his own regiment. He began by taking some captured Hessians and other German-speakers who wished to serve the United States but had not been integrated to the Valley Forge fraternity. De la Balme, offended because Congress had appointed Pulaski as chief of America's cavalry, in addition to starting to raise a similar independent regiment drew up plans to create a village for artisans just outside Philadelphia, where he would offer work to those in the countryside whose lives had been disrupted by the British occupation. In an advertisement he sought as candidates "Soldiers, Sailors, Deserters from any Troops (except the America Army and French Navy) Carpenters, Bakers, etc., of any Number" to work for "Good Wages, Victuals, Lodgings, Fuel, Candles and Washing."

Steuben, in full military dress, conducted drill exercises twice a day and became beloved by the soldiers for cursing at them in three languages while molding them into units able to obey orders, which would eventually help them perform under enemy fire without breaking ranks, which some had done at Brandywine and Germantown. Among Steuben's teachings was the use of the bayonet, which most Americans had not employed in battle even when there was opportunity to do so.

Steuben clashed a bit with Duportail on the design of the camp and its defenses, finding redoubts unfinished and other problems. Laurens wrote to his father, "The repeated cavils of some general officers have driven the engineer . . . to substitute lines to redoubts in fortifying the camp, whereby the labor of the soldier was greatly augmented." Steuben also had disagreements with a Philadelphia physician over the proper sanitary and cooking facilities for the camp, but both agreed that latrines should be at one end, near the river, and cook tents at the other.

Gates himself gave Steuben little difficulty, writing to him, just after he had begun to train the soldiers, "Considering the few Moments that is left for us for this necessary Work, I should rather recommend the Discipline of the Leggs, than the Firelocks or the Hands; the preservation of Order at all Times is essentially necessary. It leads to Victory, it Secures a Retreat, it Saves a Country."

If the wisest of leaders is the one who chooses to listen to the broadest range of counsel, then the most closely listened to of those counselors is the one who speaks the truth even when that truth is painful. On April 20, 1778, Washington, as he habitually did when faced with an important decision, requested opinions from senior officers. Which of three plans for the near future should he adopt? One was to attempt to retake Philadelphia, the second was to attack New York while the British were still in Philadelphia, and the third was "remaining quiet in a secure, fortified Camp, disciplining and arranging the army, 'till the enemy begin their operations."

The query was put at a moment when Washington finally had in camp the strategic counsel he had longed for, and it made itself known in the differing recommendations. While the American officers all urged making an attack on Philadelphia, the Europeans Lafayette, Duportail, and Steuben counseled against doing so (de Kalb was not present). The most persuasively argued of the essays was Duportail's, mainly because it was brutally honest: "We were beaten at Brandywine—we were beaten at German Town altho' we had immense advantage of a complete Surprise. . . . The diminution from Battle and principally sickness and Desertion, has been half the army." These tough truths were prelude to Duportail's recommendation, a strategy based specifically on Fabius's against Hannibal: "To defend the country inch by inch, to endeavor to hinder the enemy from rendering himself master of it, consequently never to receive him but when we are protected by a natural or artificial fortification, in other words to carry on what is styled a *defensive war*." Duportail advocated allowing the British to evacuate Philadelphia, and henceforth to give battle only under conditions that would ensure American success, namely, when small units could attack discrete sections of enemy forces.

The failure of the Albany expedition and the growing consensus in Congress that Washington needed to be supported rather than replaced persuaded Gates to resign as head of the Board of War and thereafter to attempt to be a more properly deferential subordinate to Washington. In April, after Conway wrote Washington demanding the command of a division and the chief refused it, Gates and Mifflin did not intervene on Conway's behalf. Conway submitted his resignation. This time Congress accepted it and awarded Steuben the title of inspector general, also appointing him a major general and arranging for his pay.

Late that month Simeon Deane arrived in America with the documents of the Franco-American alliance. By May 2, when Simeon reached York to officially present the treaties to Congress for ratification, news of his and their arrival had preceded him, as had the news that Great Britain had declared war on France. That last news eliminated any congressional reluctance to sign the treaties, and they were ratified on May 4. Some congressmen professed amazement at the generosity of the French terms—no territorial demands, nothing that was not commensurate with full and complete independence of the United States of America.

Washington shared the news of the alliance with his officers. Tears of joy streamed down Lafayette's face, and the reactions of the other French reflected their mingled senses of relief, pride in their country, and exultation. On May 6 a stirring daylong celebration was held at Valley Forge. Under Steuben's direction the army executed some fancy maneuvers, its divisions commanded by Stirling, Lafayette, and de Kalb. At Lafayette's request, that day Washington granted clemency to two soldiers who had been sentenced to die. There was the ceremonial *feu de joie* musket firing. Its spectacular, near-continuous noise and smoke made Gates hold his hands over his ears. At the end of the day each soldier was given a gill of rum.

Then the war council of the generals, in a unanimous decision, adopted the Duportail-Lafayette-Steuben recommendation on what to do about the British in Philadelphia: they voted not to attack them there, nor to shift their focus to New York for actions, but rather to apply their energies to augmenting and equipping the army for the approaching campaigns, in which they dared hope that the French military would join.

On May 18, at Walnut Grove in Philadelphia, the British army held an extravagant celebration in honor of the departing General Howe—and in defiance of the new Franco-American treaty. The *Mischianza,* as the event was titled, was organized mainly by Captain John André, twenty-eight, a favorite of Howe's who was also a poet, actor, and artist. It followed in a tradition of army-written entertainments for the troops, notably Burgoyne's *The Blockade of Boston*, presented during the siege of that city in 1776. The *Mischianza* (the word means "medley" in Italian) featured a parade, a regatta, a seventeen-gun salute, a jousting tournament, a dancing ball and banquet for 430, and fireworks, only briefly interrupted by a foray of a few Continental soldiers. The guests included the general's brother, Admiral Richard Howe, the general's successor, Clinton, and most of Tory Philadelphia, although not the general's mistress, Mrs. Elizabeth Loring. Much work went into painting backdrops, building wooden triumphal arches, and arranging costumes and the jousting tournament. As André described it:

> On the front seat of each pavilion were placed seven of the principal young ladies . . . in Turkish habits, and wearing in their turbans the favors with which they meant to reward the several knights who were to contend in their honor. . . . A band of knights, dressed in ancient habits of white and red silk, and mounted on gray horses, richly caparisoned in trappings of the same colors, entered the list, attended by their esquires on foot. . . . [On one's] tunic was the device of his band; two roses intertwined, with the motto, *We droop when separated*. . . . Two young black slaves, with sashes and drawers of blue and white silk, wearing large silver clasps round their necks and arms, their breasts and shoulders bare, held [a knight's] stirrups.

A display of excess, braggadocio, and nostalgia for a long-gone era, the event was far removed from the reality of the impending British retreat. When news of the *Mischianza* reached London, the *Chronicle* described the festivities as "nauseous," and the *Gentlemen's Magazine* as "dancing at a funeral, or [at] the brink of a grave."

General Howe postponed his departure from Philadelphia after a rebel turncoat revealed that Lafayette and a contingent of several thousand troops had taken a position that exposed the marquis to capture. Howe lusted after the pleasure of seizing the French firebrand and taking him back to London in irons. The general even invited some Philadelphia ladies to dine with Lafayette and him the next evening, and with his brother rode out in a carriage to be voyeurs at the hunt.

Washington had given Lafayette permission to harass the British retreat but instructed him to take extra care in doing so because the loss of the 2,200 troops he led would cripple the army. To assure Lafayette's safety Washington sent along Morgan's sharpshooters. But Lafayette's choice of encampments left him and his forces vulnerable to 8,000 British and Hessian troops and fifteen field pieces, which by dawn on May 20 had nearly surrounded the Americans bivouacked on Barren Hill, a promontory above the Schuylkill.

Lafayette, upon realizing that the enemy was near and in force, decreed several ruses to confuse the British. Parceling out small contingents of soldiers and a few cannons to each of several forested sites adjoining the barren hill, he ordered the troops to fire extravagantly at the British and then quickly move to another site and do the same. It was an attempt to trick the enemy into thinking that there were more Americans than there actually were. He also unleashed fifty warpainted Oneida to whoop as they attacked an approximately equal number of British cavalry. Lafayette ordered the main body of his troops down a defile to the Schuylkill and across the river, then running at a depth of four feet. Steuben's training made possible the troops' quick and disciplined retreat. When most had crossed to safety, Lafayette and a contingent of snipers took a position at the ford and with accurate fire deterred the British from following. So did the sound of big guns booming from Valley Forge, where officers had learned of the continuing engagement and touched off cannons to summon troops to Lafayette's rescue.

General Howe did not ignore this obvious signal; deciding not to risk a larger engagement, he ordered the British back to Philadelphia. After this failure, he departed for Great Britain and Clinton's forces prepared to leave Philadelphia. Clinton had brought with him new orders to send divisions to Nova Scotia and to attack St. Lucia, a French Caribbean outpost. Since the dispatch of these troops would seriously diminish his forces in America, Clinton decided to keep them all together until they reached New York and then to disperse them.

The Carlisle commissioners were already in New York, their ship's destination having been changed for reasons revealed to them only when they landed: Clinton was evacuating Philadelphia. They requested he delay doing so until they could present their peace plan to the Americans. He didn't give them much time. On June 9 Washington's men intercepted a messenger sent to York with that peace proposal, which was promptly forwarded to Congress. Its cover letter stated, "We trust that the inhabitants of North-America . . . will shrink from the thought of becoming an accession of force to our late mutual enemy, and will prefer a firm, free, and perpetual coalition with the parent state to an insincere and unnatural foreign alliance."

This offensive notion was echoed by others in the letter and the document, to the point that when the letter was read to Congress, the members became so outraged that discussion was halted and the proposal itself not even read until after the weekend, when Congress summarily spurned it. Laurens did not then write to Carlisle to say so, but did put Congress's reasoning in a letter to Washington: "Nothing but an earnest desire to spare the farther effusion of human blood could have induced [the Congress] to read a paper, containing expressions so disrespectful to his Most Christian Majesty [Louis XVI], the good and great ally of these states, or to consider propositions so derogatory to the honour of an independent nation."

Because circumstances prevented the Carlisle commissioners from making their entreaties in person, Congress was deprived of the opportunity of learning from them their secret instructions, which empowered the commissioners, in the event that the Americans insisted on recognition of independence before negotiations, not to reject that idea out of hand but simply to refer it to London and while waiting for a reply to agree to an armistice.

On June 18 General Clinton's troops finally evacuated Philadelphia by land and sea. He took several days to load his four hundred transports and set his troops on the road north. Washington, interpreting the slowness of the Clinton departure as an attempt to invite the Continental army into a general action that the British could easily win, refused to rise to the bait, proving yet again that one of the prime assets of a person of action is a reservoir of patience.

After the Admiralty had permitted d'Estaing's force to sail uncontested to America, it ordered Admiral August Keppel's Home Fleet to keep tabs on the substantial French fleet at Brest, opposite the southwestern corner of England at the point where the English Channel widens into the Atlantic Ocean. D'Orvilliers's fleet also had units out looking for the British, more to be aware of their movements than to engage in battle—after all, Vergennes had emphasized to him France's need to induce the British to fire the first shots, since France had not yet declared war.

The British obliged on the afternoon of June 17, 1778. The frigate *Belle Poule*, now under the command of a new captain, scouting with three other French naval vessels for the location of Keppel's fleet, found more than they were looking for: a formidable flotilla featuring twenty-one ships of the line. Keppel saw the four French vessels, but rather than surround them he directed four of his ships to intercept them individually; to the *Arethusa* he awarded the task of halting the *Belle Poule*.

While the three other French ships were quickly captured, the *Belle Poule* was not. The *Arethusa* fired the first salvo, the *Belle Poule* answered, and for four hours they engaged in an intense firefight. Each captain followed his rule book: The British aimed their cannon for the hull of their enemy while the French aimed theirs for the rigging. The result was a blood-soaked raw. The *Belle Poule* hastened toward Brest, 102 dead out of a crew of 230; the *Arethusa,* although having lost only 44 of 198, had more severe structural damage, requiring that it be towed.

A messenger from the *Belle Poule* took the action report to Versailles. Louis XVI's council heard it and concluded that the *Arethusa*'s attack on the *Belle Poule* constituted that incident of British aggression for which Vergennes had been waiting, causing a state of war to come into existence between France and Great Britain. Louis objected only to language in the declaration holding George III personally responsible for Great Britain's assaults; at Louis's insistence the wording was changed. The attack and France's declaration also meant that its secret, second treaty with the United States of America, the military one, was now in force and that the two countries had become more than trading friends; they were now military partners united against a common enemy, Great Britain.

The ship's intrepid captain was lionized as France's first hero of a new war, and some women at Versailles had their hair done up in a style thereafter known as "coëffure à la Belle Poule," bouffant, and topped by a model of the frigate with miniature red, white, and blue sails.

PART FOUR

Together: First Steps

1778–1779

11

"Concerting my operations with a general of Your Excellency's repute."
— Comte d'Estaing

The desired consummation had been effected: France and the United States of America had become allies, united against a common enemy, and they had already had a success, chasing the British out of Philadelphia in the expectation of a French fleet's arrival at America's capital.

That fleet had not yet arrived in June 1778, as the American army shadowed Clinton's British forces northward through New Jersey, the progress of both armies slowed by the unusually hot and rainy weather. Lassitude fostered speculation, in the American camp, on the future of the French officers currently serving with the Continental forces. Charles Lee, the general captured by the British early in the war and recently released from parole, was debating the matter with Lafayette. Should they fight as a group? For France or for the United States? Many were already determining their own paths. Armand, de la Balme, and Pulaski were mustering corps; Fleury was seconded to Morgan's Rangers, du Plessis to the artillery, and Gouvion "has been of a greater use to America among [the Oneida] than it is possible to say," Lafayette had reported to Congress. He thought that the remaining French officers should be in a battalion under a French commander.

Lee discussed solutions to nonexistent problems with Lafayette while to Washington he offered only obstruction. When Washington's council debated tactics against the British, Lee asserted that Washington's prior Fabianism—employing the tactics of the Roman general Fabius, who by guerilla tactics had beaten Hannibal—had not worked, but he then made a case for a very Fabian maneuver, what Lafayette called a *pont d'or* (bridge of gold), to allow the British to exit New Jersey unimpeded. However, Lafayette, as well as Washington, Duportail, Greene, Wayne, and another general, John Cadwalader, were unwilling to pass up an opportunity to deal Clinton's forces a telling blow.

Washington offered Lee command of the forces to fight Clinton's. Lee declined, so Washington awarded command to Lafayette, with Wayne as his second. The next morning Lee changed his mind and begged all to reconsider. Washington did not want to, so Lee appealed to Lafayette: "I place my honor and fortune in your hands. You are too generous to make me lose either of them." Lafayette succumbed to the flattery and Washington acceded to their decision.

As the battle of Monmouth Courthouse began, Lee led the troops in disastrous ways, giving contradictory orders and refusing to attack at a prime opportunity to capture a large Clinton contingent. Washington then rode up to Lee, cursed him out, relieved him of command, and directed the troops in retreat and re-formations, aided by Lafayette and Wayne. Steuben, who arrived moments later, rallied troops in disarray and marched them back into battle—a testament, Hamilton observed, to the value of the discipline that Steuben had instilled. A potential debacle became a battle in which the British lost twice as many troops as the Americans.

That night Clinton stole a march, taking his men through Sandy Hook and into New York, ceding New Jersey to Washington. In the morning Washington had just been apprised of this when he was handed a Lee letter of protest:

Nothing but the misinformation of some very stupid, or misrepresentation of some very wicked person coud have occasioned your

making use of so very singular expressions. . . . They implyed that
I was guilty either of disobedience of orders, of want of conduct,
or want of courage. . . . [You have] been guilty of an act of cruel
injustice. . . . I have a right to demand some reparation for the in-
jury committed.

Washington ordered Lee's arrest for insubordination. A court-martial featuring the detailed memories of Lafayette and Wayne cost Lee loss of
command for a year.

On July 4, 1778, the American forces celebrated the second anniver-
sary of the Declaration of Independence. During the festivities Cadwalader and Conway exchanged words. Conway had resigned but had
been unable to book passage home. Cadwalader managed to do what
other officers had tried but failed to accomplish: successfully challenge
Conway to a duel for his slights to Washington. In the duel Cadwalader
shot Conway through the mouth.

Conway, believing he would shortly die, wrote to Washington:

I find my self just able to hold the penn During a few Minutes,
and take this opportunity of expressing my sincere grief for having
Done, Written, or said any thing Disagreeable to your excellency.
my carreer will soon be over, therefore justice and truth prompt
me to Declare my Last sentiments. you are in my eyes the great
and the good Man. May you Long enjoy the Love, Veneration and
Esteem of these states whose Libertys you have asserted by your
Virtues.

Washington made no reply. Conway's wound was disfiguring, not fatal.
He recovered enough to sail for France, where he was welcomed back into
the military. A sizable portion of France's army was massed along the
northern coast for potential action against Great Britain. Versailles sent
Conway to that command, in a lower rank than he thought appropriate to
his experience, but he decided to keep his injured mouth shut about that.

. . .

On July 5, 1778, the long-awaited French savior knocked at America's door: Admiral d'Estaing and his fleet arrived off Virginia, and on July 7 reached the mouth of the Delaware, downriver of Philadelphia. Their presence was tremendously important, evidence to America that France's commitment consisted of more than cheers and excess inventory. And that commitment had immediate consequences; as Lord Carlisle explained in a letter to his wife, "The arrival of this [French] fleet makes every hope for success in our [peace] business ridiculous."

D'Estaing knew that the alliance partners' moment together would be brief. His moderate-size flotilla would enjoy naval superiority only until more ships from Great Britain arrived to supplement those in New York Harbor. He was also constrained by orders. One stressed caution over initiative in action, a second positioned his fleet's mission as less important than those of the fleets sent to the Caribbean, to India, and the English Channel, and a third mandated that he take his ships to the Caribbean well before the end of the year.

Before embarking for New York, at Philadelphia he sent an opening letter to Washington by the hand of a distinguished carrier, his aide, a marquis who was a relative of Sartine's. D'Estaing said he looked forward to *"concerter mes opérations avec un général tel que Votre Excellence"* (concerting my operations with a general of Your Excellency's repute), whose "talents and great actions . . . have insured him in the eyes of all Europe, the title, truly sublime deliverer of America."

Washington's response got right down to business: he was planning to cross the North River fifty miles above New York, and "shall then move down before the Enemy's lines, with a view of giving them every jealousy in my power . . . and facilitate such enterprizes as you may form and are pleased to communicate to me."

A naval attempt to take New York would depend on d'Estaing's ability to get over the sandbar at Sandy Hook. Lord Howe had positioned ships and shore batteries there to make such passage costly. Should d'Estaing's ships clear the bar, they would only be able to do so one at a time, and would then run a gauntlet of six Howe warships, "echeloned" so that their fields of fire would overlap. As d'Estaing waited outside the Sandy Hook bar for a favorable tide, he tried to slake his most urgent needs—fresh water, meat, and vegetables—his stores overly depleted by the long voyage. Washington sent him a herd of cattle. Water was harder to obtain. When John Laurens arrived, he listened to d'Estaing's problems and explained them in a letter to his father: The "disaffected inhabitants either refused their wagons, or granted them only at an exorbitant price." D'Estaing was very pleased with Laurens as an emissary from Washington, noting to Vergennes that Laurens was the son of the president of Congress, and that his officers judged the young man "actif et aimable." Only some water was obtained. Also, for want of fresh vegetables, nearly half of d'Estaing's troops and sailors were ill. And this was July, cruelest of months because food could be seen growing in the fields but was not yet ripe enough to eat.

Laurens brought a letter from Lafayette, a distant d'Estaing cousin and neighbor. To assure d'Estaing that the letter was not a forgery Lafayette included references to what only a neighbor would know, such as "M. Montboisser's good salmon fishery." He and d'Estaing, he wrote, shared a hatred of and the desire to humiliate Great Britain: "I have the honor to be as much related to you by this sentiment as by the ties of blood." The next visitor was Hamilton, accompanied by Fleury and some experienced New York pilots. By then d'Estaing had realized that his most formidable vessels could not broach the sandbar. In any sea battle d'Estaing's flagship, a ninety-gun vessel, and his eighty-guns and seventy-fours would have the advantage over Howe, whose largest were a half dozen sixty-fours. But while sixty-fours could clear the Sandy Hook bar, d'Estaing was informed that his seventy-fours might not, and there was no likelihood of bringing in the flagship, the ninety-gun *Languedoc*. He reportedly offered as much as 150,000 pounds to the pilots to take his seventy-fours over the bar but they refused.

After eleven days of d'Estaing standing off Sandy Hook, the tidal conditions changed, supposedly assuring a clearance of thirty feet over the bar, enough for the seventy-fours. The British expected d'Estaing to pass the bar and assail them in the harbor, and were astonished when the French fleet did not and instead took off to the east.

To put the best face on the action, d'Estaing had been encouraged to caution by his agreement with Washington on an alternate target, Newport, Rhode Island, toward which he now sailed. It was a good target, for a Franco-American capture of Newport's British garrison of several thousand men would be a severe blow. Clinton, recognizing this, had already dispatched additional troops to that port.

John Adams was having a very difficult stay in France. No sooner had he arrived than he learned that his task, negotiating a treaty, had already been accomplished. He considered returning immediately to Boston, but at dockside also learned of the American commission's internal problems and thought that he might be able to ameliorate them—after all, he had worked closely with Franklin in Congress, and the Lees were the Adamses' congressional partners.

Even though Deane had departed, the climate at Passy was worse than Adams had imagined. "It has given me, much Grief, since my Arrival here, to find So little Harmony, among many respectable Characters. So many mutual Jealousies, and So much Distrust of one another," Adams wrote in answer to R. H. Lee's inquiry about his brother, Arthur. Chagrined at the sloppiness of the commission's affairs—"There never was before I came, a minute Book, a Letter Book or an Account Book, and it is not possible to obtain a clear Idea of our Affairs," as Adams wrote in his diary—he took on its paperwork tasks, organizing its files and handling its correspondence. Although Franklin tried to help him by attending to John Quincy's educational needs and by introducing Adams to Turgot and others with whom he could converse on elevated subjects, Adams chafed at the voluptuous luxury of his surround and the nonessential character of the commissioners' mission. "This is an ugly situation for me who does not abound in philosophy and who cannot and will not trim," Adams wrote to his cousin Samuel. He tried to cut the Gordian knot by inviting Lee to move into the capacious Valentinois, touting it as a way to save the public's money and "cultivate a harmony" among the commissioners. Lee refused, and with that refusal the last vestiges of amicability vanished.

Presented at court, Adams formed good opinions of Louis XVI and Marie Antoinette, the latter the focus of added attention for her very visible pregnancy. As Adams's stay in France wore on he became increasingly convinced that a commission was superfluous and that he and Lee should be recalled, leaving Franklin as America's sole representative. But equally, as he wrote to a close friend, "The more I consider our Affairs, the more important our Alliance with France appears to me. It is a Rock upon which we may safely build."

On July 11, 1778, when d'Estaing's fleet stood off Sandy Hook, still hoping to do battle with Howe's, three thousand miles away the prelude to a naval engagement of great moment to the American Revolution began at the spot where the English Channel meets the Atlantic Ocean. That day Admiral Keppel's Home Fleet left port, looking to fight d'Orvilliers's French squadron, whose officers' eyes also gleamed with the anticipation of battle.

Keppel, a lifelong naval officer, was a Whig MP who had opposed the North government's strategies regarding the American colonies to the point of having refused to serve in American waters. He took the Home Fleet post despite his conviction that Sandwich, First Lord of the Admiralty, whom Keppel had relentlessly criticized in Parliament, hoped that he might fail at it and cease being a viable critic. When the Admiralty dispatched Admiral John Byron to chase d'Estaing, Keppel protested: "Taking eleven of the finest ships from under my command . . . leaves me in a situation I must think alarming for the safety of the king's home dominions." He refused to sail until he had thirty capital ships. By July 11,

1778, he had them and set out, his flag in the one-hundred-gun *Victory*. But his captains had never drilled in unison and were unused to complex maneuvers, and his rear was under the command of a political enemy.

Twelve days later the British and French fleets espied each other, sixty-six miles west of the island known in Great Britain as Ushant and in France as Ouessant, and in midafternoon on a foggy day the action began.

Maneuvers lasted into the evening. D'Orvilliers could then have used the cover of night to sail out of reach, but instead did something difficult, sailing around the British and obtaining the weather gage, the position with the wind behind them, which was considered the best for mounting an attack. He was able to complete that maneuver because he had experienced captains, including La Motte-Picquet and François-Joseph-Paul de Grasse, both recently promoted to commodore. During the maneuver, however, two of d'Orvilliers's capital ships strayed, so at dawn he had fewer ships and fewer cannons than Keppel.

As firing commenced, both sides employed the tactics characteristic of their respective royal navies, the British aiming low and firing as their ships dipped, sending their carronades into the opposing hulls, and the French aiming high and firing, as their ships rolled back, with langrage to shred the enemy's masts and sails. The action produced more than one thousand casualties, but the British ships emerged more battered and unseaworthy than the French ones. During the next night d'Orvilliers doused his ships' lights, except for three sets—one appearing to be on each edge of his squadron and the third in the center although they were only three vessels—and in darkness managed to slip away with the rest of his fleet. At dawn Keppel realized that the French lights had been a ruse and that it was too late to catch d'Orvilliers.

While neither combatant fleet had subdued the other, England, as Ségur would later write, "too long accustomed to naval triumphs, considered it a defeat, because we had not been beaten; while France seemed to claim the victory, because she had not received a check." Keppel had wasted the opportunity to destroy the French fleet; he had not sunk or captured a single French vessel. Recriminations followed. He and the commander of the rear third of his fleet accused each other of cowardice and dereliction of duty. The French celebrated because d'Orvilliers had demonstrated that the Royal Navy was not invincible. As for the United States of America, its future as an independent country was made more certain by the outcome of this faraway battle.

In late July 1778, near Newport, Rhode Island, a first land and sea battle pitting the allied French and United States forces against their British enemies was shaping up—and the American commander was not ready for it.

Two years earlier the British had occupied Newport, on Aquidneck Island in Narragansett Bay, an anchorage that British naval commanders considered the best on the eastern Atlantic Coast, able to accommodate even the largest-draft ships and ideally situated to control the rebellion, for in a day or two's sail a flotilla could be at Boston, New York, or Philadelphia. Since then American forces had threatened but not recaptured the town. On March 10 Congress permitted Washington to relieve the Newport area commander and appoint Major General John Sullivan, thirty-eight.

A lawyer and New Hampshire member of the Continental Congress, Sullivan was one of a dozen brigadiers, each from a different colony, appointed to high command. He had seen action at Bunker Hill and was captured on Long Island, reportedly with pistols in both hands until surrounded. Sullivan was known as a fierce fighter, but in March 1777, after he had complained to Washington more than a few times, the commander had to set him straight: "Do not my dear General Sullivan, torment yourself any longer with imaginary slights, and involve others in the perplexities you feel on that score—No other officer of rank, in the whole army has so often conceived himself neglected—slighted, and ill-treated, as you have done—and none I am sure has had less cause than Yourself to entertain such ideas." After Brandywine, when other officers accused Sullivan of not performing adequately, Washington came to his defense and during the long winter at Valley Forge put him in charge of building a bridge over the Schuylkill. Sullivan completed that task and then beseeched Washington for a post "where there was Even a probability of Acquiring Honor." Washington awarded him Newport.

When Washington had first discussed Newport as a target with d'Estaing, he had an eager candidate to replace Sullivan, Horatio Gates. "A certain Northern heroe gave His Excellency several broad hints that if he was sent upon the Newport expedition great things would be done," Nathanael Greene wrote to Sullivan. "But the General did not think proper to supercede an officer of distinguished merit to gratify unjustly a doubtful friend." Leaving Sullivan in place, however, saddled Washington, as a recent Sullivan biographer puts it, with a commander "admitted to be temperamental, overly sensitive, and hot-tempered, even by his contemporary friends and subsequent admirers." Perhaps Washington was relying on Sullivan's good relationship with Lafayette, his subordinate at Brandywine, whom Washington was sending to Newport at the head of a phalanx of troops, or on Sullivan's knowledge of the French language. Still, in expecting d'Estaing to share command with the roughneck Sullivan—and the wet-behind-the-ears Lafayette—Washington was presuming too much on his partner's reserves of benevolence. On the other hand, the target, Newport, became a motivating factor for d'Estaing when he learned that its garrison was commanded by the brother of the man who had jailed him in India.

Sullivan and his senior officers, who had had only a few days' notice of the imminent arrival of the French, agreed that even their combined forces would not be ready to attack Newport—they must wait until they were joined by Lafayette's men and the militias. These were coming, but slowly, the muster including a Rhode Island unit of blacks to whom the legislature promised freedom in return for service.

Laurens waited for the French at Point Judith, forty miles south of Providence at the mouth of Narragansett Bay, accompanied by pilots and escort whaleboats to assist d'Estaing's fleet when it appeared. On the morning of the twenty-ninth, the fog lifted and the appearance of the French fleet "was as sudden as a change of decorations in an opera house," Laurens wrote. He delivered to d'Estaing a Sullivan letter containing a plan for a joint attack, which had the French coming from one side of Aquidneck and the Americans from the other, first assaulting Butts Hill, the high point, and then turning against the garrison.

This was a reasonable plan but an affront to the French as it had not been made jointly and disregarded protocol and right of precedence. As a modern biographer of d'Estaing comments, matters involving Sullivan and d'Estaing, from the first moments "revealed difficulties, stemming as much from the character of d'Estaing as from the jealousy of Sullivan." D'Estaing wanted to land his marines immediately and challenge the British garrison. A believer in the value of surprise, he was frustrated because the Americans would not join an immediate attack; he wrote later that the days lost in waiting for the militia and Lafayette's troops "were the most favorable ones, the precious moments of the arrival, when all are astonished, and most frequently no one resists." D'Estaing used the time to obtain water, food, and hospital beds for the ill French—nearly half of his forces.

Lafayette's arrival on August 4 was a conundrum for d'Estaing, since as a loyal officer of the French court he was duty bound to arrest Lafayette and return him home in irons. But in the year since Lafayette had fled France, news of his battlefield exploits at Washington's side had made him a hero to the French populace. Moreover, in Narragansett Bay Lafayette was acting as an American officer. So d'Estaing welcomed Lafayette, and he, aware of the difficulties occasioned by his presence, became inordinately helpful to the admiral, aiding in establishing the hospital and transferring sick troops. He also worked hard at assuaging d'Estaing's amour-propre, almost giggling with him as he contended that Sullivan's plan of attack would be just a "comedic" opening act to the "grand spectacle that your fleet and troops will provide."

Lafayette ran into resistance from the American officers with his own plan for the attack, to have the best of the American troops join with him and the French marines. When the American officers objected that this would force their overreliance on untrained militias, as Laurens told his father, the marquis became "dissatisfied" with the discussion and "withdrew his attention wholly from the general interest." D'Estaing raised the stakes on the joint venture, warning Sullivan: "I dare hope that Your Excellency . . . will put it in my power to give an account to the King and to the Congress of the Number and goodness of the troops that you shall have joined to the French," adding that it would be a first occasion to provide Louis with "authentic proof of the value which [the Americans] set upon the alliance of His Majesty."

Sullivan then willfully usurped French privilege. A day in advance of the scheduled joint attack, upon learning from a British deserter that they had abandoned Butts Hill and withdrawn to Newport, Sullivan landed his troops and occupied that high point. This annoyed d'Estaing, more so than Laurens could bear. He wrote to his father that the French officers took "much umbrage" and "talked like women disputing precedence in a country dance instead of men engaged in pursuing the common interest of two great nations." D'Estaing, suppressing his irritation, conceded that the high point needed to have been seized, and landed his troops. Together the French and Americans readied themselves to begin a siege.

Almost as soon as they did, the curtain of fog lifted to reveal another dramatic sight: an enormous British fleet standing off the bay. Admiral Howe had arrived with thirty ships including eight ships of the line, some from Byron's squadron that had been redirected from New York to Newport.

D'Estaing was incensed that the Americans had not warned him of the imminent arrival of a fleet that they had been closely watching for in New York. Fleury, one of the translators on scene, in a report to Sartine said nothing about that anger, commenting only that the admiral, having "sensed the gravity of the situation," decided to take the battle to the open sea, where he could bring to bear his own capital ships, which were larger than those of the British. Sullivan was of course disappointed in d'Estaing leaving port to fight at sea—any delay in the allied assault would allow Clinton to send more land forces to frustrate it—but understood. Fleury wrote that d'Estaing "did not hesitate to give chase" to Howe, and Sullivan soon informed Washington, "I had the pleasure of seeing [the British fleet] fly before [d'Estaing]," after the count had promised that once he had defeated Howe, he and his ships and marines would return and help Sullivan capture Newport. By the next afternoon, d'Estaing's fleet was in position to do battle with Howe's squadron. Then a hurricane struck and blew both fleets to pieces.

Fleury wrote that before that storm had arrived d'Estaing had been about to win the battle, but a less partisan post-battle assessment judged that while "the British admiral [had] maneuvered adroitly, d'Estaing— an army officer who comprehended very little of the complexities of maneuvering at sea"—had not.

For ten days Sullivan, Laurens, Fleury, Lafayette, Greene, and the American troops had no idea where the French fleet was, and spent their time attending to the damage on land from the two-day hurricane, which had upended tents, ruined ammunition, and otherwise caused great destruction. Sullivan commented to Washington:

> To combat all those difficulties and to surmount all those obstacles, require a degree of temper and a persevering fortitude which I could never boast of, and which few possess in so ample a manner as your Excellency. I will however endeavour by emulating the excellence of your example, to rise superior to the malevolence of fortune.

On August 20 parts of the French fleet reappeared. Laurens met them and was soon writing a long report to his father explaining that the *Languedoc* was dismasted and rudderless, and had had to resist a British fifty in that condition. "Imagine the cruel situation of the Count to see his ship thus insulted, after having arrived in the midst of the English squadron and preparing for a combat in which victory was inevitably his."

He then broke off the letter because "The council of war on . . . the French vessels have determined the squadron ought to go immediately to Boston to refit. I am going on board with a solemn protest against it." Laurens and others pleaded with d'Estaing for two more days so that their combined forces could win Newport. D'Estaing demurred, believing that the well-entrenched enemy could not be ousted in two days. When Sullivan continued to protest, Estaing informed him: "The express orders I have from the King direct me in case of [facing] a superior force to retire to Boston."

Sullivan sent d'Estaing's letter with that phrase to Washington, along with his own assessment of what actually drove d'Estaing's retreat: "It Seems That the Captains of the French Fleet are So Incensed at the Count Destaings being put over them he being but a Land officer that they are Determined to prevent his Doing any thing that may Redound to his Credit or our advantage." More likely in this instance was that d'Estaing, as a recent biographer suggests, was a "victim of the state," keenly aware that disregarding instructions and engaging in battle would get him pilloried at home. But d'Estaing also understood, as he had written to Gérard in advance of action in America, that in collaborating with the Americans "The least act of feebleness or timidity might be very fatal."

Exiting Newport abruptly certainly had the appearance of timidity, regardless of d'Estaing's reasons for doing so, and the action quickly drew from Sullivan a letter that assailed d'Estaing with the worst charges he could level—"abandoning" the Americans, an action "derogatory to the Honor of France . . . & destructive in the highest Degree to the Welfare of the United States of America & highly injurious to the Alliance." Sullivan added, "This must make such an unfavorable impression on the minds of Americans at large, and create such jealousies between them and their hitherto esteemed allies, as will in great measure frustrate the intentions of His Most Christian Majesty and the American Congress."

D'Estaing read the letter and underlined the words, "hitherto esteemed allies," a phrase that encapsulated Sullivan's insults.

"Would you believe," Lafayette wrote d'Estaing after the admiral's departure for Boston, "they dared summon me to a council where they protested against a measure taken by the French squadron? I told those gentlemen that . . . whatever France did was always right . . . and that I would support those sentiments with a sword that would never have been better employed." Lafayette's next letter was less irate, having understood the deleterious consequences of the fleet's abrupt withdrawal, which caused disheartenment and desertion in the American militias. He advised d'Estaing that the incident "need not mean falling out with General Washington and Congress, the two great movers of all our undertakings." D'Estaing must hasten his return to Newport, for only then would the French be "able to revenge ourselves on the English by punishing their insolence and on the Americans by forcing their admiration."

Washington, apprised of what happened, acted very much as the only adult in the room. He wrote to Lafayette:

> I feel myself hurt also at every illiberal and unthinking reflection which may have been cast upon Count d'Estaing. . . . In a free & Republican government . . . every Man will speak as he thinks, or more properly without thinking—Consequently will judge of Effects without attending to the Causes. It is in the nature of Man to be displeased with every thing that disappoints a favourite hope, or flattering project, and it is the folly of too many of them, to condemn without investigating circumstances.

But Sullivan had already sent copies of his letter to the newspapers. In Boston it spurred street fights with French soldiers and sailors. A French naval lieutenant attempted to intervene in one brawl after two of his sailors were grievously hurt defending a bakery they had set up on shore. It remained unclear whether the instigators of the fracas had been British provocateurs, British sailors from American privateers in port, or Americans; in any case the fight ended with one French lieutenant's skull smashed in. The stunned city fathers apologized for the death, tried to curtail further ruffian activities, and pledged to build a monument to the lieutenant bearing the inscription, "May any comparable efforts to separate France from America have a similar outcome."

On August 26 Sullivan, at Lafayette's urging, sent new orders to his men: "It having been supposed by some Persons that the Commander in Chief meant to insinuate that the departure of the French Fleet was owing to a fixed determination not to assist in the present enterprize. . . . The General would not wish to give the least colour for ungenerous and illiberal minds to make such unfair interpretations." He sent Lafayette to Boston to hurry the French fleet's return. The ships were not ready. D'Estaing offered to lead his troops overland from Boston to help Sullivan—to himself "become a colonel of infantry, under the command of [Sullivan] who, three years ago, was a lawyer, and who certainly must have been an uncomfortable person to his clients." The offer was not accepted.

Sullivan decided anyway to make an attempt on Newport. His troops, under Greene, some led by Laurens and other seasoned officers, did not take the garrison but acquitted themselves well. After Washington ordered a full retreat because British naval reinforcements were en route, Sullivan accomplished it without incurring additional bloodshed. In these battles the daredevils Laurens and Fleury were again wounded, and the Rhode Island black unit performed with valor. The morning after the American retreat, one hundred British ships did appear off Newport.

Steuben, who had also undertaken at Washington's request a mission to Newport to calm Sullivan, returned to headquarters and wrote a note to Gérard perfectly summing up the Franco-American alliance thus far: "America has declared herself independent and France has recognized that independence; but it seems to me that neither one nor the other has taken solid enough measures for the conservation of that title."

12

"Take a bit of courage, have a bit of patience, and all will go well."
—José Moñino, Count of Floridablanca

The partners had had the sort of falling-out—a result of pique, missed signals, and unfortunate circumstances—that makes both partners miserable but does not obviate the bond that initially connected them or their hope that it will do so again.

Vergennes was still attempting to buttress the future of that alliance. His efforts centered on inducing Spain to join it. The initial roadblock was an unexpected Spanish offer to France and Great Britain to mediate the American war. Was this a genuine proposal to end the war or a ploy to postpone what Vergennes believed to be Spain's inevitable entrance to that war at the side of France? His annoyance had risen in midsummer of 1778, when Floridablanca hinted to London that Spain's neutrality could be bought. France had little to gain by entering a bidding war for Spain's participation, so Vergennes bided his time, and in the fall Floridablanca let Vergennes know that Carlos III had become impatient at the slowness of Great Britain's response to the mediation proposal.

Yet the Spanish king and his first minister were not unhappy at the lackadaisical pace of affairs because they knew that in Spain as a whole there was a notable dearth of enthusiasm for entering a war on the side of America. The Spanish populace feared the potential spread of American-style rebellion to South America—in Quito, Ecuador, there had already been tax revolts against Madrid similar to those that preceded the American Revolution. Also, neither Spain's army nor navy was as fully recovered from the devastations of the Seven Years' War as France's. When Montmorin, France's ambassador to Madrid, tried to learn whether Spain would eventually enter the war, Floridablanca offered only a cryptic message: *"Prenez un peu de courage, ayez un peu de patience, soyez sûr que tout ira bien"* (Take a bit of courage, have a bit of patience, and be certain that all will go well).

Lafayette was trying to help the alliance too. In the wake of the Newport debacle, he planned a voyage home to France to obtain additional troops, ships, and money for America. Congress commissioned a ceremonial sword for him; he accepted the honor with his usual grace, asking only that his workmen in France be permitted to fashion the sword, as they better knew the family's devices. While waiting to depart, he issued a personal challenge to Lord Carlisle over the insults to Louis XVI contained in the Carlisle commission's letter to Congress. Carlisle refused the duel on the grounds that the offending language had not been personal but was part of a diplomatic argument.

Lafayette's other task before leaving was to keep the Canadian pot simmering.

He distributed a letter to "my Children the Savages of Canada," saying that he was returning home for a bit but that he would come back to lead them to freedom. Your American and French "fathers," he wrote, "want to take the thirteen states with one hand and Canada with the other in order to join them together against our enemies." While still in Boston awaiting a ship, Lafayette discussed an invasion of Canada with d'Estaing, who apparently did not dismiss the notion out of hand despite having instructions to do so. He dutifully matched Lafayette's proclamation to French-speaking Canadians, exhorting them: "You were born French [and] you have never ceased to be French." Not long afterward d'Estaing and his squadron departed for the Caribbean, aiming for St. Lucia, toward which, he had been recently informed, a British squadron had just sailed from New York. The admiral vowed to Washington and Congress to return next year and help rid America of the British.

By year's end, Steuben was almost finished writing and illustrating a manual of regulations, drills, and model orders for the Continental army. Washington believed that his forces had been overreliant on British army rules that were wildly inappropriate to a citizen-filled army in a republic, and had given Steuben the task of constructing a new set. Steuben could have used as his only source the Prussian regulations that he knew well and prized, but as a student of military affairs he recognized that the most recently overhauled code was France's, and sought to incorporate French regulations in the manual. He hired Fleury to help interpret those rules, du Ponceau to translate his prose into English, and L'Enfant to illustrate it. The manual's practical aim was to guide field commanders during combat, but the document was also deeply philosophical: The first objective for a captain "should be, to gain the love of his men, by treating them with every possible kindness and humanity." The resulting "blue book," so named for the color of its cover, was a testament to the professionalizing of the Continental army and its debt to America's French partner.

First impressions often capture the essence of a situation better than longer immersion, whose plethora of detail can obscure. Conrad-Alexandre Gérard landed in the United States with deep positive feelings for America based on his reading of English literature and his exposure to Franklin and Deane; but he was not in Philadelphia an entire week before writing to Vergennes that there reigned in America's deliberative body "*un esprit de parti*" (a spirit of partisanship), with one group constantly negating the activities of the other while all the members were attempting to assure their reelection—activities that made them seem to Gérard as though they were aspirants for places in a permanent aristocracy, not in a democracy. Congress, he concluded, was no longer the institution that Franklin had so lovingly described.

Some of Gérard's instructions were straightforward: have Congress ratify the alliance and sign a document stating that neither country would agree to a separate peace with Great Britain, and to deal with loans and currency questions. More important was Gérard's hidden agenda: to dissuade the United States from any attempt to annex Canada, and thereby to allow Great Britain to make of that territory a buffer to American expansion; and for the same reason to encourage Congress to yield to Spain's wishes to control the Mississippi River and the Gulf of Mexico.

This was a rather stunning program. While France desired that its partner obtain full independence, at the same time France wanted that partner, after independence, to be geographically hemmed in, fearing that if it were not, it would become the next great power and threaten France's resurgent dominance. In Gérard's first few months at Philadelphia he had to push aside this agenda while he dealt with more immediate problems, such as Congress having neglected to officially turn down the Carlisle commission proposals. In September he convinced them to do so, and also prevented Congress from openly discussing Sullivan's rash letter of anger at d'Estaing; he reported to Vergennes that he had "neglected nothing . . . to establish a just opinion of the conduct of the Comte d'Estaing."

Then Gérard had to direct his energies to the plight of Silas Deane.

For three weeks after landing in Philadelphia, Deane had basked in the glow of a warm welcome home from Washington and Congress, but the latter's benevolence began to fade once he formally asked to make his report. He appeared in front of that deliberative body by invitation on August 14 but was not permitted to utter a word; his testimony was delayed, rescheduled, and tabled until the late fall, by which time the full scope of the Lee-Adams attack on him had become apparent. The accusations against Deane echoed two recent imbroglios involving other former members of Congress, one in which a quartermaster general was accused of abusing his post for profit, and a second in which the chief of the medical division was charged with selling army hospital supplies to private buyers. In treating Deane poorly, Congress disregarded his having facilitated the military supply of America at a critical moment in the Revolution, his negotiating of the Franco-American alliance, and the contract that entitled him to a fee on transactions he made on behalf of the American government.

Deane had done nothing more untoward in mixing private and public business than had every quartermaster, procuring agent, and commissary chief in charge of securing goods for the Continental services. His pillorying by Congress was not so much about his perceived lapses of financial rectitude as it was a fight between Congress's "Gallician" and "anti-Gallician" factions. Gérard became involved in it because the question was raised as to whether Deane and Beaumarchais had laid out money for supplies and were now owed for them, or whether these activities had been funded by Louis XVI as a gift to America. The emissary could not allow Congress to mistake the intentions of his sovereign. But he needed an opening to make his case, and Deane provided one in December 1778. After five months of being prevented from presenting his report to Congress, he decided to issue a public explanation to end the rumors of dereliction of duty. In the *Pennsylvania Packet* he accused the Lees of trying to destroy him and of being anti-French and of seeking reconciliation with Great Britain, and he charged Congress with partisan unfairness in its refusal to let him report. Congress then entertained a motion to condemn Deane. It failed by one vote. Asked in another motion to allow a rebutting letter, already printed in the *Packet,* to be read aloud, the members defeated that motion, too, by the same margin. These impasses upset Henry Laurens, who denounced Deane's comments as derogatory to

Congress and resigned as president. To replace him Congress settled on a compromise candidate, a former member from New York, absent for two years but just returning: John Jay.

The brouhaha also occasioned a step over the line of propriety by Tom Paine. Writing in the *Packet* as "Common Sense," in an open letter to Deane and in seven follow-up articles Paine cited supposedly secret letters to the Committee of Secret Correspondence, for which he served as secretary, to contend that "the stores which Silas Deane and Beaumarchais pretended they had purchased were a present from the Court of France, and came out of the King's arsenals."

Such disparagement of France's intentions spurred Gérard to enter the controversy. For him to remain on the sidelines would have allowed Congress to impute the wrong motives and actions to Louis XVI, so he asked Paine to retract his statements. Paine wrote back:

> My full opinion is, that whether Mr. Deane had been there or not, those supplies would have found their way to America. . . . It is my wish, it is my earnest desire, to lead the People of America to see the friendship of the French Nation in the light they ought to see it; they have deserved much from us of friendship and equal benevolence.

For a day Gérard was relieved, but then Paine returned to the attack in a new "Common Sense" article that continued to muddy the distinction between Deane's alleged improprieties and French goodness. The emissary's formal protest quickly resulted in Congress summoning Paine and the publisher of the *Pennsylvania Packet* to testify. Morris, whom Paine had also taken to savaging in the later articles of his series, demanded that Paine be fired as secretary of the committee. Ten days of very public accusations and recriminations followed, in which Paine had cause to rail about precisely the sort of treatment that Congress had visited upon Deane, a refusal to permit him openly to state his case and have it debated. During this period, Paine indignantly refused a bribe of one thousand dollars a year to write articles lauding France. On January 16, 1779, Paine felt forced to resign to avoid being fired. Congress's secretary then wrote to Gérard that the legislative body rejected Paine's negative claims about the work of Deane, and reaffirmed the sanctity and generosity of the Franco-American alliance.

Gérard took this acknowledgment as opportunity to successfully lobby Congress to pass a resolution, on January 7, 1779: "Resolved . . . these United States will not conclude either truce or peace with the common enemy without the formal consent of their ally first obtained." Although this understanding had been implicit in the Franco-American treaty, to have it so baldly stated in an official congressional resolution was a notable Gérard accomplishment.

"Why was not Gen Washington pursued after Brandywine," Carlisle had pressed the British generals in New York before departing for home. "Why was nothing done against him all the winter [of 1777–78] when he was so near with an inferior force. Why was nothing done in May when his force was dwindled and not above 4000." Not receiving acceptable answers, when Carlisle returned to London he exhorted the government to action on what he considered the more perilous problem, "the French interference":

> The Question is no longer which shall get the better, Gt. Britain or America, but whether Gt. Britain shall or shall not by every means in her power endeavour to hinder her colonies from becoming an accession of strength to her natural enemies, and destroy a connection, which is contrived for our main ruin and might possibly effect it, unless prevented by the most vigourous exertions on our part.

That fitted well with the proclivities of George III. Despite the British public's eagerness for peace with America so that British energies could be wholly devoted to beating the French, the king still wanted to crush the American rebels. The cabinet devised a way to do both. Great Britain would direct most of its military might toward the wider war, while utilizing in America resources already in place and shifting their focus to the South. Its "Southern strategy" was built on a pyramid of assumptions. The base was the belief that Georgia and South Carolina were full of Loyalists and therefore could be easily reconquered. Once the British were in control, the Loyalists there would readily take over the tasks of governing—a second assumption—freeing the troops for the next-level task, ousting the Americans from North Carolina and Virginia. The third assumption was that total control of the southern states would so substantially cut the Continentals' funding that it would end the rebellion.

In mid-December, taking advantage of the restored British naval supremacy along the Atlantic Coast from Nova Scotia to Florida, Clinton dispatched a convoy to Savannah bearing 3,500 New York Loyalists, Hessian mercenaries, and the Seventy-First Highlanders. Earlier in the war the British had tried and failed to capture Charleston, a similar coastal city one hundred miles north of Savannah. To avoid repeating the mistake of a direct assault on such a city, the British troops were landed south of Savannah and trekked through concealing swamps until they emerged within striking distance. The American commander spotted the British, realized he was badly outnumbered and outflanked, and ordered Savannah evacuated. The British forces marched in on December 28, and then pursued the Continentals, killing 83 and capturing 483. A few weeks later, joined by other British forces that had been roaming north Florida, they marched almost unopposed to Augusta and took that state capital. Modest numbers of Loyalists did apply to join the British military ranks, which seemed to validate London's "Southern strategy" for winning the war against the rebels and breaking up their alliance with France.

D'Estaing arrived in the Caribbean in January 1779 as he had at Philadelphia the previous July—too late to accomplish his mission. The British had already seized St. Lucia. He proceeded to engage Admiral Byron's fleet in a series of battles. Each side sought to protect its most recent conquests, the British of St. Lucia, and the French of Dominica. In these encounters, d'Estaing was once more quite cautious, spurring Bougainville to complain to his diary, "What comfort our indecision, our endless delays and our wasted maneuvers are giving to the enemy!" In the naval encounters the French suffered seven hundred casualties, far more than the British, but there was very little net effect on either side's control of territory.

Once de Grasse came on the scene, however, Byron made no further successful moves on French possessions. Later in the spring, a small squadron under the Marquis de Vaudreuil and a larger one under La Motte-Picquet joined d'Estaing and de Grasse.

The Caribbean was now well defended by the French.

The cost of doing so was high, but it was not the largest fraction of France's naval budget, the bulk of which, many tens of millions of livres, was being spent to protect French territory, a fact that finance minister Necker emphasized as he attempted to fill the treasury with lottery receipts. His appeal to the public to buy the tickets stressed that the lottery revenues would go toward protecting the patrimony and specifically not to underwrite the American partnership. Actually, figuring in the cost of the fleets and the bill for bivouacking twenty thousand French troops on France's northern coast to protect it and for a potential invasion of the British Isles, the total amount of money committed solely to defending French territory dwarfed the amount of livres France was extending to supply the armed forces of the United States. Moreover, much of that latter sum was being spent in the place and in the manner that foreign aid almost always was, in the home country, in this instance to buy outmoded French armaments.

The importance attached by the American government to Lafayette's return to France to obtain more help was emphasized by the resources committed to it—America's largest warship, the *Alliance*, captained by Pierre Landais, a French naval officer who had been serving with the American navy. The voyage was not an easy one. Off Newfoundland the *Alliance* nearly foundered, and when it was approaching the European coast, Lafayette and Landais were threatened by a plot of some sailors and junior officers (none born in France or America, Lafayette would note) to take over the ship and deliver the famous passenger to Great Britain. "Only an hour before the plot was to be carried out, we called together the officers and a few trustworthy men and climbed, sword in hand, up to the deck while others among us seized the cannons."

On arrival in France Lafayette sped to Paris, where he was relegated to "the confines of the Hôtel de Noailles [which] were thought preferable to the honors of the Bastille, which was first proposed." Still a criminal in the eyes of Versailles, he nonetheless held interviews with Franklin, Adams, and others on schemes to aid the United States and punish Great Britain, and assured Vergennes and Louis XVI, by separate letters, that he was his majesty's "very humble and very obedient and faithful subject." A slap on the wrist for his prior disobedience followed; there could be no harsher punishment because his popularity had become immense.

Nor could Vergennes do much to punish Spain for its truculent neutrality or to move it toward the American alliance. "I will not dissimulate, Sire," Vergennes wrote to Louis XVI. "The views and pretensions of Spain are gigantic." When he had pressed the Spanish to name their price for war, he was told that Carlos III desired a large-scale, joint invasion and conquest of Great Britain, utilizing the combined Bourbon fleets. This was anathema to Vergennes's vision of a war undertaken to reduce but not eliminate British power. However, since France had little to lose and much to gain from humoring Spain, he went through the motions of planning an invasion, down to advising Floridablanca that the combined fleets would have 107 capital ships to Great Britain's 92.

Spain, still playing the would-be-mediator card, had requested definitive bottom-line demands from France and Great Britain. France had only one, and it was furnished early and it was nonnegotiable: the guarantee of the independence of the United States of America—this, for France was "a point of honor," as Montmorin told Floridablanca. The British demands, when they finally arrived, were that France must stop all aid to the United States, summon home d'Estaing's fleet, and agree that Britain would continue to control New York, Newport, and other areas of America. There was not a word about American independence.

The belated and inflexible nature of the British response finally convinced Floridablanca, in January 1779, that Great Britain did not seriously desire mediation. Accordingly, he told Vergennes, Spain would now negotiate the terms on which Carlos III would enter the war at the side of his nephew, Louis XVI, and only incidentally at that of France's partner, the United States of America. Since Floridablanca refused to draw up a list of what Spain wanted as the price of alliance, Vergennes, Maurepas, and the king made one for them. It included plans for an invasion of Ireland by a combined thirty thousand Franco-Spanish troops, and a guarantee that neither Spain nor France would lay down arms until American independence was achieved.

Floridablanca deemed the demand for American independence "useless" and "out of place," and the invasion proposal insufficiently large. Vergennes continued to plan an invasion that he hoped would never occur: "If we succeed [by our preparations for invasion] only in interrupting Britain's trade, you may depend on it that the resultant alarm and despondency will be as great as if we had landed in some part of that island," he told a confidant. When he demanded that Spain provide half the troops, Floridablanca responded that Spain would pay more but would furnish no soldiers. Lacking enough troops to conquer England, Vergennes proposed to start with Ireland, where the Irish hated British rule. "They may be won with the bait of establishing that democracy which they worship so fanatically," Vergennes noted. To hurry that plan along he sent over to Ireland, as a spy and emissary to rouse the Irish to revolt, an American in Paris who had Irish roots, and whom he and Lafayette agreed was perfect for the job: Dr. Edward Bancroft.

. . .

In February 1779 Gérard in Philadelphia had an unpleasant task, to put to Congress Spain's insistence that America declare its willingness to accept a truce in which the opposing armies would remain in control of the territory they currently occupied so that Spain could negotiate a peace. He tried to position this demand as a de facto Spanish recognition of American independence, which it was not. Gérard stressed to Congress that the United States must prepare for peace even while waging war. A few days' discussion should settle the American agenda for peace, he thought, and urged the Americans to constrain their demands to the physical boundaries of the original thirteen colonies, plus any additional land held when negotiations began.

He was surprised when Congress embarked on a very protracted debate. The northeast states wanted Newfoundland and Nova Scotia included in American demands, while Virginia and Pennsylvania wanted the Mississippi River. Gérard worried to Vergennes that underlying all was a growing American dissatisfaction with the new country's finances, as exampled by depreciating "Continentals" (the government-issued currency) and rising taxes. He forwarded a copy of a Maryland resolution in which that state refused to become a signatory to the Confederation so long as the tax moneys it would pay in were to be spent out of state. If France and Spain were to rescue the American Revolution, Gérard advised, they had better act soon, and together.

By March 1779 Vergennes and Floridablanca were close to a deal but they fundamentally disagreed on an article in the compact that in Vergennes's wording would have Carlos III declare, "He will recognize the independence of the United States of America, either by acceding purely and simply to the [Franco-American] treaty . . . or by some other pubic act." Floridablanca crossed that out but substituted a pledge that Spain would procure for the United States "all the possible advantages" from U.S. conquests and not stand in the way of France fulfilling its treaty obligations to the United States. Other Spanish provisions called on

France not to sign a peace treaty until Spain obtained Gibraltar, Minorca, and the American Floridas, and had kicked Great Britain out of all enclaves in the Gulf of Mexico.

On April 12, in the royal palace at Aranjuez, south of Madrid, Floridablanca and Montmorin signed the alliance. Its existence was kept so secret in Spain that only the king and Floridablanca knew of it, and they persuaded Louis and Vergennes not to discuss the alliance with the French military, pending receipt of the British final response to Spanish mediation. Six days later Louis XVI ratified the treaty.

Vergennes worried about the remaining hurdle, the Spanish ultimatum to Great Britain, because the Spanish proffer was so reasonable: separate cease-fires, one for Great Britain and France, and another for Great Britain and its former colonies, neither of which truce could be broken without a year's prior notice; general and mutual disarmament on lands and seas; and a peace commission to negotiate changes in territorial boundaries.

In early May of 1779, Montmorin had good news for Vergennes: "Fortunately . . . England . . . has cut through all the difficulties" by rejecting the Spanish ultimatum. The signing of a treaty to end the Bavarian succession crisis cleared additional potential obstacles to joint Franco-Spanish action, as it freed the Bourbon powers to focus on a new enemy. Spain would now enter the war against Great Britain. It would not be directly allied with America, but its participation was expected to benefit the United States. As that news reached America, Washington learned from Gérard that d'Estaing would soon be returning and had requested suggestions as to where to direct his force. In response Washington invited Gérard and Spain's representative, Juan de Miralles, to visit him at Valley Forge, promising that they would receive a thirteen-gun salute, review the troops, and with him plan for d'Estaing's return.

In the summer of 1779, while awaiting d'Estaing the American forces feinted and clashed with the British on land, mostly in small encounters. One had as its focus Stony Point, a dozen miles downriver of West Point, seized during the spring from Continental hands. The fort, on a promontory 150 feet above the river, was approachable only through an underwater marsh and a steep slope. Atop the British had added abatis—felled and sharpened branches—and redoubts whose cannons could rake climbing attackers. "I do not think a Storm practicable," Wayne advised the commander, and Washington agreed. But a new series of provocative British raids changed his mind; he authorized a sally, put Wayne in charge of it, and assigned Fleury to assist.

Steuben had trained the American battalions in the use of the bayonet, which the silence and darkness of the attack's design would require. To induce the men to undertake such a high-risk attack, awards of up to five hundred dollars would be given to the first five men to enter the inner redoubt. "Forlorn Hope" trailblazer battalions, twenty men in each, would carry heavy axes to dismantle the abatis. Fleury would lead one trailblazer. They found the underwater marsh to be chest-deep rather than the expected two-foot depth, but managed and ascended the slope without incident. Fleury was the first through the abatis. Surprising the British, he quickly seized and hauled down the Union Jack, then yelled to the men, "The fort's our own!"

Fleury and four Forlorn Hope companions received the promised prizes, plus bonuses based on the capture of the fort's two hundred thousand dollars' worth of provisions. That Stony Point was less an important military victory than a high-value morale builder was underscored by Washington's decision, a few days later, to abandon it as requiring too many scarce resources to defend. Congress recognized the battle's importance, however, by authorizing Fleury to receive one of the very few medals it awarded to military personnel during the entire Revolutionary War. Like Lafayette's sword, this token of esteem was also to be made in France, and to receive it Fleury was granted leave to return home.

The Abbé Raynal's *Two Indies* book, with its extensive sections on America, had continued to sell briskly and had become the major reference for literate French and Spaniards on their new ally—Lafayette, for example, had read it on his first crossing to America. Franklin and Deane met Raynal in Paris; Deane pointed out to the abbé several egregious factual errors in the book; and Franklin told him that an American speech that Raynal had cited, supposedly made by one Polly Baker, who had birthed a handful of illegitimate children, had been fined each time for doing so, and sought mercy from a court—a speech admiringly cited through the decades by many writers on American social conditions before Raynal had put it in his book—was a hoax that he, Franklin, had concocted. "My word," Raynal reportedly responded. "I would rather have included your tales in my book than many other men's truths." Raynal's and the encyclopedist Denis Diderot's meetings with Franklin and the American commissioners resulted in some changes in the 1779 edition of the *Two Indies* book. One was particularly noted, a caution, based on the American Revolution's illumining of the contrasts between the hope of the New World and the oppression of the Old World to which France, Spain, and Great Britain belonged:

> A mine is prepared under the foundations of our abuses, the materials for the collapse are gathered together and heaped up, formed out of the relics of our laws, of the clash and ferment of our opinions, of our lack of valor, of the luxury in our cities, of the misery in our countrysides, of irreconcilable hate between the vile men who possess all the riches, and the vigor of those who have nothing to lose but their lives.

Though France was not named as the locus of those observations, in the kingdom of Louis XVI they were close enough to the bone to be considered treasonous, forcing Raynal to have the new edition printed in Geneva. Booksellers in France were forbidden to carry the work, and troops were forbidden to read it.

13

"What a wonderful opportunity is slipping from our grasp."
—Comte de Vergennes

Each new war expends a great deal of effort to undo the results of the previous one. D'Estaing could not return to the American coast until he had carried out orders to recover territory in the Caribbean lost by France to Great Britain in the Seven Years' War and to acquire equivalent new territory from Great Britain. In an attempt to capture Barbados, one of the largest British wealth generators, in June 1779 d'Estaing sailed in strength, his twenty-four ships of the line incorporating the de Grasse, Vaudreuil, and La Motte-Picquet squadrons. They carried 5,500 marines; among them was Lafayette's brother-in-law Noailles, finally getting into the action—ostensibly on behalf of America—that he, Lafayette, and Ségur had long ago imagined.

The winds were unfavorable to invading Barbados so d'Estaing went after Grenada, at the southern end of the Lesser Antilles, French until 1763. His marines stormed Grenada's Hospital Hill, overwhelming the outnumbered locals and causing the desertion of many slaves to the French ranks. In the notice of the feat sent to Sartine, d'Estaing recommended Noailles for the Croix de Saint-Louis, one of France's premiere medals for military valor.

Admiral Byron, upon learning of the recapture of Grenada, sailed to counter d'Estaing. A large-scale battle ensued. The British seized the weather gage, but the French, maneuvering smartly, were able to severely damage six British vessels, one limping into port with "ninety-five Holes intirely through her Sides," as a newspaper account put it. The day's action was later deemed the greatest setback for the Royal Navy since 1690, for d'Estaing had also taken the Grenadines, a chain of small islands between Grenada and St. Vincent.

He then headed to defend Guadeloupe, French since 1763. Byron's fleet had already occupied that island's harbor and could not be easily dislodged or lured out to fight by the French insultingly parading their ships just outside the anchorage, all flags flying. D'Estaing shifted to another of his missions, to ferry convoys of merchantmen to a point in the Atlantic from which they could cross to Europe untroubled by privateers. This duty, too, Versailles had dubbed essential, since the merchantmen's cargoes would translate into the most important annual infusion of treasure to the treasury.

Only after shepherding those convoys could d'Estaing set sail for America. He was returning to the United States because he felt morally obligated to do so, not because of orders, since Sartine had directed him to come back to Europe, if possible conquering along the way Nova Scotia and Newfoundland. D'Estaing interpreted his instructions to mean that he could voyage near the coastal United States, where he knew he might bump into the enemy and aid the ally. D'Estaing tried to excuse in advance, to Sartine, a dalliance in America by suggesting that "if we only go [to Savannah and Charleston] and show ourselves, this will produce an effect which I believe will be of the greatest importance."

But he thought he could do more. "There is every reason to believe," Washington had written Gérard in a letter for forwarding to d'Estaing, that in Georgia the admiral "would with great facility capture & destroy the enemy's fleet & Army." And d'Estaing was also influenced by a missive from a former musketeer who was now the leader of his paid troop in South Carolina: "It is necessary to defend [this area] against its enemies and against itself. All is in lamentable condition, few regular troops, no assistance from the North, a feeble and ill-disciplined militia, and a great lack of harmony among the leaders." Thus summoned and enticed, d'Estaing departed on August 16, 1779, for Savannah, with twenty ships of the line, seven frigates, other troop transport ships, and 3,500 troops.

Just then, a potential invasion of Great Britain's home islands was taking shape in the English Channel. It had been awhile in coming. Lafayette had learned of an invasion in the late winter, at Versailles, perhaps from Louis XVI as the returned prodigal and his king hunted together, or from Marie Antoinette, who was quite taken with the marquis and liked to trade in secret information. But the precise plans for the grand invasion were taking so much time to come to fruition that Lafayette suggested to Maurepas he first attempt small-scale raids of England with a highly trained force of fifteen hundred. Lafayette's model, then the talk of Versailles, was a similar-size French force known as Lauzun's Legion—for its leader, a nobleman of equally distinguished lineage, the Duc de Lauzun—which had just wrested Senegal from British control.

Franklin, not privy to the grand invasion plans, was enthusiastic about the modest Lafayette caper, and added a most important element: "Much will depend, on a prudent & brave Sea Commander who knows the Coasts, and on a Leader of the Troops, who has the Affair at Heart," he wrote to Lafayette as prelude to recommending John Paul Jones, then upgrading the old ship that Jones had renamed in Franklin's honor the *Bonhomme Richard*. Jones told Lafayette: "I shall expect you to point out my Errors when we are together alone with perfect freedom. Where men of fine feeling are concerned there is seldom misunderstanding." It was in regard to this mission that Jones had recently boasted to Chaumont, "I wish to have no connection to any ship that does not sail fast; for I intend to go in harm's way," a sentiment likely to flutter the heart of a Lafayette. The marquis wanted Pierre Landais to accompany them, having developed a high respect for the captain when together they had quelled the mutiny aboard the *Alliance,* and he also wanted the fast-sailing *Alliance.* The French navy lent an additional complement of ships. But Chaumont warned Jones, "You shall not require from [these extra] vessels any services but such as will be comfortable with the orders that [their captains] shall have," which included making no changes to the French vessels' crews or armaments, since those captains must be fully "answerable to those who have armed them."

On May 22, Lafayette's part of the adventure ended, and for the best reasons. As he explained to Jones, the king had reassigned him to a larger command in a full-scale invasion of Great Britain, scheduled for summer. Jones quickly redefined his mission and on June 19 departed Lorient in the *Bonhomme Richard* with the *Alliance* and the rest of his train. Problems began immediately, as Landais steered his ship into Jones's, and more arose when it became apparent that the *Bonhomme Richard* was too slow. Changes at sea to the rigging and ballast added a half knot to its speed, but not enough to allow Jones to give proper chase to two British convoy escorts. As he wrote to Franklin, the British "courage failed, and they fled with precipitation, and to my mortification outsailed the Bonhomme Richard and got clear."

The much larger invasion mission was experiencing even greater difficulties in getting to the point of weighing anchors. Even before the signing of the Aranjuez treaty, Vergennes had tried to hurry military preparations for the grand armada and the invasion of Great Britain, despite not wanting such an attack. It became an essential part of the deal with Spain, and so after the signing he redoubled his efforts, keenly aware that for the invasion to succeed it must take advantage of two rapidly closing windows: The combined Bourbon fleets' superiority over the British navy, which would be eclipsed within six months by the frenetic pace of British capital shipbuilding, and the six weeks of relative calm weather that the English Channel experienced in the early summer, which would dissipate with the onset of an annual series of harsh storms on August 1.

Louis XVI, king of France (top),
and his foreign minister, Comte
de Vergennes (bottom), decided
to aid the rebels in America even
before the Declaration of
Independence was signed.

Charles Gravier   Comte de Vergennes

The playwright Caron de Beaumarchais (top left), through a fictitious company underwritten by France and Spain, worked with Silas Deane (top right) to supply munitions that enabled the American victory at Saratoga in the fall of 1777. Then negotiations in Paris by Benjamin Franklin (bottom left), Arthur Lee (bottom right), and Deane rapidly led to the Franco-American pacts of February 1778.

At Brandywine Creek (top left), Americans were joined by French officers, several of whom were wounded during the defeat. In a lesser-known but important action, Major François de Fleury held Fort Mifflin on Mud Island (bottom) long enough to delay the British for the winter. Fleury's later heroics at the Battle of Stony Point won him a Congressional Medal, one of only six awarded in the war (modern version, top right).

General George Washington, pictured reviewing troops at Valley Forge with the Marquis de Lafayette (top), had earlier longed for strategic counsel. Broadly experienced advice from Brigadier-General Louis Duportail (bottom), who became chief of the American Army Corps of Engineers, and from other French officers, helped him avoid mistakes and fashion a Fabian strategy to preserve the army.

Coeffure à la Belle Poule

The *Belle Poule* incident at sea in June 1778 gave France reason to declare war on Great Britain, and was celebrated at Versailles by a coiffure (top). That summer, the Comte d'Estaing, seen here in a cartoon as the preserver of America (bottom), led French naval forces in a failed attempt to oust the British from Newport, Rhode Island.

The Comte De Grasse's victory in the Battle of the Virginia Capes (top), and French naval control of Chesapeake Bay allowed Franco-American land forces to surround Cornwallis's at Yorktown. In the culminating siege, French cannon (center) played an important role. French casualties at Yorktown on land and sea exceeded American ones. The Rochambeau, Washington, and De Grasse joint victory of 1781 was commemorated in a 1931 stamp (bottom). Placement of French and American forces (map, opposite) reflected strict instructions from Louis XVI that French forces allow precedence and the right side of the battlefield to American command.

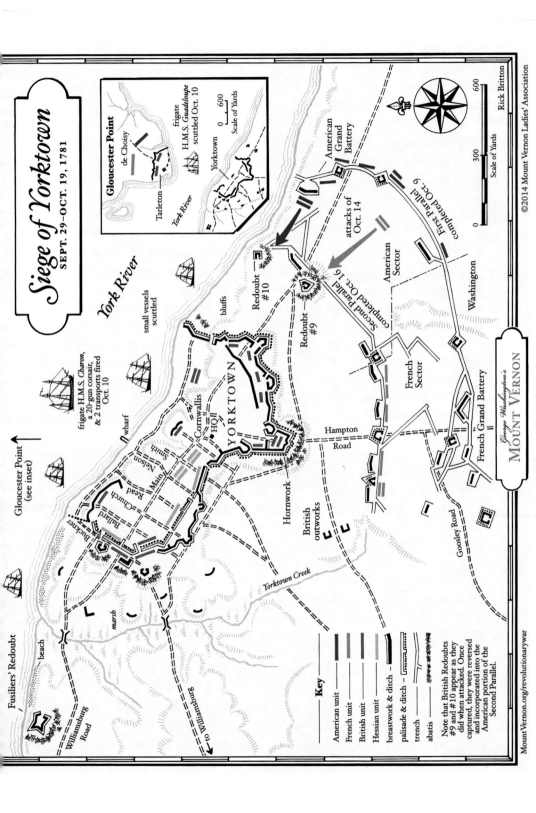

Siege of Yorktown
SEPT. 29–OCT. 19, 1781

York River

Gloucester Point (see inset) →

Gloucester Point (inset)
de Choisy
Tarleton
frigate H.M.S. Guadeloupe scuttled Oct. 10
Yorktown
York River
0   600
Scale of Yards

frigate H.M.S. *Charon*, a 20-gun corsair, & 2 transports fired Oct. 10

small vessels scuttled

bluffs

wharf

YORKTOWN

Cornwallis
HQ
Nelson
Smith
Main
Read
Church
Ballard
Buckner

American Grand Battery

First parallel completed Oct. 9

attacks of Oct. 14

Redoubt #10

Redoubt #9

Second parallel completed Oct. 16

American Sector

Washington

French Sector

French Grand Battery

Hampton Road

Hornwork

British outworks

Goosley Road

Yorktown Creek

marsh

Williamsburg Road

to Williamsburg

Fusiliers' Redoubt

beach

Key
— American unit
— French unit
— British unit
— Hessian unit
‑‑ breastwork & ditch
▭ palisade & ditch
▬ trench
abatis

Note that British Redoubts #9 and #10 appear as they did when attacked. Once captured, they were reversed and incorporated into the American portion of the Second Parallel.

Rick Britton

©2014 Mount Vernon Ladies' Association

0   300   600
Scale of Yards

George Washington's **MOUNT VERNON**

MountVernon.org/revolutionarywar

In 1782, peace negotiations to end the Revolutionary War began in Paris, between America and Great Britain, and separately among France, Spain, and Great Britain. Benjamin West's painting of the Anglo-American negotiations remained unfinished because the British contingent refused to sit for it. From left to right: John Jay, John Adams, Benjamin Franklin, Henry Laurens, and William Temple Franklin.

Initial plans called for the French to sail first, from Brest, in early May, to meet up in Spanish waters with the Spanish fleets by midmonth, and then to spend a couple of weeks perfecting joint maneuvers before in June all moved toward the English Channel and from there made a rapid strike; the expedition was not a "question of a *guerre de campagne* [an extended campaign] but only of a *coup de main* [a surprise attack]."

Among the many factors affecting the attack's potential success was the presumed willingness of the Irish to throw off the British yoke and join with the invaders. Bancroft, sent to assess that possibility, returned with the disappointing news that the prospect of a Franco-Spanish invasion had driven the Irish back into the embrace of Great Britain. No help could be counted on from that quarter.

Naval delays of the armada were initially due to Carlos III's insistence that military officers in both realms not be made aware of negotiations before the treaty was signed. Additional delays resulted from the Spanish admirals' resistance to having the French fleet guide their actions, and from Spain's ships being far less ready for battle than those of France. A military aide to Montmorin toured the ports where the Spanish ships were being readied, and his assessment was dismal: crews recruited from convicts; old Scottish cannons that few knew how to maintain; poor-quality supplies from Russia; flimsy hemp from the Netherlands; and admirals either over the hill or known to be irresolute.

Delays mounted when Spain categorically refused to sail until war had been declared, something that could not occur prior to the completion of the time-honored sequence of delivering an ultimatum, having it rejected, and then withdrawing ambassadors. The Madrid government wasted time accumulating a list of grievances for the British to reject and then dallied in its deliverance. Finally Vergennes realized that Madrid would not hand over that list unless and until the French fleet had left Brest.

Then it was the French fleet causing the delays: D'Orvilliers told Versailles that he was unable to sail in May because of an incomplete upgrade to the *Ville de Paris*, from ninety guns on two decks to one hundred ten on three, necessary to counter the largest British ships. On June 4 the French fleet finally sailed, and six days later reached the rendezvous off Spain's Atlantic Coast, but during the next six weeks the Spanish fleets did not join them. The discouraging delay was attributed partly to the weather but more to the Spanish admirals' distaste for the French. Then, too, Spain decreed it necessary to wait not merely for the list of grievances to be delivered and rejected in London but for the news of the rejection to travel to Madrid and then to the port and the ships. Moreover, Spain's prime target for invasion had shifted: It was much more interested in a joint Franco-Spanish attempt on the island of Gibraltar. That action began on July 11 and involved fourteen thousand Spanish troops and fifteen warships.

On d'Orvilliers's ships, during six weeks under the broiling sun off Spain's western coast, pestilence broke out—smallpox, dysentery, and scurvy, made worse because there were no surgeons; in the haste to depart Brest they had been left behind. Some 12,000 of the 23,750 men aboard became seriously ill, and there were many deaths. Then d'Orvilliers discovered that the Spanish ships did not have the agreed-upon signals to enable him to direct them during a battle.

As for the army of invasion, by July its 31,000 French soldiers had been distributed into dozens of camps in Normandy, with embarkation positions at Le Havre and Saint-Malo. De Broglie did not like the altered invasion plans and had refused to lead it. After his departure that army, nominally under the command of a seventy-four-year-old marshal, was actually led by Rochambeau, whose warrior single-mindedness provoked Lauzun to write that he "talked only of feats of arms, and demonstrated positions and executed movements out-of-doors, indoors, on the table, or on your snuff-box if you took it out of your pocket; without an idea outside of his profession, he had a marvelous grasp of that."

Everyone in the nobility wanted in on the invasion, even the Chevalier d'Éon, who offered to ditch his petticoats and again don a military uniform—a violation of the conditions that had let him return to France as a female. That request was denied, just as his earlier one, to serve in America, had been. Lafayette advised Vergennes that he was providing "twenty million to support the paper currency, ten million to pay for an expedition, and ten to pay the interest on a general repayment" of the loan floated to buy supplies for the invasion.

Near the end of July a series of gales blew sails to shreds and kept the fleets from the Channel. Vergennes wrote to Montmorin: "Blackness overwhelms me. . . . What a wonderful opportunity is slipping from our grasp, without anyone being to blame! England, without resources or allies, was on the point of being taught a lesson; success seemed within our grasp . . . but the elements are arming themselves against us and staying the stroke of our vengeance."

"The disunion of the two parties who divide the Congress increases and exasperates each other more and more. They lose on both sides the points of view of discretion and moderation," Gérard was writing to Vergennes just then from Philadelphia. He had been recalled, but before returning home the emissary was determined to settle America's peace terms. The Lee-Adams faction continued to insist on Newfoundland's fisheries being included on the list, and to threaten that the New England states would leave the confederacy if they were not. Gérard cautioned Congress that the fisheries were not a part of the Franco-American pacts. When he queried Vergennes on the matter, the foreign minister's response was quite tough:

> 1) that the King is actually the only guarantee of the Independence of the thirteen United States; 2) that this guarantee is only eventual as regards their possessions; 3) that the United States have no actual right to the fisheries; 4) that the King neither explicitly nor implicitly contracted an obligation to let them participate in them; 5) that they can have a share in them only insofar as they assure themselves of them by arms, or through a future truce or peace.

On July 24, after both Samuel Adams and R. H. Lee had left the deliberative body, Congress voted to omit the fisheries from the list of conditions for peace but, as Henry Laurens suggested, to make them essential in postarmistice discussions.

In mid-August the sizable Franco-Spanish armada entered the western end of the English Channel, expecting to engage and conquer the British Home Fleet and clear the way for the invasion. D'Orvilliers wrote to the ministry: "The combined [fleet] is at present anchored in calm waters within sight of the tower of Plymouth. . . . It is most important to hasten the battle, particularly as the condition of the French ships is worsening daily, as regards both the disease running rampant in them and the small quantity of water and rations they possess."

While the land troops waited for the armada to do its work, Franklin dispatched to Le Havre his seventeen-year-old grandson, William Temple Franklin, bearing the ceremonial sword commissioned by Congress for Lafayette; Temple wanted some military glory for himself, and Lafayette obliged, attempting to obtain Franklin's consent for the boy to be his aide-de-camp during the invasion. In another letter Lafayette advised, regarding a feeler Franklin had received to go to London to negotiate a peace, that the offer would result in nothing because "whatever is prudent for [the British] to do, they will omit; and what is most imprudent to be done, they will do it." He could have cited as the latest evidence of this that the British had passed over experienced, aggressive commanders to appoint as the new head of the Home Fleet Admiral Charles Hardy, sixty-five, who had not been to sea in twenty years.

And that, despite London having been aware of French and Spanish invasion designs since early spring and having obtained such specific information as the names of troop unit commanders, the number of troopships, the quantity of stores aboard them, and the main targets, Portsmouth and Plymouth.

The British preparations were almost as inept as the French and Spanish. Lord North had sent the information about the French-Spanish plans to George III in a locked box; the king had lost the box's only key, and a locksmith had to be summoned to break it open. Once the king read the materials in the box and understood the danger from the combined fleets of France and Spain, he offered to take active command of the British forces on land during the invasion.

That proved unnecessary. No large-scale invasion of the British Isles took place. Nor did any climactic sea battle, although the combined French and Spanish fleets did get into the Channel and sail about in late August and part of September, when, infrequently, they could best the wind. Fogs contributed to the absence of action. On several occasions, the Franco-Spanish fleet and the British one narrowly missed each other. As significant a contributing factor was the commanders' timidity. A tough observer aboard Hardy's flagship wrote of him, in words that could also be applied to the French and Spanish admirals in this endeavor, "He means to take as small a share of responsibility upon himself as possible . . . to procrastinate as long as he can and when he is obliged to act he will make Ministers responsible for the consequence if he fails."

The largest armada assembled since 1588 for invading Britain came to naught—at a cost to France of one hundred million livres, much more than had been expended to aid the American rebels. Lafayette, summing it up in a letter to Congress, acknowledged that the Franco-Spanish invasion of Great Britain had failed, but at least it had "exhausted England and detain'd at home forces which would have done much mischief in other parts of the world."

The big invasion produced nothing, but John Paul Jones's was still in the offing, though it had been delayed. In June and July, while the *Bonhomme Richard* was being repaired in Lorient, Jones had taken on additional hands, including former British sailors, and had to put down a potential mutiny by some of them. He also became ill. In early August, Sartine had dispatched Chaumont to the port to hasten Jones's departure—and to meddle in the captains' willingness to obey Jones's commands. On August 9 Jones quickly left dockside and on August 14 passed the outer anchorage with the *Bonhomme Richard,* the *Alliance,* two French privateers, and three other French warships.

Once the small squadron was out of the harbor, one French privateer decided not to continue. Jones was powerless to halt his defection. The remaining six ships proceeded toward the Irish coast, taking several merchantmen. Problems cropped up everywhere, from Landais, whose ship fired at Jones's, from the polyglot crew—the Irish members stole the flagship's barge and rowed themselves ashore—from the desertion of another French naval vessel, and from the veering off of the second French privateer after capturing a prize and wanting to get it into port.

Jones, at odds with Landais, nonetheless continued to take merchantmen and menace the coast. "Not a day passed but we are receiving accounts of the depredations committed by Paul Jones and his squadron," according to a letter that soon appeared in the *London Evening Post.* Jones then landed at Leith, Edinburgh's seaport, aiming to exact a two-hundred-thousand-pound ransom in exchange for not burning the town, which was defenseless; but when the wind died suddenly Jones and his captains decided to return aboard and row themselves away, lest they be caught by the Royal Navy. Similar attempted raids and narrow escapes followed until September 22, when off the Yorkshire coast Jones spotted a fine target, a convoy of forty merchantmen. Able to seize some of them immediately, Jones learned that they were being guarded by two Royal Navy vessels, the larger being the *Serapis,* listed as forty-four guns but that Jones believed had between forty-six and fifty, mounted on two decks. In the ensuing fight off Flamborough Head, *Serapis*'s cannons ripped through the *Bonhomme Richard* so thoroughly that it was close to foundering, causing the British captain to ask Jones if he had struck his colors; he famously replied: "I have not yet begun to fight." Ramming his ship into the *Serapis,* Jones then had his men grapple on, and they fought the British hand to hand in one of the most sanguinary close encounters of the war, which left nearly three hundred of the six hundred men dead. An exploding American grenade ignited gunpowder kegs and put *Serapis*'s cannon out of action. Its captain surrendered just in time for

Jones to transfer into it with what remained of his crew and their prisoners, which he did because the *Bonhomme Richard* had become unstable.

An isolated victory, Jones's feat was militarily insignificant, but in a season in which the larger invasion of Great Britain and the Franco-Spanish armada had come to such utter failure it was a notable success. The feat transformed John Paul Jones into a hero and it justly celebrated his crew, which included many French sailors as well as those of a dozen other nationalities.

Among the British reactions to the Franco-Spanish near-invasion were doubling the size of the militias, eliminating many loopholes through which young Britons had been able to avoid military service, and making conciliatory overtures to Ireland to abate rebellion, including the easing of exclusionary practices against Catholics. In France the combination of Franklin, Adams, and finance minister Necker—Protestants all—began to advocate for similar elimination of second-class treatment of Protestants, and progress was made on that front.

Liberalizing in France had repercussions in America. It assisted congressional supporters of the Franco-American alliance by stripping from the anti-Gallicians the use of the canard that they intended to take over America and force Catholicism on its citizens. The anti-Gallicians found another opening when it became necessary to dispatch a plenipotentiary to Madrid. Jay was nominated, but the antis kept bringing up various objections that became confabulated with the Silas Deane/Arthur Lee impasse and took time to resolve. Finally Jay was approved, Lee was dismissed from his previous post, and Deane was offered a payment of $10,500, which he rejected as an attempt to buy him off for a few cents on the dollar.

In October 1779 Jay and his wife embarked for Spain on the same ship returning Gérard to France. Jay had decided that because of Lee's poor reception by Madrid he must now approach Spain gingerly, going first to Paris and from there applying for entry. Once at sea, a storm necessitated changing course; in the argument over whether to head for the Caribbean or reattempt a more direct crossing, Gérard and Jay disagreed, and finished the voyage as less than friends.

"I don't know what can be done regarding America," Vergennes wrote Lafayette in the fall of 1779 at Le Havre, where the marquis had remained. "Our plans can no longer be unilateral; they require a preliminary agreement. It is obvious that the concern for America's welfare requires that troops be sent, but that alone would not be doing enough." He added a complaint about the Americans: "We hope they will have exerted themselves more than they have done up to now." He excepted from this complaint the John Paul Jones victory, and the one at Stony Point that, he noted with pride, had been led by Lafayette's colleague and friend Fleury.

Shortly Fleury returned to France and at Lafayette's urging completed a memo of his time with the Continental forces, to which he appended comments on what should be done next. It echoed Vergennes in contending: "America is in a state of crisis that is alarming but not hopeless," and went beyond the minister in its insistence that France could best prevent the states' reconciling with Great Britain by "sending arms, clothing, money, or more assistance."

To combat the British danger to the southern states, the American Congress passed an act authorizing South Carolina and Georgia to "raise three thousand able bodied negroes" to supplement the states' regulars and to pay slave owners a thousand dollars for each slave who passed muster. A New Hampshire delegate recognized the implications of the congressional edict as laying a "foundation for the abolition of slavery in America." To lead the new regiment Congress tapped John Laurens. His father allowed him to use in this regiment as many of the family's slaves as circumstances permitted. But John was sidetracked in the establishing of the regiment by the need to defend Charleston from British sorties, and was joined in this effort by Pulaski's cavalry, which had also been sent south. Throughout the summer of 1779 the American forces managed to keep Charleston in American hands and to reject the British demand for surrender. Still, the civilian leaders of South Carolina refused to go along with using the state's slaves in a Continental regiment. His father wrote to John, "I learn your black Air Castle is blown up, with contemptuous huzzas."

In mid-August 1779, Admiral d'Estaing was about to depart the Caribbean for America. "I know I have been disobedient," he wrote to Maurepas after being accused of breaches of protocol in the conquest of Grenada. "I beg you to recommend that [the warden of the Bastille] give me, upon my return, commodious lodgings."

Such insolence was characteristic, and was further expressed in d'Estaing's attitude toward his forthcoming American mission: He was willing to help, but not to do too much. Although Washington had deemed it well within the d'Estaing force's capabilities to wrest Savannah from British control, the admiral committed himself only to staying at Savannah for a week before going on to Halifax and Newfoundland. But on September 1, when upon reaching the mouth of the Savannah River he was able to surprise and capture a few British vessels, he decided he might do a bit more before moving on. Then a hurricane struck, wrecking d'Estaing's fleet. Several weeks would be required, he learned, to obtain adequate new timbers for the repairs. "The damage done to my ships," he wrote to Sartine, "has imposed on me the melancholy necessity of acting where I should not and did not wish to act."

But he did not act immediately, thus disobeying for the second time his own tenet that surprise was the best asset of an attacking force. He also made only a halfhearted attempt to avoid repeating another Newport mistake, disregard of an ally's needs. Although he sent Major General François de Fontanges to Charleston to consult with General Benjamin Lincoln, he didn't wait long enough for Lincoln's response. In Charleston, Fontanges and Lincoln had fixed the day of a joint assault on Savannah for September 11, but Lincoln was delayed in reaching Savannah because the Charleston civilian authorities had not wanted him to leave. While Lincoln was en route, d'Estaing, who had not learned of the delays, decided to act unilaterally.

He was encouraged to do so by his progress thus far. After managing, despite a lack of pilots, to broach the mouth of the Savannah River, d'Estaing found the guard island abandoned. The British had withdrawn eighteen miles upriver to the city itself. Upon reaching there, the French counted twenty-three cannons behind the city's barricades, and soon saw that the number was growing daily as General Augustine Prevost augmented his fortifications through the work of several hundred of the city's slaves, which went on day and night. As a French officer wrote, Prevost's situation was fortunate, since by virtue of having swamps on two sides of the city, and British cannon-laden ships in the river, Prevost "had nothing to fear from the rear, or from the right and left. It was necessary therefore to provide for the defense only of the front or southern exposure of the city." Nonetheless, d'Estaing demanded that Prevost surrender the city to the forces of Louis XVI. Prevost had not yet responded to the surrender ultimatum when Pulaski's cavalry arrived in the Savannah area, ahead of Lincoln's troops from Charleston and also of another small American army that was coming from mid-state. Pulaski did all that was possible to overcome such obstacles as a dearth of ferryboats—he had his men dismount and swim their horses across the river, after which they "so thoroughly cleared the way, and broke up all the enemy's advanced posts, as to afford Major General Lincoln the opportunity of an interview with the French General . . . on the 16th." Before that interview could take place, Prevost stalled and d'Estaing did not press. The stalling paid off, for the very next day eight hundred British troops from Beaufort managed to slip through both the American and French lines to join Prevost inside the city.

Only then did Lincoln arrive. Apprised of the situation he expressed annoyance that d'Estaing had asked for surrender in the name of the French king only, which brought out old American fears of the French taking over. Lincoln demanded the sending of a new surrender note with his signature added to d'Estaing's. The admiral obliged, but now the reinforced Prevost rejected the ultimatum. French and American leaders then blamed one another for having allowed the extra British troops to slip into the city, Fontanges in such a blistering way that d'Estaing was certain that John Laurens, his hotheaded American friend, would surely challenge Fontanges to a duel. Laurens did not rise to that bait, having learned better than d'Estaing the third lesson of the Newport debacle, the peril of taking undue offense at an ally's remarks.

The American and French commanders then jointly made a poor decision, to besiege the city rather than storm it, even though they had better resources to storm it, 7,000 men to the defenders' 4,800. Their siege began classically with the digging of entrenchments, the time-honored tool for creeping ever closer to barricaded positions. British sorties destroyed almost all trench progress as soon as it was made, and at one point caused French and American troops to mistakenly fire on one another, with resultant casualties. When Noailles and his unit attempted to storm a British redoubt, mistakenly aimed French firebombs forced them to retreat.

Lincoln and d'Estaing did not get along, although for different reasons than those that had set apart the French nobleman from Sullivan at Newport. The admiral, according to one of his officers at Charleston, "always knows how to make jokes in the least amusing circumstances," in contrast to Lincoln, who neither drank nor cursed and was notably fastidious, much more so than the raucous Sullivan. D'Estaing contemplated abandoning the siege but understood, as he later wrote: "If I had not attacked Savannah, I would have been considered a coward. London, America, and even Paris would have done more than dishonor me. They would have supposed I had secret orders not to assist the Americans."

The poor results of the allies' sporadic sallies seemed to justify d'Estaing's reluctance to attack in force. During one sally, on September 22, the diarist officer noted that a Noailles lieutenant, "carried away by his courage, disregards the instructions . . . and, being incautious, rushes straight upon the enemy, attacking with full force a post that should have been taken by surprise." On the twenty-fourth, a larger endeavor also met with disaster:

"Our imprudence in leaving our trench to pursue [six hundred British troops] exposed us to the artillery fire of their redoubts and batteries, and caused the loss of seventy men killed or wounded."

On October 4 d'Estaing began a bombardment by fifty-three heavy cannons and fourteen mortars, "with more vivacity than precision," the diarist wrote, attributing the miscues to the gunners having imbibed too much rum the previous night. They took great return fire, too, not only from the 23 emplacements that the French had seen upon reaching Savannah but also from the 123 that Prevost had since amassed. On October 6, as the Franco-American bombardment continued Prevost asked for permission to remove women and children from the city; d'Estaing and Lincoln refused, fearing another stalling ruse. By then, a month since the hurricane, d'Estaing's ships had been somewhat repaired, and he felt the need to soon set sail or be bottled up by worsening weather. Seven of his ships had already lost their rudders, and scurvy and other ills were consigning some thirty-five men a day to watery graves. Moreover, as the diarist noted, "We begin to lose confidence upon discovering that all this heavy firing will not render the assault less difficult. We should not have constructed works. In doing so, we afforded the English time to strengthen theirs. We regret that we did not attack on the very first day."

Both d'Estaing and Lincoln continued to assert that the siege and bombardment would soon produce surrender. Laurens sent word through a messenger to Washington that it would only be a matter of two or three days. On October 8 L'Enfant, serving under Laurens, attempted with a small group to set fire to the abatis. The wood was still wet and the fire did not take. He suffered burns.

D'Estaing called a council of war at which his chief engineer said that he required ten more days to complete the entrenchments, which time d'Estaing could not afford. Lincoln insisted that they now either make a direct assault on the defenses or abandon the siege. D'Estaing agreed to the assault and to personally lead some troops, as Laurens and Pulaski would also do. Fontanges's corps of volunteer black Haitians was to be in the thick of the battle; a d'Estaing written order called for people of color to "be treated at all times like the whites," because since they aspired "to the same honor, they will exhibit the same bravery." Also in the mix would be a French regiment composed of Irishmen, and another of Hessians and British deserters.

On the eve of the attack d'Estaing decided suddenly to reorganize the French troops, putting many of the soldiers under new officers. The ensuing muster was sloppy and delayed the attack beyond the most advantageous hour.

Prevost was more than ready for them. Acting on information from a deserter as to the location of the emphasis of the impending Franco-American attack, he replaced Loyalist militia with seasoned British troops at that vulnerable point. His cannons fired grapeshot, which killed many attackers and mangled even more, including d'Estaing. Fontanges was also grievously wounded, along with many Haitians. Of the Americans, Laurens was one of the first to reach the redoubts, but he and his group were repulsed, along with most other units. As Pulaski and his cavalry were preparing to breach an area between redoubts, the Pole was fatally wounded. After that his men refused to continue. A Noailles-led retreat avoided even more carnage in the French-American ranks. The entire Franco-American attack ground to a halt. It had lasted less than an hour.

During a four-hour truce the combatants collected their dead—in the hundreds for the French and Americans, less than a hundred among the British. D'Estaing, himself among the wounded, vetoed a Lincoln request to renew the assault. The admiral did continue the siege for another week but then felt compelled to reboard his troops and sail away. Shortly, several of his ships foundered in hurricanes and were lost with all hands. Additional large lots of French solders and sailors died from disease even after the fleet separated into several squadrons, some returning to the Caribbean, others (including d'Estaing's and Noailles's) to Europe, with three ships directed to winter over in Chesapeake Bay. De Grasse, upon reviewing the whole d'Estaing expedition, wrote, "Great God! It would have been necessary to have seen it to believe it, and in not saying the

half, we would be thought to exaggerate and be partial. . . . The navy suffered a long time the fruits of that campaign."

The failure to take Savannah put an ignominious end to the Franco-
American campaign of 1779. In a report to Gérard, d'Estaing launched
barbed arrows in every direction—at the former musketeer for the advice to go to Savannah, at Fontanges for telling him the American troops
could do the job, at Lincoln for poor preparation and for not taking out
the garrison at Beaufort, and at his own troops—he complained of not
having enough regulars and having been forced to rely on *"700 mulâtres
et 200 hommes levés dans le rebut des vagabonds de St. Domingue"* (seven
hundred mulattoes and two hundred men lifted from the ranks of vagabonds at Saint-Domingue).

Lincoln, in his report to Congress made a point of lauding d'Estaing
for bravery, courage, and for bothering to make the assault at all.

Because news from Savannah did not travel quickly, Clinton in New
York, upon first learning that d'Estaing was near that city and figuring
that he would next come north, made three decisions: First, not to dispatch four thousand men to the Caribbean, even though that would leave
Jamaica undermanned in case of a potential Franco-Spanish assault. Second, to direct Admiral Mariot Arbuthnot's fleet not to sail to the rescue
of West Florida or British enclaves on the Gulf Coast but to remain in
the New York area and prepare once more to defend Sandy Hook. Third,
to abandon the garrison at Newport without a shot being fired.

But several months later, upon learning that Savannah remained in
British hands and that d'Estaing's fleet had once more quit the Atlantic
Coast, Clinton and Arbuthnot made another decision: to mount an expedition aimed at wresting from rebel hands Charleston, the queen city
of the South and the hub of its economic activity. On December 16, 1779,
the vanguard of eight thousand British, Hessian, and Loyalist soldiers
began to move onto transport ships in New York for a voyage that would
take them to Savannah, from which they could mount an assault on
Charleston.

PART FIVE

Together:
Struggling Through
1780–1781

14

"The country that will hazard the most will get the advantage in this war." — George III

By the turn of 1780 Lafayette had tired of living in Brest among idling troops and returned to Paris to do more to advance the American cause. Frustrated twice in attempts to visit Maurepas, on January 25 he pressed his case in writing:

> The miscarriage of our great preparations in Europe, the defeat at Savannah, the [British] reconciliation with Ireland, perhaps the taking of Charleston: these are the events that will affect the credibility of the cause and the condition of American finances. The total ruin of commerce, the devastation of the coastal cities undertaken by small English corps, the *very dangerous extension* of British power in the southern states, offensive operations undertaken from New York. . . . These considerations . . . make our aid *almost indispensable*.

He was not asking for much for America, in his view, merely a well-equipped corps of six thousand in an appropriate number of warships—after all, France had allocated thirty thousand troops for the aborted invasion of Great Britain. He was less modest in suggesting for this corps a leader who knew both the French armed forces and the peculiarities of American commanders and political representatives—himself.

America needed the help. After five full years of war it teetered on the brink of exhaustion, the states unable to meet their quotas of new soldiers, and with many current ones unwilling to serve beyond their term of enlistment unless paid in a currency they could redeem for a reasonable amount of goods, something they then could not do because of the drastic devaluation of the Continental paper money. Beyond that problem was the resigned cynicism and spreading lethargy that William Bingham had found when after three years in the Caribbean he had recently returned to America: "The sentiments of the people in this country I found surprisingly altered since I left it," he wrote to John Jay, lamenting citizens "no longer governed by that pure, disinterested patriotism, which distinguished the infancy of the contest; private Interest seemed to predominate over every other Consideration that regarded the public weal."

As Lafayette intimated, Charleston was indeed in grave danger, now that Savannah had been taken and no French fleet prevented the British from moving troops along the Atlantic Coast. Having spent time in Charleston on first landing in the United States, he knew of its position in the country's economy—one of the largest ports, a principal gateway for exportation of rice, tobacco, and indigo; should the British take Charleston, they might strangle the United States economically and push for an end to the war on their terms.

Lafayette's friend John Laurens was just returning home to Charleston's defense. The city had less protection from a seaborne invasion than did Philadelphia or Boston, mainly the natural barrier of a sandbar, augmented by a few cannons on a small fort on a peripheral island—no match for determined warships. The resident American navy squadron, even after the addition of the ships left by d'Estaing to overwinter in Chesapeake Bay, was only eight vessels. Three thousand Continental troops were on the way under the direction of de Kalb, but their march had been slowed to a crawl by the most terrible winter in America during the entire eighteenth century. Adding to Charleston's woes, the South Carolina legislature again rebuffed Laurens's proposal to enlist slaves in the army, even though the proposal would have freed the slaves only after they finished their service.

Laurens persuaded the American navy to sail him about to search for the British approach. They found it. Capturing horse transports and reading their manifests, Laurens learned that Clinton was on the way, with 140 vessels and many thousands of men—such a large force that Laurens considered the information suspect. When in mid-February the British fleet was sighted off Charleston, frantic exertions on the defenses followed, directed by two French engineers. In a March 4 note to Lincoln, one echoed the prevailing despair: "It is sorrowful for me to think that I will not be able to do more for this momentous place . . . with the means I have." The navy fled, its commander contending that he could not adequately defend the sandbar. Washington in effect agreed, writing to Laurens, "The impracticability of defending the [sand]bar, I fear, amounts to the loss of the town and the garrison." On April 8, at the time of the highest monthly tide, the unopposed British ships, after offloading cannon to lighten their drafts, passed the sandbar, entered the inner part of Charleston's harbor, took up positions out of range of American cannon and began bombarding the city.

On April 25, Duportail, chief of America's fledgling engineer corps, arrived at Charleston. A few Continental units had threaded their way to the city, but the British had been augmented by a second contingent from New York. Charleston was "in a desperate State, allmost intirely invested by the British Army & Fleet," Duportail later recalled for Washington, adding that he had deemed the fall of the town "unavoidable" unless an Army arrived to the rescue.

Washington had advised Lincoln to trust Duportail completely, but when Duportail counseled Lincoln to evacuate the city because its safety could not be assured, Lincoln could not agree. He had already offered to surrender the city, so long as the Continental forces were permitted to leave it with their weapons, and had been rebuffed. Duportail then asked permission to leave town. Lincoln refused—the engineer's departure would dishearten the troops—so Duportail settled in to do what he could. Among the soldiers he discovered Pierre L'Enfant, still recovering from his Savannah burns. "I attached myself wherever I could do the most service," L'Enfant recalled, working with Duportail and Laurens.

De Kalb's troops were stuck in Virginia, more than four hundred miles north. Trying to acquire provisions, de Kalb, who had been a quartermaster in Europe, complained of the whole enterprise being "attended with many difficulties and delays which it was not in my power to remove as soon as I could have wished."

On May 9 in Charleston, after a terrifying British bombardment, three hundred civilians begged Lincoln to renew negotiations. The Clinton and Arbuthnot surrender terms were very bad: the British forced the Continentals to march out on May 12 with their flags furled rather than unfurled, a procedure that rejected the usual military courtesy, and the British refused another usual courtesy, the parole of senior officers to their country's capital, Philadelphia.

The loss of Charleston was the most devastating defeat for the Continental forces since the war began, with more than 5,500 regulars and militia taken prisoner, including Lincoln, Duportail, Laurens, and many other officers.

Laurens was granted a parole in place instead of being permitted to return to Philadelphia. It reduced him to a "state of inactivity [that was] the greatest and most humiliating misfortune of my life," he wrote Washington. Many French officers were similarly paroled in place and endured what L'Enfant described as "hard captivity." Although they did not have as harsh an imprisonment as the French and American soldiers who languished on prison ships in the harbor, they too were plagued by mosquitoes, inordinate heat, thirst, and hunger. "How many people have reproaches to hurl at Congress, at the state of Carolina, at Lincoln—I do not know who should consider themselves most to blame," Duportail wrote to the French legation in Philadelphia. "Charleston could have been saved or, if the enemy was absolutely determined to have at it, at least they could have been made to evacuate New York. . . . In the sad situation in which I find myself such things become the objects of my meditation and the indignation they give me prevents me from falling into lethargy."

Bingham wondered to Jay if losing Charleston was the "signal misfortune" that would finally rouse the populace to reinvigorated action. He himself took such action, in conjunction with Robert Morris and two other wealthy men; the four Philadelphians and eighty-eight more chipped in 315,000 pounds to create a Bank of Pennsylvania to act as a purchasing agent for the American military. Its first purchase was flour for General Greene's army. Within weeks the banking idea was replicated in Boston and Baltimore. The French were impressed; they could no longer accuse their American partners of being unwilling to truly pledge their fortunes as well as their lives and their sacred honor.

While Americans on the Atlantic Coast thought Spain's entry into the war in the summer of 1779 was an empty gesture, they were mistaken, for that action soon had a direct impact on Great Britain's ability to wage war, through Spain's efforts along the Gulf Coast and in the adjacent lower Mississippi delta. The governor of Cuba transferred Spanish troops to New Orleans for use by Bernardo de Gálvez, and in September Gálvez's Spanish-led force of 650, which included some Americans, some French military, members of several Native American tribes, and freed slaves, attacked British enclaves north of New Orleans, at Natchez achieving a victory without firing a shot. Seized letters confirmed Gálvez's suspicion that the British were reinforcing Mobile, and accordingly in February 1780 he attacked that city. During a bad storm he lost four hundred men and had four ships run aground; undeterred, he salvaged materials and made scaling ladders to reach the fortifications. His siege of Mobile exhausted the British defenders' ammunition and food supplies, forcing a surrender on March 14, 1780.

In April a large convoy of Spanish warships and supplies departed

Cádiz, headed for Havana and to reinforce Gálvez for his assault on the next most important British-controlled target, Pensacola, which he hoped to take in the fall. That spring other Spanish troops at St. Louis, with the assistance of an American army contingent, defeated a substantial British attack by troops from Canada and members of various Native American tribes. On the British retreat north from St.Louis, they raided towns with what the Spanish commander, upon viewing disemboweled and severed corpses, labeled "unheard-of barbarity."

Although these Spanish actions had the effect of helping the cause of the United States by keeping British troops and resources occupied outside the Eastern Seaboard, they had been undertaken by Spain primarily for the purpose of consolidating hegemony over the Mississippi and the Gulf Coast. In Philadelphia, the Chevalier de La Luzerne, the new French plenipotentiary, cheered on every report of these Spanish victories. He had been instructed to tell the Americans that France agreed with Spain that the United States had no right to Florida or to control navigation on the Mississippi, and to warn that in peace negotiations the U.S. would probably have to settle its western boundary at the Ohio River. Congress fumed at this notion. La Luzerne beseeched them "not to lose sight of the principle of equity and moderation which alone could render the Alliance desirable."

In the early spring of 1780, Lafayette's dream team of troops and ships, called the Expédition Particulière, was being readied at Brest, its men under the command of Rochambeau and its warships in the care of Admiral Charles-Henri-Louis d'Arsac de Ternay. The commanders had been told that their destination was America, but they did not tell the troops, claiming that the destination was in sealed orders to be opened only after being at sea ten days. The soldiers and sailors could deduce by the quantity of laded matériel that the goal was far away, but it could as readily be India, Africa, or the Caribbean as North America.

Among the officers was Fleury. On the eve of leaving Paris for Brest he had written Franklin that since he would be unable to receive the medal promised for his heroics at Stony Point, Franklin should please hand it to his father; and also, "The medall voted for me by congress, is a silver one; but I could wish, besides, to have one of gold struck at my own expences. It will not hurt the dies; I leave the money for that purpose in the hands of the medaillist. He will keep the gold medall for me till my Return. I hope you will not have any objection." Franklin had none. Delays in departure allowed Fleury to receive the silver medal; thereafter he wore it constantly.

The single-minded devotion to war that Lauzun ascribed to Rochambeau was also applied by his comrades to Ternay; and a description of Ternay's character as composed of "pride, hauteur, and almost of severity" fitted Rochambeau just as well. At Brest the commanders clashed on what should go aboard, Rochambeau arguing for artillery and horses and Ternay protesting that too much artillery was unwarranted and that horses required too much forage and water. Ternay won on these matters. Rochambeau had wanted eight thousand troops and Ternay, twenty ships of the line, but both had to be content with less. Rochambeau's 6,000 were just four divisions out of more than a hundred, a small fraction of the 250,000 troops of the French army, beyond whom were 50,000 reserves, plus members of the coast guard who could be called to service.

The most precious item carried by the ships would be money, mostly in Spanish pesetas, the rest in letters of credit drawn on Chaumont's accounts in America. It was expected to do more than pay for the French troops; Louis XVI's council understood that financial assistance to America was as necessary to its survival as military assistance.

The yearly cost to the French treasury of the officers in France's military services was 46 million *livres*, and that of the remainder of the soldiers and sailors another 44 million. Those proportions were reflected in the top-heavy Rochambeau army, whose five hundred officers included the son of de Castries, Rochambeau's son and nephew, and kinsmen of other nobles. Only a few spoke English, notably the writer François Jean de Chastellux, the Duc de Lauzun, Noailles (who had spent time abroad), and Rochambeau's aide Baron Ludwig von Closen, and even fewer had past experience serving with American troops. These latter veterans included du Bouchet and Fleury, but not Conway. It had become obvious that Conway would not be welcome in America, so he had been billeted for India. So had Bonvouloir, who had finally obtained a naval commission.

George III also did not know where the Expédition Particulière was heading. "The more I reflect on the fleet now equipping at Brest under the command of M. de Ternay, the more I am led to fix on North America as the most probable object," he wrote, adding, darkly, "The country that will hazard the most will get the advantage in this war." George's encomium to aggressiveness did not stir his Admiralty; while it directed Admiral Thomas Graves to collect a fleet at Portsmouth to counter Ternay's, it did not clear his way. In addition to having problems of supply similar to those of Ternay at Brest, Graves had one more, directly traceable to the Admiralty: The sailors had not been paid, so "There is a disposition in my ships' company to require two months' advance before they go to sea," Graves noted. His impecunious tars mutinied, barricading themselves belowdecks. To pry them out consumed many days. So on May 2, when Ternay and Rochambeau got under way, the Graves fleet was not yet ready, which allowed forty-six French vessels to sweep into the Atlantic unopposed. Only after most of France's sea "horses" had bolted did Great Britain shut the watery "barn door," blockading Brest to prevent the remaining troops from going to America.

By then Lafayette had sailed ahead. To formally take leave of Louis XVI he had worn his American officer's uniform, and in *l'Hermione* he was accompanied by officially provided munitions, including fifteen thousand rifles, shot, and uniforms for the Continentals. The formality, openness, and positive sanction of this 1780 departure were in pronounced contrast to his disobedient, surreptitious escape of 1777.

Lafayette's most audacious recent accomplishment at Versailles had been to dictate Rochambeau's instructions on conducting combat in America. Mirroring the language of earlier Lafayette letters to the ministry, these were repeated in a Montbarrey letter to Rochambeau on behalf of Louis XVI. The most important directive: "The general to whom His Majesty entrusts the command of his troops should always and in all cases be under the command of General Washington."

Here was a stunning instruction to which any French commander might have objected had it not been issued over the seal of the king and stated in such unequivocal terms. The directive was aimed at preventing a recurrence of the mistakes at Newport, in which Lafayette had been a participant. That intent was made even clearer by accompanying instructions: "The French troops, being only auxiliaries, should on this account, as was done in Germany in the campaign of 1757, yield precedence and the right to the American troops." The sentence was specifically designed to resonate with Rochambeau, who had participated in that campaign against Frederick the Great. Standard orders were that during an assault, the right-hand side always had precedence; Montbarrey's letter emphasized this by explicitly stating that on the American battlefield, American officers of equivalent rank to the French would have command.

While the Expédition Particulière was in the mid-Atlantic, Louis XVI sent a message to the French clergy, then holding a "quinquennial" conclave. He demanded a gift of 30 million livres to prosecute the war. Since a year earlier he had asked for and received 7 million from the clergy, this new demand, according to an attendee, "produced at first the most profound astonishment." The king's messenger explained that the various economies introduced by Louis had made it possible to sustain the greatest navy that France ever had, currently fighting in many places throughout the world, at the same time that "the people have been preserved . . . from new taxes." The king required assistance to continue doing both wonderful things. The clergy cried poor but then saw the need to "concur in obtaining liberty of commerce and the safety of the seas."

Near the American coast, Ternay and Rochambeau learned that Charleston had already fallen. Changing course, they arrived at Chesapeake Bay on July 4, 1780. During the night Ternay glimpsed in the fog

unknown ships moving among his; he deduced that they were Arbuthnot's, returning Clinton's men to New York from Charleston—and did
not fight them. Ternay "chose to pass up an engagement that would have
gained nothing [for the expedition] other than personal glory," Rochambeau remembered, and concluded that Ternay was "always occupied
with his main task of convoying the troops to their destination." In the
morning, the interlopers gone, the French fleet proceeded to Newport,
Rhode Island. Arrangements had been made through Lafayette for the
Americans to set signals for them at the edges of Narragansett Bay. If
the French were clear to land, they would see the French flag already flying, but if the British had chosen to return and give battle, then there
would be only the American flag. The incoming ships spied the fleur-de-
lis flag, and with no opposition began to disembark.

15

"My command of the F–Tps at R Is-d
stands upon a very limited state."
—George Washington

When a war widens, its original intent is inevitably subjected to new and different pressures. In 1780, Great Britain's war against its rebelling colonies burst the boundaries of a familial dispute, as British forces had to fight those of France and Spain, in addition to those of the United States, off the northern and southern coasts of Europe, in the Caribbean, in the Gulf of Mexico, on the Mississippi, and off Africa and India. The fate of the American Revolution had always hung in the balance in this war, but now, so also did Great Britain's decades-long dominance of the European powers.

The two became closely linked in the spring. Great Britain had been wooing Empress Catherine II of Russia to become an ally, promising her that at the war's end she would receive such spoils as the Mediterranean island of Minorca. Now, Catherine did more than spurn Great Britain's suit; she declared that henceforth her ships at sea would act as armed neutrals, authorized to resist attempts by any belligerent power to examine their cargoes for contraband and confiscate them, something the British had been doing with impunity. For years Vergennes had urged Russia to defend its honor on those grounds, and now he had further reason to cheer as Denmark and Sweden joined Russia in the League of Armed Neutrality. Very quickly France and Spain agreed to abide by the league's freedom-of-the-seas principles. Great Britain did not. The Netherlands asked the league to guarantee its colonies, which Russia would not do, and so the Netherlands did not immediately join the league. Although the northern powers' strength at sea was negligible compared to that of the Royal Navy, by declaring their neutrality Russia, Denmark, and Sweden deprived Great Britain of allies.

Britain's sea power was also being compromised by its ministers, whose disagreement on where and when to use it occasioned several failures, principal among them permitting the Ternay-Rochambeau fleet to escape from Brest. Another French fleet, led by the Comte de Guichen, seventeen ships of the line, and a convoy of sixty other vessels carrying 4,400 troops, was similarly able to make an unmolested journey to the Caribbean because the fleet of Admiral George Brydges Rodney was busy relieving Gibraltar.

A third significant missed British opportunity allowed a Spanish Caribbean resupply fleet to leave Cádiz on April 28 with twelve ships of the line, eleven thousand troops, and 146 merchantmen and transports. During the six weeks that it took the fleet to cross the Atlantic, it was not harassed, and upon reaching the Caribbean it was shepherded to port by Guichen's ships. This arrival gave to the French and Spanish in the Caribbean a combined superiority of troops and ships, stymieing British plans to capture the French and Spanish sugar islands.

During the summer of 1780, British unwillingness to detach ships of the line to escort British convoys across the Atlantic also resulted in the Spanish capture, near Cádiz, of a convoy of sixty-one British merchantmen whose combined value was put at 1,500,000 pounds.

Another Admiralty failure was having kept Rodney out of action for the previous four years, and for an odd reason—his indebtedness. Early in his career Rodney had made a fortune in the same way that most British naval commanders had done: by being entitled to part of the value of the goods he confiscated on ships that he had captured. But then he had overspent on his estate and in pursuit of a political seat, and in 1774 had had to flee to Paris to escape creditors. Four difficult and fallow years followed for him because of Lord Sandwich's insistence that Rodney repay his debts before being recalled to action, and Rodney's lacking the money to do so. Then in 1778, to Rodney's amazement, just after the signing of the Franco-American alliance but before Great Britain declared war on France, a French marshal offered to pay Rodney's debts, a gift from one gentleman to another. Maurepas and Louis XVI agreed to this extraordinary offer, which enabled Rodney to return to Great Britain and to command.

He began in a spectacular way, encountering and destroying a Spanish squadron on the way to Gibraltar, seizing several ships of the line and causing another to blow up. He then provisioned Gibraltar, which had been on short rations, opened supply lines for that island with Tunisia, and went on to relieve Minorca before proceeding to the Caribbean. News of these Rodney victories cheered London.

John Adams's hiatus from diplomatic work lasted only six months after his return home following a frustrating year in Paris. In the fall of 1779, Congress appointed him minister plenipotentiary, empowered to negotiate peace with Great Britain on terms that Congress had spent the better part of a year debating. Adams considered this appointment as the highest civilian position that the government could then bestow, and delayed his departure only to participate in the Massachusetts convention, for which he had written the state constitution. Before he sailed, he thoroughly researched American documents bearing on matters likely to come up in a peace negotiation, such as America's northern and eastern boundaries, and fishing rights off Newfoundland and Nova Scotia.

Disembarking in Spain toward the end of 1779, Adams, his two older sons, John Quincy and Charles, and his secretary, former representative Francis Dana, made their way overland to Paris. To prevent a repetition of prior cavalier treatment, Adams attempted to have Congress specifically instruct Franklin to pay his expenses and to order all American ship captains to take him wherever he needed to go without checking with Franklin. He also chose to reside in Paris so as not to be under Franklin's thumb at Valentinois.

On February 11, 1780, Adams and Franklin met with Vergennes, and the next day Adams wrote the minister, "I am the only person who has the authority to treat of peace," so "if any propositions on the part of Great Britain should be made to his Majesty's ministers . . . they [should] be communicated to me." For Vergennes this rang a very loud alarm. It reinforced his suspicion, earlier voiced by Gérard, that the Lee-Adams contingent in Congress was attempting to reconcile America with Great Britain. Adams denied that to Vergennes directly, and La Luzerne, when consulted, advised that Adams had become so avidly anti-British that the British should fear him in negotiations.

Balance had seemed about to be restored to the Adams-Vergennes relationship when news arrived in May that further upset it. Congress had radically devalued the American currency, pegging it at forty new Continental dollars to one old one. Chaumont protested to Adams, seeking an arrangement by which the Continental would be devalued at home but remain at par in repaying France for loans and goods previously advanced—a distinction between foreign and domestic creditors that European nations had frequently honored. Adams derided the idea. Then Vergennes agreed with Chaumont, telling Adams, "While I admit, Sir, that [Congress] might have recourse to the expedient [of devaluation] in order to remove their load of debt, I am far from agreeing that it is just & agreeable . . . to extend the effect to strangers as well as to citizens of the United States."

It was a critical moment in the affairs of the two allied countries, a clash of conflicting narratives about a single event; and, as often happens in romantic partnerships, the point of disagreement was money. Each had assumed that the other felt the same way about the debt obligation, and now that assumption was shattered by their disagreement—and the crisis went beyond the money problems and the personal acrimony between Adams and Vergennes. It concerned the future sovereignty of the United

States and its position in the postwar world, matters that Adams had specifically addressed in his model treaty of 1776 and that Vergennes had purposefully ignored in his writing of the 1778 Franco-American pacts. As Adams continued to spar with Vergennes, his xenophobia and rudeness poisoned the atmosphere. Vergennes, the seasoned diplomat, parried Adams by citing his rudeness as reason for Congress to recall the seeming Francophobe as a danger to the alliance. For that purpose, on June 30 Vergennes handed Franklin copies of all of his Adams correspondence and a request to transmit them to Congress and recommend Adams's recall. Franklin too was angered at Adams but would not undermine his colleague with such a recommendation.

But Adams had a way to make a riposte to Vergennes. Henry Laurens, given the task of obtaining a loan from the Dutch, had been captured at sea en route to the Netherlands and was now imprisoned in the Tower of London. Adams had been designated to take over that task. In his last letters to Vergennes before he left for Amsterdam, he hinted that he would use the Dutch city as a base from which to negotiate peace with Great Britain. This, finally, was too much for Vergennes. He informed Adams that he would henceforth deal only with Franklin. By then Adams had departed, telling Franklin that his objective in Amsterdam was learning "whether something might not be done to render us less dependent on France."

When Franklin finally read Congress's actual instructions to Adams (forwarded by La Luzerne to Vergennes, who gave them to Franklin), he apologized to Vergennes: "The Sentiments therein express'd are so different from the Language held by Mr. Adams . . . as to make it clear that [his conduct] was from his Indiscretion alone. . . . It is impossible that his Conduct . . . Should be approved by his Constituents." Then, in a letter to Congress, Franklin rejected Adams's way of dealing with the French:

> This Court is to be treated with Decency & Delicacy. The King, a young and vigorous Prince has, I am persuaded, a Pleasure in reflecting on the generous Benevolence of the Action, in assisting an oppress'd People, and proposes it as a Part of the Glory of his

Reign; I think it right to increase this Pleasure by our Thankful Acknowledgments; and that such an Expression of Gratitude is not only our Duty, but our Interest.

Adams's difficulties with Vergennes were exceeded by Jay's with Floridablanca. Jay's original plan had been to come to Paris and from Paris apply for Spanish credentials. But when his ship was forced by bad weather to Cádiz, he decided it would be silly to exit Spain only to then seek admission, and so sent missives to Madrid saying he was America's official representative. Floridablanca replied that until "the manner, the forms, and the mutual correspondence" concerning the relationship of Spain to the United States had been established, "it is not proper for your Excellency to assume a formal character." As a sop, Floridablanca encouraged Jay to come to Madrid anyway. When Jay did, he and Floridablanca clashed, partly because Jay said just the wrong thing to him: Jay tried to press Congress's wish to control navigation on the Mississippi. This ran afoul of Spain's desire to do so, already buttressed by its military triumphs in that region. As an internal Spanish document put it, "Since His Majesty's armed forces had captured all that territory [on the Mississippi] from the English . . . the Americans have no settlements in it and therefore are totally without any right to the slightest claim."

Part of the reason for Floridablanca's distancing of Jay came from Spain's continuing diplomatic attempts to obtain Gibraltar from Great Britain. To hasten the end of the war, Spain did many things, among them participating in talks with unofficial and semiofficial British emissaries in Madrid, and encouraging the efforts of Russia and later Austria to act as mediators, even as Spain suspected that all such mediation efforts were only being kept afloat by the British to detach Spain from France and the United States.

In the early summer of 1780, coursing south through Virginia and the Carolinas toward Charleston, Baron de Kalb and his several thousand men were in agony from "the intolerable heat, the worst of quarters, the most voracious of insects of every hue and form," including ticks, whose bites had the baron black and blue. Moreover, he wrote home, "of the violence of thunderstorms in this part of the world Europeans cannot form any idea." "I meet with no support, no integrity, and no virtue in the state of Virginia," he wrote a friend, and the same had been true in North Carolina. His orders were to continue the march south even after the loss of Charleston, his original objective. But because of the difficulties when word reached de Kalb, just after crossing into South Carolina, that he was to cede command to Horatio Gates, he was grateful.

"Take care lest your northern laurels turn to southern willows," Gates had been warned (by Charles Lee) on learning of this appointment. But in the South Carolina camp, Gates's arrogance continued unrestrained. Even though de Kalb agreed to stay on as Gates's second in command, neither the baron nor any other officer was able to influence Gates as the small army kept moving in a search for Lord Francis Rawdon's British forces. When Gates's officers complained of needing to halt to wait for supplies, or to find places to forage, Gates insisted that supplies would follow them, and "plenty will soon succeed the unavoidable scarcity." He appeared not to have learned from his Saratoga victory that an army without supplies is doubly vulnerable, both to the lack of sustenance and to the mistakes that scarcity exacerbates. He regularly and repeatedly refused to colloquy with his ranking officers or read their written suggestions. Among his unilateral decisions was, on the night before the expected battle near Camden, since there was no rum to serve the soldiers, he gave them molasses, which made many of them ill.

Around midnight on August 15, 1780, the British and Americans tried to attack each other, making first contact but then retiring to wait for dawn. Only then did Gates learn from a captive that he was facing not only Francis Rawdon's troops but also Cornwallis's three thousand—the two British contingents, which had been marching separately, had finally combined. "The general's astonishment could not be concealed," an officer later wrote about Gates. Only at this penultimate moment did he ask his senior commanders for their opinions. Most considered it too late for a retreat. De Kalb, whose counsel Gates had so often overruled, said nothing.

Shortly after dawn, Armand's cavalry advanced and was beaten back. The British and Hessian troops soon overwhelmed the American troops, which aside from de Kalb's and a few other units were rural militia, almost 2,500 of whom "threw down their *loaded* arms and fled in the utmost consternation," as an American officer wrote. De Kalb and his seasoned troops held fast but to no avail. His horse was killed and he was sabered on the head. Bloody and on foot, he suffered ten more wounds by bayonet thrusts, saber cuts, and bullets; grievously hurt, he was assaulted by British and Hessians coveting his elegant uniform and boots until his comrade shielded his body with his own, and the two were found and rescued by Cornwallis. After three days, and despite the attentions of Cornwallis's surgeons, de Kalb died. Rawdon learned from the comrade, himself wounded four times, of the tactics that de Kalb had suggested to Gates: a surprise attack when first apprised of Rawdon being in the area and before Cornwallis's troops had joined with them. Rawdon later wrote that Gates, by rejecting de Kalb's very good idea, "gave us three days to meet him in a country favorable to me."

Gates was then 180 miles away. Before the battle at Camden had ended, he had begun his flight, riding some 60 miles from the site before night fell, and equally far each day for the next two. Only then did he stop his flight to write a self-exculpatory report to Congress. Such reports often ruined subordinates' careers, as this one did for Armand, faulted by Gates for what was, in essence, Gates's own failure. Although other officers at Camden did not share the commander's bad opinion of Armand, the Frenchman thereafter had difficulty restoring his reputation. American losses at Camden were nine hundred killed or wounded and one thousand taken captive; it was among the worst American defeats.

The Chevalier de La Luzerne was more gregarious a plenipotentiary than Gérard and worked assiduously at things that Gérard had not. He paid the Reverend Samuel Cooper of Boston and a prominent Philadelphian to write pro-French articles. Cooper, who had recycled his sermons of the French and Indian War era, replacing anti-French with anti-British rhetoric, further influenced New Englanders in articles and sermons espousing the alliance. He was particularly helpful in countering the anti-Gallicians' attempts to push matters detrimental to the interests of the alliance and to France.

La Luzerne also developed a conversation circle that included most of the French officers serving in America, with whom he met with regularly, and a correspondence circle with French-speaking American enclaves.

Mottin de la Balme was an avid member of the inner group. In the spring of 1780 de la Balme needed to call on La Luzerne for assistance. The previous year he had been captured in Maine during a debacle, the Penobscot expedition, and then exchanged. By spring he had no new assignment and had lost his letters of recommendation; Luzerne helped him obtain a copy from Congressman James Lovell. With it and other papers, de la Balme took off for the Indiana territory town of Vincennes and its French-speaking population.

There he intended to meet up with, or at least to work in the same vein as, George Rogers Clark, who had liberated Vincennes in 1779. Claiming to be a *pensionnaire* of Louis XVI, de la Balme used that supposed authority to collect Native American allies for a punitive expedition against the Miami, allies of the British, with the aim of seizing the great prize of the area, Detroit, the British stronghold. From Vincennes, in the early summer of 1780, de la Balme sent a petition to La Luzerne on behalf of the city, asking for closer ties with the government of France; and from a headquarters in a local tavern with a French name he issued certificates of appreciation to various Native American leaders. To induce the braves to join his troop he threw alcohol-fueled orgies during which he also took part in drunken rapes.

By the fall de la Balme and a band that included Native Americans from various tribes and French-speaking settlers from Vincennes and nearby French settlements began to raid small towns in the Wabash River valley, freeing cattle and stealing horses in the name of liberating the towns from British control. However in November, Little Turtle and his main band of Miamis ambushed de la Balme, and in a pitched battle over several days he lost thirty men and was taken prisoner. Notice of the encounter, and de la Balme's papers, were sent to the ranking British army officer in Detroit; it was clear from the official-looking papers that de la Balme was not an ordinary settler. The British looked forward to questioning him, but he died before reaching Detroit, either from his wounds or by being summarily executed.

French finance minister Necker saw no end in sight to the rising costs of arming France and fighting the British in the Caribbean, Africa, and India as well as in America. Prior to the war, France had been paying 30 percent of the government's annual budget for debt service on the Seven Years' War loans; now, with the added expense of waging war, the debt service was approaching 50 percent of the annual budget. Great Britain's debt service was at the same fraction of the national budget, but the British had more efficient and sustainable ways of taxing the populace, and ready lenders in the London capital market, while Paris had to go to Amsterdam for loans. After France's lottery ran its course, producing 85 million livres but promising 105 million in prize money and repayments, in 1780 Necker turned to a different funding tool, *rentes viagères*, government-backed annuities, to be bought by healthy individuals and only paid out upon their reaching old age or to their heirs at their deaths. Previously he had decried such a scheme but now embraced it, using it to raise 260 million livres—on the promise of paying back, in the future, almost double that amount. Most of the income went to fund the government's everyday and military activities; the loans made to America were a small fraction of the total, usually doled out in the single millions of livres at a time, with the largest lot being 10 million. France's navy alone was costing more than 120 million a year, up from 28 million annually in the prewar period.

As financing became more important, Necker's power grew. It also brought him to a clash with Sartine; when Necker allotted 120 million for naval operations in one year, Sartine needed 20 million more and raised it privately. The next year Sartine told Louis that if he did not get his extra money only sixty of eighty vessels could sail. Louis asked Maurepas: "Shall we dismiss Necker, or shall we dismiss Sartine? I am not displeased with the latter. I think Necker is more useful to us." When the king would not decide, Necker convinced Marie Antoinette in his favor. In the fall of 1780, to the chagrin of Vergennes, Sartine and Montbarrey were replaced by the Marquises de Castries and de Ségur.

Philippe-Henri, the Marquis de Ségur, a long-serving senior officer in the army, had lost an arm in an early military encounter and was the third generation of his family to achieve the rank of lieutenant general; he was also the father of Lafayette's friend. The Marquis de Castries was a soldier of similar age, service, and nobility, and had administrative experience from his years as a governor. De Castries's understanding of the faults of the military promotion system made him overrule precedent to accelerate elevations for men of proven naval leadership ability—de Grasse, Barras, and Bougainville.

Ségur, though committed to continuing the reforms begun under Saint-Germain (who had died, but whose papers Ségur often consulted), nonetheless reintroduced the requirement that officers aspiring to the very top ranks of the armed services be able to document four generations of noble forebears. The minister also thought that all the various classes of nobility would serve more usefully if "distributed in the military in an order more analogous to the places they occupied in civil society."

That supposedly profligate spender, the Rochambeau-Ternay expedition, arrived at Newport on July 10, 1780. The commanders were acutely conscious of what had happened near Newport in 1778, and Rochambeau used d'Estaing's fiasco as chapter and verse on how not to go about Franco-American relations on American territory. Although

Rochambeau was not considered much of a diplomat, on arrival he played that role well, serenading Newporters with his military bands, decreeing parades for their benefit, and above all spending hard cash with them. His success in gaining the approbation of the local citizenry became visible when he asked for help in moving his ill, and five thousand locals responded.

Rochambeau's first letter to Washington announced that the king had ordered him to give his fealty to the American general. He added his own words of admiration; after all, to a seasoned combat veteran any general who had successfully fended off the British for five years, kept his army together, and had not been replaced by his political superiors had accomplished quite a bit. To "have no secrets" from Washington, Rochambeau enclosed a copy of the Montbarrey letter, plus another with his secret instructions, which featured such mundane matters as not permitting any part of his corps to be detached from the main body except for brief assignments. All this was prelude to the bad news he had for Washington. Because Rochambeau had been deprived of additional warships by the sending of the Guichen fleet to the Caribbean, and because his viability in Newport was threatened by Arbuthnot's expected return to New York waters, Rochambeau asserted that his French troops and ships would not be ready to conduct offensive operations in America for at least another month.

Washington's equally courteous welcome to Rochambeau, written before receiving the French general's letter, announced that Lafayette would meet Rochambeau to discuss plans. "As a Genl Officer I have the greatest confidence in him—as a friend he is perfectly acquainted with my sentiments & opinions. . . . All the information he gives, and all the propositions he makes, I entreat you will consider as coming from me."

Washington assumed that sending Lafayette would smooth the way for joint Franco-American operations. It did just the opposite. Even though Rochambeau decided not to take umbrage at Washington for not coming himself to Newport, Lafayette's arrogance during their meeting taxed his courtesy, and he was riled even more by the marquis's subsequent twelve-page letter. Rochambeau judged Lafayette's communications insolent and said so in a biting response. His slap had the desired effect: Lafayette apologized and asked forgiveness. This charmed Rochambeau. "Permit me, my dear marquis, to respond to you as would an old father to a son he loves and esteems," Rochambeau's next note to Lafayette began, and it went on to offer fatherly advice: After forty years at war he had concluded that the French were not invincible, and so even they should not go into battle against overwhelming odds. He pledged to Lafayette that they would see grand action together—just not now.

Then the British fleet appeared outside the harbor and Rochambeau had to deal with that, and with the need to care for his ill and wounded—a quarter of his forces—mostly alone, as Ternay was increasingly feeble. The French defended themselves aggressively, defeating British land forays and holding their sea lines, which extended from Narragansett Bay across to Long Island. Rochambeau's footing in Newport received an unexpected setback when the French agent in Philadelphia refused to honor the Chaumont letter of credit, insisting that Chaumont's accounts in America were empty, and causing the more rapid than anticipated depletion of the cache of specie that Rochambeau and Ternay had brought with them. Supposedly to compensate for the unavailable credit, the agent then bought cash in Philadelphia, ostensibly for the troops, at a low rate of exchange, but instead of delivering it to Rochambeau at Newport he sold the cash for more than he had paid for it. La Luzerne heard the Newport quartermasters' howls over this gouging and had Paris recall the agent, but not before considerable damage had been done.

Rochambeau did not then comprehend the worst of the French forces' problems: the sorry state of their intended partner, the Continental army—so enfeebled that Washington had felt he could not leave his command, even for a brief meeting with Rochambeau, lest it fall apart. Part of the difficulty was structural. While the individual states continued to keep their heads above water financially, the credit of the central government had been completely destroyed, and as a result it was unable to supply or pay the troops. Congress, having exhausted its means of supporting the Continental army had shifted this burden to the states, only some of which were fulfilling their share of the army's needs. The underlying reason for all of these difficulties was the weakness of the Continental dollar. Farmers chose not to plant more than their families could use for fear of any excess being confiscated or paid for in near-worthless paper money. Half the enlisted men would have the right to quit service at year's end, and this time they were expected to do so.

Supplies compromised, and having lost six thousand soldiers at Charleston, and with Gates mired in South Carolina with several thousand more—Washington had not yet learned of the captures at Camden—America's forces were at their lowest ebb. Nonetheless he and Rochambeau made plans to meet halfway between their respective headquarters. By mid-September, when both contingents set off for Hartford, news had reached Rochambeau of the British blockade of Brest, preventing the sailing of the remainder of his troops, and Washington had received word of the Camden debacle.

That set the context for, and served to dampen enthusiasm at, the September 20 meeting of Rochambeau, Ternay, Rochambeau's son, and several other French aides, with Washington, Lafayette, Knox, Hamilton, and Gouvion. The commanders' business at Hartford was, first, to find ways to get along. Ternay, ailing, did not play a role. Rochambeau and Washington were quite alike: military-minded to the core, with a firm grasp of the common objective, and always well prepared. Rochambeau had a neatly drawn document with propositions to put to Washington and space allotted in which to record his responses. Rochambeau's ten questions were a Socratic progression designed to lead the student to agree with the teacher's preferred conclusion. When to the first of these questions Washington responded, "There can be no decisive enterprise against the maritime establishments of the English in this country, without a constant naval superiority," his direction was sealed. From then on he could not help but answer the other questions with responses that cumulatively undermined his own multipage plan for a fall attack on

New York. Thus, step-by-step he was led to make the conclusion that Rochambeau desired: There could be no joint attack on New York until the arrival of more French troops and ships. Washington and Rochambeau then jointly signed an appeal to Louis XVI for such units.

A major accomplishment of this meeting was the satisfying of each commander as to the mettle of the other. An additional result, no less salutary for cooperative purposes, was that the French staff emerged impressed with Washington, whose courtesy and consideration of subordinates presented a contrast to their gruff and often cantankerous chief. But Washington also understood, from this meeting, as he put it in a note to Lafayette, that despite Rochambeau's orders from Louis XVI to treat Washington as his superior officer, "my command of the F-Tps at R Is-d stands upon a very limited state."

Benedict Arnold used the Hartford conference as the moment to attempt to turn over West Point to the British. The genesis of his plan dated to early 1779, when he had gotten in touch with Major John André. The contact had been made through Arnold's wife, the former Peggy Shippen, who had known André when Howe's forces were in Philadelphia. On May 23, 1779, Arnold told André, who had since become Clinton's adjutant general, "I will cooperate when an opportunity offers" to betray the American cause, in exchange for "some certainty, my property here being secure and a revenue equivalent to the risk and service done." When the French fleet was welcomed at Newport, Arnold informed André that Washington would go to meet Rochambeau, and that "I have accepted the command at W[est] P[oint] as a post in which I can render the most essential services, and which will be in my disposal."

To General Clinton, possession of West Point was "an object of the utmost importance" to the British war effort, since the combined French and American force threatened to oust his army from New York and end the war. The French presence in the area made it imperative for Arnold's plot to succeed now, or it might never do so.

Arnold made certain that West Point's readiness declined, that its defensive works—drawn up mainly by Duportail, Kościuszko, and other French engineers—were not completed, and that many of its troops were dispersed to other locations. When Washington departed for Hartford, Arnold set his plot in final motion and persuaded André to perform his part in it in civilian clothes. Only the chance stopping of André by militia near Tarrytown and the discovery of incriminating papers on him prevented the handover of West Point. Arnold escaped just minutes before Washington arrived at the home that Arnold and his wife had been using. Washington had no idea what Arnold had been up to until Hamilton, who had gone in search of Arnold, returned with the papers taken from André. Washington immediately recognized these as descriptions of West Point and notes from an American council of war, in Arnold's handwriting. Washington was aghast at the treachery, a very personal blow from a man whom he had repeatedly protected and promoted.

Because André had been in civilian clothes, had used an alias, and had intended to meet Arnold, he was charged as a spy and could have been summarily executed, but Washington decided to hold a court-martial. André was found guilty. Hamilton pleaded with Clinton to exchange André for Arnold, but got nowhere. Then, and despite André's exemplary behavior in captivity, Washington had no choice but to order André's death. The creator of the *Mischianza* was hanged.

André was mourned by his British colleagues, but their leaders celebrated the arrival of Arnold, America's most aggressive general, who would now take the field for them with the added motivation of craving revenge on Washington, whom he blamed for André's death.

In the halls of power in France and Spain, Arnold's perfidy was looked upon as another instance of loutish British behavior, of a piece with their use of torture, their overly punitive raids against civilians, and their appalling mistreatment of prisoners.

16

"Siberia alone can furnish any idea of Lebanon, Connecticut."
—Duc de Lauzun

When the League of Armed Neutrality had been formed, the Netherlands sought to protect its shipping by joining. The British objected to the Dutch doing so on the grounds that their 1678 treaty required the Dutch to stay out of such alliances. On November 20, 1780, the Netherlands brushed that notion aside and became a signatory. Immediately the British cabinet drew up reasons for declaring war on the Netherlands. Among them were that the Dutch had provided France with war matériel, allowed John Paul Jones to bring captured British prizes into Dutch ports, offered a first salute at the Caribbean island of Saint Eustatius to an American ship, and, based on a draft of a treaty seized when Henry Laurens had been taken prisoner, that the Dutch were planning to ally with America. The cabinet considered irrelevant that the draft treaty was unauthorized by Congress and had been drawn up by private citizens.

In the same fast frigate to the Caribbean that carried the British declaration of war on the Netherlands, the North government sent Rodney instructions to attack Saint Eustatius, the Dutch "golden rock," an entrepôt through which had passed half the military supplies sent to America. He was to attack before the Dutch learned they were at war. Two days after receiving the message, Rodney's squadron, with three thousand troops aboard, entered the Saint Eustatius harbor in such strength that he was able to persuade the governor to surrender the island without a battle; in the succeeding days he took the neighboring Dutch islands of Saint Martin and Saba.

In the Saint Eustatius harbor Rodney seized 130 ships, and for the next three months under his explicit direction the British forces avidly confiscated those ships' property and the island's. Moreover, by keeping the Dutch flag flying over Saint Eustatius he lured in many other ships that did not know he had taken control of the island, and seized them too.

As 1781 began, a weary Washington, with an assist from Hamilton, put in writing to John Laurens, who was going to France, a commander's understanding of the current difficulties of the young United States of America. These were traceable to "inexperience in affairs . . . the want of sufficient stock of wealth, the depreciation of the currency, the general diffidence that has taken place among the people, the calamitous distress to which the army has been exposed." The army's "discontents," now "matured to an extremity," had brought the country "to a crisis which renders immediate and efficacious succors from abroad indispensable to its safety." Laurens was being sent to secure loans from France, loans that the general emphasized must be "large enough to be a foundation for a substantial arrangement of finance, revive fallen credit and give vigor to future operations." Without that money "we may make a feeble and expiring effort [in] the next campaign, in all probability the period to our opposition," adding that it would be "better to diminish the aid in men . . . than diminish the pecuniary succor."

"I suspect the French Ministry will try your temper," Hamilton warned his close friend, Laurens, "but you must not suffer them to provoke it." On Laurens's way to a ship in Boston he was taught the same lesson by

Washington's way of dealing with mutinous Pennsylvania troops. Although Laurens, who had visited them earlier, had advocated subduing them by force, Washington, who understood the deprivation of the soldiers that had spurred the revolt, defused the crisis through a combination of permitting Pennsylvania's civil apparatus to judge the ringleaders, and a personal appeal to Congress to generously assuage the mutineers' needs.

Tom Paine accompanied Laurens as an unofficial adviser after declining a request to come along as his secretary. Colonel Armand joined them on board, having decided that he would be better off raising a new legion in France, where his nobility as the Marquis de le Rouërie was more respected than it had been thus far in America.

The visitors found the climate in Paris in the spring of 1781 not as dire as in America, but still worrisome. Dissent was being actively suppressed. A Beaumarchais screed regarding his activities in London was viewed by Versailles as antiadministration and the copies confiscated. Necker was forced to resign from the council for publishing the *Compte rendu au Roi*, a detailing of the government's income and outgo—which almost inadvertently revealed the instability of the country's finances. Raynal was arrested for publishing a new edition of his *Deux Indes* book; it contained two new chapters by Diderot on North America and its Revolution, in which the parallels between the need to overthrow an old British government and the activities of France's thousand-year-old monarchy were underscored: "There is no form of government with the prerogative of being immutable; no political authority which created yesterday or a thousand years ago, cannot be abrogated in ten years or tomorrow; no power, however respectable or sacred, that is authorized to regard the state as its property." The book's most shocking passages were those addressed directly to Louis XVI, and which committed the further crime of using the intimate pronoun *tu* rather than the properly distant *vous*:

Cast your gaze upon the capital of your empire, and you will find two classes of citizens. The one, glutted with riches, displays an opulence which offends those it does not corrupt; the other, mired in destitution, worsens its condition by wearing a mask of prosperity. . . . Fix your gaze upon the provinces, in which industry of every description is dying out. You will see them bowing under the yoke of taxation and the harassment of the tax agents.

That spring, when a long-serving popular curate used his pulpit to direct similar truths at an audience that included Louis XVI—the information that half of the thirteen thousand foundlings in Parisian hospitals had died from neglect—the preacher was banished from the pulpit for the next several years.

For Laurens's direct affronts to Louis XVI, he ran a similar risk of ostracism. Franklin told the young man, upon arrival, that his mission was useless because he, Franklin, had already applied to Vergennes for additional loans and had been rejected. Vergennes claimed that the American currency had depreciated too far for loans, Franklin reported, but had nonetheless dispatched 1.5 million livres to America and had also promised a 6 million livre gift from the king. Laurens insisted on seeing Vergennes, and in that meeting protested that the gift was not enough, warning that unless Versailles was also willing to grant a substantial loan, America would have to end the war, and America's commerce and resources would be "restored to the tyrant of the European Seas, the ancient rival of France."

Some accounts have Laurens antagonizing Franklin by such bluntness and by usurping Franklin's position as negotiator with France, while others suggest that Laurens accomplished what Franklin could not. Such readings misinterpret the Franklin-Laurens relationship: In dealings with the ministers Vergennes, de Castries and Ségur, the Americans played good cop and bad cop, Laurens issuing demands and taking the hard line to make Franklin's softer requests seem more reasonable. "Mr. Lawrens is worrying the minister [Vergennes] for more money," Franklin wrote to Jay, "and we shall I believe obtain a farther sum."

On April 8 Vergennes informed Laurens that the king had agreed to guarantee the principal and interest on a 10 million livres note that would come from the Netherlands. Given an inch, Laurens instantly asked for the mile—for the sum to be provided, in advance, from the French treasury. Laurens wrote directly to the king. He conveyed "the homage of the most ardent gratitude" but claimed "that although his Aid goes to the objective which His Majesty proposes, it is proved that in the state of things it is insufficient in view of the urgent needs . . . and [of] the exhaustion in which America finds itself, the absolute lack of Resources and Specie, and the enormity of the outlays necessary to make war with vigour."

Vergennes complained to Franklin, Lafayette, and La Luzerne of Laurens's effrontery in writing to the king in a manner "not . . . suited to the nature of his mission." Laurens continued to press. Coordinating his efforts with Adams's in the Netherlands—Adams had already applied for an extensive loan there—Laurens succeeded in obtaining more than the six million livres that Franklin had accepted prior to Laurens's arrival. Evidence that Laurens had not overreached came in the form of a diamond-encrusted snuff box presented to him on behalf of Louis XVI, similar to the one previously given to Deane, and a testimonial from Franklin, who, far from resenting Laurens, suggested in a letter to him that if he could tear himself away from military affairs and the pursuit of glory, he would be an ideal replacement for Franklin as minister to France, as Congress "could not put their Affairs in better hands."

During John Laurens's very public visit to France, the British authorities made life worse for his father, Henry, in the Tower of London, and then suggested that Henry could lessen his troubles by condemning John's mission or pressuring him to abort it. "I know [John] is so full of love and Duty to me, he would sacrifice his Life to serve me rightly," Henry responded, "but he would not sacrifice his honor to save my life; his Maxim is my Country first and then my father. & I applaud him."

De Grasse, taken ill during the latter part of his participation in the d'Estaing expedition in America, had been happy to reach Europe, landing at Brest in January 1781. At Versailles he was granted permission to add to his name "des princes souverains d'Antibes, marquis de Grasse-Tilly." Shortly thereafter de Castries named three new commanders: Barras for taking over the Ternay fleet, Suffren for India, and de Grasse for the Caribbean. De Grasse returned to Brest on February 26 to take command of a convoy of 150 vessels including many ships of the line. His flag would be in the 110-gun, three-decker *Ville de Paris*, formerly Guichen's flagship, and from whose top deck d'Orvilliers had fought Keppel at Ouessant. When de Grasse's sailors threatened to mutiny because they had not been paid, like Graves's in Portsmouth a year earlier, de Castries did for his men what Sandwich had not done for the British tars: The minister came to Brest and knocked on what de Grasse remembered as a hundred doors to obtain private loans to pay the sailors. De Grasse, for his part, showed up at the dock every morning at five to hurry repairs and lading. On March 22 he was elevated to the French equivalent of rear admiral, given the Croix de Saint-Louis, and with a very large fleet left for the Caribbean, under orders not to injure his health or tie up his ships in a "long and troublesome campaign."

A week out to sea, Suffren's squadron veered off to go to India, and a day later de Grasse dispatched the *Sagittaire* toward Boston, with thirty other vessels bearing additional troops, Rochambeau's son, and more treasure.

Part of the reason that the winter of 1780–81 had been difficult for the French in Newport was being out of touch with Versailles, and a larger part was due to the uncomfortable situation. While several hundred senior officers secured billets in Newport's homes, it was not palatable to the citizenry to house four thousand ordinary soldiers that way—the imposition on the populace of an occupying British army had been a prewar flash point. Special barracks were constructed for the soldiers but were not adequately outfitted for the rigors of a New England winter.

The Duc de Lauzun's veteran hussars, with the steeds they had bought, were housed separately in Lebanon, halfway between Newport and Hartford. "Siberia alone can furnish any idea of Lebanon," Lauzun grumbled to his diary; he didn't like being away from the gaiety that he knew would attend the French officers in Newport, and pined for that of Versailles, where he had been a favorite of Marie Antoinette and rumored to be her lover. Lauzun hunted squirrel with the visiting Chastellux and made the occasional raid while awaiting the summons to greater action. His legion was an odd bunch, only a third of them French, mostly from the Alsace region, and the rest from fourteen other countries including Sweden, Russia, Poland, Hungary, and Ireland; in camp their designated language was German. Lauzun's men, more so than Rochambeau's, were prone to desert, and Lauzun had two deserters shot dead.

The basic problem for the French troops, according to Rochambeau's aide Comte Axel von Fersen, was that they "vegetate . . . in the most sinister and horrible idleness and inactivity. . . . We are a burden to [the American army]; we are not reinforcing [them yet] they are having to pay for us, too, as by increasing consumption we are making supplies more scarce, and by paying coin we cause their paper money to fall." The British tried to exacerbate the chafing by publishing in a New York newspaper intercepted letters from French officers deprecating their American colleagues as "ignorant, superstitious, without education, without taste, without delicacy or honor," and by insisting that the French had given Washington sixteen million livres so he could declare himself king of America.

On February 25, 1781, the *Astrée* made it into Boston's harbor with the much-needed 1.5 million livres sent by Vergennes, but also the news that the second division was likely not coming to America. Rochambeau and Washington would have to make do with those French forces already in place.

Just as that news arrived in Newport, so did a welcome sight, the forty-four-gun British *Romulus*, now flying the French flag. Earlier in the month the Chevalier Destouches, who had taken over the Newport fleet after the death of Ternay, had dispatched four warships to Chesapeake

Bay to counter the British troops. They had forced the British to retreat somewhat and had seized several British prizes while losing one of their own ships.

On the strength of this success, Washington urged Lafayette, in Virginia at the head of fifteen hundred troops, to try to further assail the British there, then led by William Phillips, who had been captured at Saratoga, exchanged, and promoted to command of a substantial army. Lafayette was keenly aware that Phillips's father had fired the cannon shot that had killed his father, and was determined to avenge that deed.

In the Virginia campaign of the spring of 1781, Lafayette did heroic work defending Richmond. Then, facing a larger force, Lafayette hid Richmond's munitions and abandoned the city to Cornwallis. The British in Virginia kept shifting leaders, as Phillips died and Clinton did not permit Benedict Arnold, Phillips's temporary replacement, to retain command for more than a few weeks before ceding it to Cornwallis, a man generally acknowledged as Great Britain's best field commander. To counteract Cornwallis, Lafayette solicited advice from Greene, Morgan, and "swamp fox" fighter Francis Marion, a hero at the battle of Camden, all of whom suggested tactics that were beyond Fabian and constituted guerrilla warfare. To blunt the effectiveness of Cornwallis's cavalry, led by Banastre Tarleton, Lafayette's men lured them into the woods where snipers picked them off. Locals outraged by Cornwallis and Tarleton's rapacious treatment of the countryside and its inhabitants helped Lafayette's army stay alive and gain reinforcements. His confidence grew: "The enemmy Have Been so Kind as to Retire Before us. twice I gave them a chance of fighting . . . But they Continued their Retrograde motions," he wrote to Washington in late June, adding,

Our little action more particularly Marks the Retreat of the ennemy—from the place He first Began to Retire to Williamsburg is upwards of 100 Mile. . . . His Lordship did us no Harm of any Consequence lost an immense part of his former Conquests and did not make any in this State—general greene demanded of me only to Hold my ground in Virginia—But the Movements of Lord Cornwallis May answer Better purposes than that in the political line.

No sooner had Lafayette made that boast then he made a mistake. Trying to trap Cornwallis near Williamsburg, Lafayette sent Wayne's division against the British rear, and they were nearly overwhelmed. Lafayette rode personally to the rescue. He had his horse shot out from under him but reached Wayne, and the two leaders managed to get themselves and most of the men to safety. That day was lost by the Americans, but Cornwallis did not consolidate his victory; rather, he continued on the move, first abandoning Jamestown for Portsmouth, and then at Clinton's instruction leaving Portsmouth too, for Yorktown.

Many Saint Eustatius warehouses and companies had been enriched by the trade of transferring goods from Europe to the nearby French-controlled islands and to America. Rodney plundered Saint Eustatius on such a large scale that he soon ran into difficulties. Much of the property at Saint Eustatius belonged to British residents of other Caribbean islands, and some of it to Quakers in Philadelphia, who complained to La Luzerne that Rodney's confiscations had caused them to lose 2.5 million livres, mostly garnered in illicit commerce with the English. They and ninety other Jewish and other Dutch, French, and British merchants sued Rodney for unlawfully confiscating their property.

He fought back, and his overinvolvement in the court cases distracted him from making further raids in the Caribbean. It also made Rodney unwilling to leave the Caribbean and sail to the American coast to assist Arbuthnot—and this cost the British during what could have been a decisive battle for them, off Chesapeake Bay.

Early in March 1781, Destouches, at Washington's request and after having learned that three of Arbuthnot's larger warships had been damaged in a storm, took off from Newport for the Chesapeake, aiming to prevent the British from reinforcing their army. Arbuthnot learned of this sailing and in his faster, copper-bottomed ships reached the bay first. When Destouches arrived, a battle ensued. Although the two fleets did considerable damage to each other, the engagement was judged a draw. Destouches was unable to prevent the British fleet from investing the bay, but he was able to get away with his ships—if Rodney's had also been present to help Arbuthnot's, the outcome would likely have been a disaster for the French squadron.

At the conclusion of de Grasse's Atlantic crossing to the Caribbean, when his lookouts spotted the isle of Martinique they also saw a British frigate, frantically signaling others. As the French soon learned, Admiral Samuel Hood's squadron was lying in wait for them. After a dawn mass the following day, the British and French fleets lined up opposite one another and commenced firing. In that battle de Grasse's forces seriously damaged six British capital ships, including Hood's flag, *Intrepid*. But the British ships all managed to escape, giving the austere de Grasse reason to chastise his captains for not obeying signals. The next day the French did better in communicating, but were unable to reach the enemy. On the third day, a squall obscured de Grasse's ability to see Hood's vessels. Once it stopped, "I saw with grief that it was only too true that the sailing of the English was superior to ours," de Grasse wrote to de Castries. "There were with me only eleven ships in range to attack; the others . . . were very far in the rear. Some even were out of sight."

De Grasse returned to his main task, ferrying into Martinique the huge convoy that he had brought across the Atlantic without having lost a single vessel. He next sent several ships and thirteen hundred marines to take Tobago, where they captured twelve hundred soldiers and their munitions. Rodney's squadron, which had not arrived in the area in time to fight alongside Hood's, tried to engage de Grasse but soon backed off. De Grasse, now master of the Caribbean, was then able to turn his attention to North America.

. . .

A new phase of the Franco-American alliance was marked by the arrival of the *Sagittaire* in Boston in May 1781. On board was Rochambeau's son, as well as additional troops, treasure, the good news that de Grasse was on his way to the Caribbean and would then come north, and the bad news that no second division was being sent. Donatien Rochambeau told his father that the king's brothers were laughing at Louis XVI for the inaction of the Rochambeau forces in America. In the packet of instructions for Rochambeau was a letter from Louis XVI saying that had Rochambeau been in France he would have been offered the post of minister of war. His ambition had "never aspired to such an important function," Rochambeau would recall, but just then the scantiness of his resources and the difficulty of the situation produced a pang of regret at not being home to accept this plum.

The remainder of the *Sagittaire*'s contents fired him up, though, and he quickly fixed with Washington a time and place for another formal meeting: Wethersfield, on Monday, May 21, 1781. Both set out for it, Washington accompanied by Knox, Duportail, and others, but not by Hamilton.

For some time Hamilton had been agitating for a field command, and Washington, who had granted such posts to other aides, had refused, insisting that Hamilton was too valuable at headquarters. In February, after the Americans had returned from the Newport meeting with Rochambeau, Hamilton had kept the commander waiting once too often; Washington rebuked him for disrespectful behavior, and Hamilton quit on the spot.

At Wethersfield, Rochambeau was accompanied by Chastellux but not by Ternay's replacement, the Comte de Barras, who had arrived in Newport recently and taken command from Destouches. Barras did not attend because the British fleet had reappeared and he felt he must remain with his ships in case of an attack. Six weeks earlier, during Washington's flying visit to Newport—an occasion mainly notable for its lavish reception and dinners—the American commander had urged that the French sail their troops to Chesapeake Bay to harass the British there. Barras, apprised of that plan, did not want to chance such a maneuver against a recently enlarged British fleet, and when the subject was brought up again at Wethersfield, and Barras's reasoning became known, Washington yielded gracefully: "However desirable such an event might have been, the reasons now assigned by the Count de Barras are sufficient to prove its impracticability."

The Wethersfield conference was further impacted by Washington and Rochambeau's needs to conceal secret knowledge from each other. Rochambeau knew that the de Grasse fleet, then en route to the Caribbean, would definitely come to the Atlantic states after action there, but he had been enjoined by Ségur not to say so. Washington knew more about de Grasse's plans than he could let on, thanks to Chastellux, who had become an admirer and was chagrined at Rochambeau's treating Washington with "all the ungraciousness and all the unpleasantness possible." Just prior to the conference, Chastellux had written to Washington what "may be considered a transgression," a private note conveying that de Grasse's fleet would indeed join Barras's.

Washington and Rochambeau shared a laugh over captured correspondence between the British Lord Germain and General Clinton that equally disparaged both French and Continental troops, morale, finances, and courage.

At Wethersfield, Washington proposed that the armies join now for action against the British, with American militia left behind to defend any French ships remaining at Newport. Barras had objected to this proposal in advance, believing that the ships would not be safe in the care of such a guard, and threatening that if the action were undertaken anyway he would obey prior orders to sail to Boston. Go ahead to Boston, Washington responded; if the fleet's moving to Boston was the price of having Rochambeau's forces join his at the North River, he'd bear it. Rochambeau immediately deflected that notion by breaking the news that de Grasse was expected momentarily in the Caribbean and would come to America in the summer, so "What are the operations that we might have in view at that Epocha?"

"Should the West India Fleet arrive upon this Coast—the force thus Combined may either proceed in the operation against New York, or may be directed against the enemy in some other quarter, as circumstances shall dictate," was Washington's ready answer. New York was preferable to Virginia as a target because of "The great waste of Men (which we have found from experience) in the long Marches to the Southern States, the advanced season now to commence there in—and the difficulties and expence of Land transportation thither." Six years into the war, Washington believed New York to be the only stronghold whose recapture could end the conflict. The United States would win the war eventually if it could hold out, and if British patience could be exhausted prior to that of the American public and of Congress. But for a quick ending to the war only the taking of New York would suffice; recapture of Charleston or Savannah would not be as productive. More as a sop to Rochambeau than as a firm conviction, Washington did agree, as he told his diary, to "extend our views to the Southward as circumstances and a Naval superiority might render more necessary & eligible."

The decision to fight the British at Yorktown did not come out of the Wethersfield conference. Rather, as Washington wrote in his diary, at that conference he had "Fixed with Count Rochambeau upon a Plan of Campaign" against New York, to begin once the French had marched across Connecticut to join him. Within a week of the conference Washington received John Laurens's note about Louis XVI's gift of six million additional livres. Two days later he directed Duportail to "make the estimates of the articles in your department necessary for the operation [against New York] that the previous arrangements for the siege . . . may be put in the best train." Within a few weeks he moved headquarters from New Windsor southward twenty miles to Peekskill, to be in a better position to attack New York when Rochambeau arrived.

Shortly before the French troops were to depart Newport, Rochambeau's nephew made an offer to buy du Bouchet's horse, commenting that du Bouchet would have no use for it as he was scheduled to remain behind, in charge of the heavy artillery. Du Bouchet took the comment as an unnecessary slap and forced a duel. The nephew's saber stuck under du Bouchet's collarbone and was difficult to remove, but du Bouchet's honor was salvaged by his lost "grand quantity of blood." And so on June 10, when Rochambeau and his train began to leave Newport, du Bouchet was not with them.

The French forces departed at the rate of a regiment a day—approximately one thousand soldiers and officers—for four days. The forces were understrength; some detachments had been used to replace ailing sailors, and still others were unavailable as soldiers either because they were still in hospitals or were employed as teamsters. The contingents continued westward in their thousand-man groups, each succeeding regiment occupying the beds that the previous one had been in the night before. Engineers and sappers forged ahead to prepare and repair roads. Rochambeau's army trailed eight twelve-pound cannons and six mortars, but not the largest cannons, the twenty-fours—there had not been time to construct the heavy carriages necessary to transport the twenty-fours over America's terrible roads. That the twenty-fours would have to be shipborne to the eventual battle site was evidence that Rochambeau knew they would not be used against New York but against a target in coastal Virginia.

PART SIX

A Triumph and
a Fare-Thee-Well

1781–1783

17

"Could not waste the most decisive opportunity of the whole war."
—Francisco de Saavedra

While the French troops were marching across Connecticut to link up with the Americans at the North River, preparatory to attacking either New York or another target, in Philadelphia La Luzerne was completing a conquest of Congress. At the start of 1781 he had had an important instrument all but drop into his lap: former general and current New Hampshire representative John Sullivan. He and Sullivan had been acquainted, but their relationship changed when Clinton decided to send to Philadelphia Sullivan's brother Daniel, a prisoner in New York, ostensibly to obtain his own exchange but really to suborn John; a note that Daniel carried, supposedly from a British Loyalist admirer in New York, extolled his brother as "a gentleman of the first abilities & Integrity in the Government. . . . Much I think is expected from you in this matter . . . pray save the further Effusion of the Blood of your Countrymen[.] Step forth & let Negotiation Originate." John Sullivan was being asked to sponsor the reconciling and reuniting of America and Great Britain. He tore up the note, sent Daniel back to New York, and gleefully related the story to La Luzerne, who offered him cash to be his man in Congress. Sullivan accepted and was soon helping La Luzerne realize his goals.

Some were salutary for America and some were not. La Luzerne argued to Congress that the United States must become more federalized; he assisted in persuading the last state holdout, Maryland, to sign the Articles of Confederation; and he championed the establishment of centralized ministries of finance, state, and war. Morris became the finance chief, Knox the war department head and, with a strong assist from La Luzerne, Robert Livingston became secretary of state for foreign affairs. La Luzerne pushed hard to prevent Arthur Lee from being awarded the foreign affairs post or an appointment to represent the United States in expected peace negotiations. He backed John Jay for that post, and also to have Congress retain Franklin, whose allegiance to the alliance and to France had been strong, and to ditch Adams. Congress refused the last notion, reconfirming Adams as a minister for peace negotiations to be held in Russia, so La Luzerne managed to have others appointed to surround and outvote Adams, namely Jefferson and Henry Laurens, the latter still in the Tower.

Then La Luzerne went even further. Since France through its good offices was to handle American participation in the Russian mediation, he asked that the instructions to the "ministers plenipotentiary," adopted on June 15, 1781, read:

> You are to accede to no treaty of peace which shall not be such as may 1st effectually secure the independence and sovereignty of the thirteen states according to the form and effect of the treaties subsisting between the said States and His Most Christian Majesty; and 2ndly in which the said treaties shall not be left in their full force & validity. . . . You are to undertake nothing in the negotiations for peace or truce without [the French ministers'] knowledge and concurrence and ultimately to govern yourselves by their advice and Opinion endeavouring in your whole conduct to make them sensible how much we rely on His Majesty's influence for effectual support in every thing that may be necessary to the present security or future prosperity of the United States of America.

This was an extraordinary coup: At a stroke Congress had taken from its emissaries the power to themselves determine the future destiny of the United States of America, while instructing them not to act without first obtaining the permission of the king of France. "I regard the negotiation as now being in His Majesty's hands, save for independence," La Luzerne bragged to Vergennes.

The biggest loser, as a result of these instructions, was Congress; for either they would permit France to unilaterally take over negotiations for ending the war, or force Congress's own emissaries to reject the instructions. As Jay put it upon reading the new instructions, "As an American I [feel] an interest in the dignity of my country, which renders it difficult for me to reconcile myself to the idea of [our] ministers to be absolutely governed by the advice and opinions of the servants of another sovereign." Vergennes was miffed that any American might misperceive the benevolence or sagacity of Louis XVI in future negotiations—or the weakness of America's own position; after all, he wrote to La Luzerne, there was "no province [of America] in which the English do not have some sort of establishment." But since the Russian and Austrian wouldbe mediators had been pushing Great Britain, Spain, and France to agree to a plan in which the United States was specifically not considered to be an independent country, nor invited to be part of the largecountry discussions, he worried that the American commissioners would not agree to the condition. Accordingly he took the emotionally difficult step of asking Adams, with whom he had so deeply clashed, to return from the Netherlands to discuss the matter.

When Adams arrived in Paris in July 1781, he had not seen the new congressional instructions and was acting only on the old ones. Once apprised of the Russian mediation scheme, which was in the form of a proposal, he translated it from the French, made notes, and in a pointby-point letter to Vergennes, rejected every iota of it:

As there is upon Earth no judge of a sovereign State but the Nation that composes it, the United States can never consent, that their Independence shall be discussed or called into question by any Sovereign or Sovereigns however respectable, nor can their interests be made a question in any [Peace] Congress, in which their Character is not acknowledged and their Minister admitted.

Adams was willing to be a party to a peace conference, but only if Russia and Austria would, as a preliminary, "acknowledge . . . the Sovereignty of the United States." This was expressly what Russia and Austria did not want to do. Two days later Adams amended his ideas to say that independence did not have to be established prior to discussions but would have to be an expected outcome. Then he changed his mind again. By the time he returned to The Hague he felt so in the grip of a nervous disorder that after five or six days in which he had totally lost awareness of the world, it brought him to "the Gate of Death." Among the contributing factors was his fear that peace for America on good terms was a long way off. His recovery was slow.

Silas Deane, no longer an American agent but having returned to Europe, seemed also to be close to mentally ill, writing letters to everyone he could think of, pointing out what he saw as the perfidy of France toward America, France's growing despotism, and the need for the United States to immediately end the war and begin a new and better relationship with Great Britain. He left France for the Netherlands and expressed his desire to return soon to London.

Once Rochambeau's troops had encamped near the North River—on the left, as the Montbarrey orders had dictated—they and the Continental troops meshed somewhat. There were nightly dinners attended by top officers from both groups, but the midlevel officers and the troops of each army were kept separated.

Rochambeau and Washington spent days together on horseback, with Duportail and Chastellux to interpret, making reconnaissance patrols of New York. They edged ever closer to Manhattan. At dawn one day they rode to a point at which at low tide they could cross to an island just off Long Island; they did so in strength, including some ninety horses. While Duportail and his colleagues made measurements for potential emplacement of batteries, the two senior commanders took a nap. When they awoke, they realized that the tide had come in more rapidly than expected. They could be trapped or drowned. Fortunately some soldiers had also realized this and had brought a boat into which the commanders, along with their bridles and saddles, were taken back to safety, while the horses were swum across. Duportail's report judged that a siege of New York would be almost as difficult to accomplish as a frontal assault, and would require about twenty thousand troops—more than twice the number then available to Washington and Rochambeau.

A third matter of importance to the Revolutionary War also came to fruition in the same time period, early summer of 1781, while Rochambeau was marching across Connecticut to link with Washington, and while La Luzerne was persuading Congress to allow Louis XVI and Vergennes to negotiate America's future. In June, in a harbor in Haiti, the Comte de Grasse and the Spanish nobleman Captain Francisco de Saavedra, thirty-five, sat down aboard the majestic *Ville de Paris* to decide where in North America de Grasse's fleet would go.

Saavedra had credence in this meeting because he had recently been involved in successfully besieging a British stronghold in North America, Pensacola. Saavedra, a special emissary from Carlos III appointed to coordinate the activities of France and Spain in the Caribbean, had put together the forces for the Pensacola attack—the Spanish and French soldiers, the vessels, and their commander, Gálvez. Back in May, that Spanish fleet and polyglot army had started to attack that Gulf Coast city. Bernardo de Gálvez's 1,315 troops had been ferried there on Spanish ships from Havana, some of those ships and troops having recently crossed the Atlantic to reinforce the Spanish Caribbean fleet.

The first Spanish ship to enter Pensacola Bay had run aground and the fleet commander refused to attempt the bar with any of his other vessels. Gálvez was furious, and his situation was shortly remedied by the arrival of more ships sent by grateful American residents of New Orleans, ships that were put under his sole command. With these he passed the sandbar, and then needled the Havana-based ships into following him through. During the ensuing siege he was wounded twice. Saavedra then arrived with more reinforcements, Spanish regulars accompanied by eight hundred French troops and some free blacks. By May 1781 in Pensacola Bay Gálvez commanded seven thousand men—more soldiers than Rochambeau had at Newport. On May 8, a Spanish cannonball pierced the walls of Crescent Fort and hit the powder magazine, which exploded, killing 105 men and making it possible for the Spanish to fire without opposition at the main Pensacola defensive works, Fort George. Two days later the British surrendered. It was a major victory. Together with the Spanish-led takeover of the lower Mississippi, it left control of the Mississippi Delta and the nearby Gulf of Mexico in Spanish hands. Gálvez, promoted to field marshal in charge of all Spanish military forces in the Caribbean and New Spain, elevated Saavedra to strategist of all future military activities.

Before entering the military Saavedra had been a theological student, and his intelligence had aided his rise in the Spanish government, in diplomatic and council posts, before he was sent to Havana. France had agreed that in the Caribbean, Spain's would be the dominant force and the French would be under their command. Learning of de Grasse's imminent arrival in Haiti a week in advance, Saavedra went there and was well acquainted locally by the time he and de Grasse met aboard the *Ville de Paris* on June 17.

There the leaders formulated a two-step plan. De Grasse would best the British in North America, and then in the fall return to the Caribbean to take part in a joint Franco-Spanish operation against Jamaica, the most valuable of the British possessions. In regard to the North American venture, as Saavedra put it in his diary, they "could not waste the most decisive opportunity of the whole war"—to take advantage of the British naval inferiority in the American Atlantic. The most vulnerable British point, in the view of Saavedra and de Grasse, was Virginia, because the British troops there enjoyed only sporadic naval protection from squadrons based in New York and the Caribbean. De Grasse was also not inclined to attack New York because he knew that d'Estaing had not been able to pass the bar at Sandy Hook. Letters from Rochambeau and La Luzerne championed a Chesapeake Bay focus, as did Saavedra's positive reports of the success of the action at Pensacola against a well-defended British stronghold. De Grasse would go to Virginia.

The most important strategic decision of the war, to attack the British on the Yorktown Peninsula, was made by French and Spanish military men in a Haitian harbor.

To receive permission to depart for American waters, de Grasse had to obtain his ships' formal release by Spain. Gálvez authorized that, but Saavedra vetoed allowing de Grasse to take Spanish ships with him, as de Grasse had requested, on the grounds that their fighting directly for America might be construed as de facto recognition of American independence, which Madrid was at pains to avoid. The Spanish fleet, by remaining in the Caribbean and protecting both French and Spanish colonies, would tie down Rodney's squadron, as the British admiral would not risk going to the aid of his brethren in the north for fear that the Spanish would use his absence to seize more British sugar islands.

De Grasse was under instructions from Rochambeau to raise specie to pay the French troops, whose stash was running out. He was unable to coax very much from the French Caribbean colonists, even after public notices advertising a very favorable credit exchange rate. Saavedra then stepped in. Deciding that "without the money the Conde de Grasse could not do anything and the delay . . . would put his fleet in jeopardy," the young captain told the admiral to start his ships toward America and that he would have conveyed to them at sea the needed money, which he would obtain from Cuba. In just six hours, by an "emergency appeal" to the populace in Havana, he collected five hundred pesetas and had them ferried to de Grasse. The admiral then took off northward with his fleet, sending ahead a letter that his destination was Chesapeake Bay.

Received by Barras on August 11, 1781, de Grasse's letter was sent to Rochambeau at the North River. Rochambeau received it on August 14 and showed it to Washington: de Grasse was en route to Chesapeake Bay, "the spot which seems to be indicated by you, M. le comte, and by MM Washington de La Luzerne and de Barras as the surest to effect the good which you propose."

Washington had seen this decision coming, had even somewhat prepared for it, and had come to realize that New York's fortifications and beefed-up forces made any proposed Franco-American attack there risk turning into a disaster. But he was still upset. Not only was his dream of retaking New York dashed, but the decision on where to make a joint attack on the British had essentially been made without him.

One mark of a great leader is, when definitively blocked to seize the moment by expanding into what has become the necessary direction. As soon as Washington realized that his army, and Rochambeau's, and Barras's fleet now had no choice but to go to the Yorktown Peninsula, there to meet de Grasse's fleet and Lafayette's army and Steuben's—six different forces!—and take on the British, he did not hesitate. Rather, he issued a flurry of orders. Barras had brashly suggested a sally against Nova Scotia. Washington scotched that. He told Lafayette to seal off the Yorktown Peninsula so that the British could not escape. He directed Barras to lade on board, in addition to Rochambeau's left-behind twenty-fours, which would be needed for a siege, the salted provisions that he had stashed at Newport.

Writing to de Grasse, in a letter cosigned by Rochambeau, Washington conceded that the decision not to force New York had been ratified by the arrival there of three thousand more British troops, which raised the number of the city's defenders to above fourteen thousand, more men than he and Rochambeau commanded. What Washington did not then know was that those new troops were the ones captured by Gálvez at Pensacola, who had been paroled to New York on the promise that they would not henceforth war against the Spanish, but who had made no such agreement in regard to fighting the Americans or the French.

Lafayette had previously had important assignments, but none had ever been so critical to the future of his adopted country as keeping Cornwallis bottled up on the Yorktown peninsula. The British general had boasted, "The boy cannot escape me"—echoing what General Howe had said of Lafayette in 1778—and Cornwallis's arrogance was also evident in rejecting the advice of his predecessor as head of the Virginia forces, Benedict Arnold, who had warned him not to settle at Yorktown but to pick a site further inland so that he would have more avenues by which to escape a trap. Throughout the late spring and early summer Cornwallis pursued Lafayette but was unable to make good on his boast to capture him, and in August he allowed the "boy" to turn the tables. Lafayette, by repeatedly but lightly engaging Cornwallis's men, coaxed the British into concentrating their forces to repel a full-scale attack, a massing that left the British and Hessian troops even more vulnerable to encirclement.

Among Washington's flurry of orders, issued once he had learned definitively that de Grasse was on his way to Chesapeake Bay, was an instruction to Lafayette:

> You will immediately take such a position as will best enable you to prevent [the enemy's] sudden retreat thro' North Carolina, which I presume they will attempt the instant they perceive so formidable an Armament [as de Grasse arriving]. . . . You will be particularly careful to conceal the expected arrival of the Count, because if the enemy are not apprised of it, they [will stay] on board

their transports in [Chesapeake] Bay, which will be the luckiest Cercumstance in the World.

Lafayette had already begun to take such positions, and by August 21 could report to Washington that he had stationed troops at the forks of the York River and nearer to Williamsburg, had written to the Virginia governor to raise more troops and send them his way, and to General Wayne to hurry a junction of their troops to block any Cornwallis exit. "Taking Whatever is in the Rivers, and taking position of the Rivers themselves while the Main Body defends the Bay—forming a jonction of land forces at a Convenient and safe point—Checking the Ennemy But Giving Nothing to chance Untill properly Reinforced—this is the plan," he wrote to Washington. And so far, it was working.

"Checking" the enemy at every turn had also been serving Nathanael Greene well in his battle against those British forces in the South that were not controlled by Cornwallis. Since Greene had taken over from Gates, by dividing his forces with Daniel Morgan so they would not risk another wholesale capture, Greene in a series of strategic retreats, countermarches, small picked battles, and lightning raids had evicted the British almost entirely from the Carolinas, forcing them toward confinement in the fortified cities of Charleston and Savannah.

In late August, two days after learning that de Grasse was on the way, Washington's sense of urgency was palpable as he laid out for Rochambeau a route south, noting, "I have named no halting day because we have not a moment to lose—and because the Troops will more than probably, be detained sometime at Trenton—but if you should think it absolutely necessary, Whippany will be a good place for a halt; as there is a good road leading from thence through Chatham (five Miles distant) to Elizabeth Town and Staten Island." The planned halt at Chatham was in part for the purpose of exploiting a recently discovered British weakness.

While the French army had been at Phillipsburg, along the North River, Baron von Closen, a Rochambeau aide-de-camp and a captain in the Deux-Ponts Regiment, had noted in his diary that the British sailing up the river in their direction had as their object "the seizure of some bread and other provisions . . . from Peekskill, where the quartermaster had built some ovens." Later that evening Closen learned that the British in their raid on a French warehouse had taken "1000 rations of bread," and fifty "recently-dyed" outer coats intended for the cavalry. Two days later, as the British raiders were passing back downriver, French howitzers fired at them, causing half the crew of their flagship to jump overboard. "You can be sure . . . that they will no longer crave our white bread," Closen smirked to his diary.

Closen's ability to read and speak English had helped him become an enthusiastic appreciator of the American cause and of what the Americans had accomplished thus far during the war; he had taken the time when in Boston to tour Bunker Hill and he read to augment his knowledge of America. When escorting Washington, Closen endeared himself to the commander by asking to be shown locations where events of importance to the war had occurred. Washington happily obliged.

Because the armies were to cross the North River at a point well above New York and then turn south, it became imperative to deceive the British into thinking that the armies' target was still New York. "Is it not advantageous to pursue the preparation for the attack of New yourk[?]," Duportail had written to Washington the day after the decision was made to go to Virginia. "If the enemy perceive that we give up the idea of attacking New york they will reinforce Portsmouth Virginia, may be before we can get there." Washington agreed, as did Rochambeau. The American commander then sent Duportail south with instructions to meet de Grasse the moment that the admiral hove into sight.

By this point in the war, the ruse that Washington had so often used—constructing excess tents and fires to make the British believe that more troops faced them than actually existed—was shopworn. Moreover, in this instance he felt it necessary to avoid leaks by preventing the American and

French troops from knowing precisely where they were heading or that a ruse was being constructed. So he proposed building pontoons, and taking thirty landing craft with the army as it moved, which the British (and his own troops) would reason was necessary only if the attack was to be through Staten Island to New York. Rochambeau agreed with these ruses, and proposed an additional one.

It began to take shape on August 19, when the French forces reached Chatham, twenty-five miles west of New York. Closen was rhapsodic about New Jersey's "beautiful country . . . a land of milk and honey, with game, fish, vegetables, poultry, etc.," which made quite a contrast to New York State, "where misery is written on the brow of the inhabitants."

If the British believed that French were making a permanent camp at Chatham, Rochambeau figured, they would reason that such a camp meant that the French were aimed at New York, not only to attack there but to be available to support de Grasse should he appear at Sandy Hook. But if the French forces were headed south, Rochambeau believed that the British would conclude, the French camp at Chatham would only be a temporary one.

So Rochambeau dispatched his quartermaster to buy up all the spare bricks to be found along the Raritan River and in the vicinity, as he later wrote, for the purpose of "establishing a *boulangerie* at Chatham." The quartermaster did as ordered and was fired upon while doing so, which pleased Rochambeau. The ovens were constructed and put to work baking batches of aromatic, crusty French bread. Washington ordered an American unit to guard the ovens. All was done, Closen reported to his diary, "to make Clinton believe that we were seriously considering an attack on New York and that the army would remain camped in the region." As a Washington aide-de-camp also noted in his diary, other ovens were ordered built even nearer Sandy Hook, contracts given for forage, and preliminary settings for emplacing batteries were made, so that "By these maneuvres and the correspondent march of the Troops, our own army no less than the Enemy are completely deceived."

By a few days after the *boulangerie* was in place in Chatham, guarded by an American unit, the bulk of the French and American troops were well down the state toward Philadelphia. "This maneuver prevented General Clinton from sending forces to the rescue of Cornwallis," Rochambeau would state. Letters sent by Clinton in this period reveal his belief that the French and Americans were still in Chatham. Also, since New York could be de Grasse's target, Clinton was not prepared to do much but to remain where he was. Not until August 28 did Clinton learn definitively that Washington's troops were nearing Trenton, thirty miles from Philadelphia, that Rochambeau's troops were not far behind, and that Barras had sailed southward from Newport. On September 2 Clinton finally informed Cornwallis that Washington's forces were on their way toward his, accompanied by Rochambeau's substantial French forces and expecting to meet Admiral de Grasse's force there.

Neither at that time nor later did Clinton ever acknowledge that at the most important moment of the war, he had been effectively tricked into complacency by the British taste for French bread.

18

"The measures which we are now pursuing are big with great events."
— George Washington

In mid-August 1781, Admiral Hood's fleet was at the northern edge of the Caribbean, looking for the arrival of de Grasse's, when Hood learned from a messenger ship sent from New York that de Grasse was likely to attack New York. The message said that de Grasse would first go to Newport, join with Barras's fleet, and then both would attack the British stronghold—so Hood should hasten to New York to help fend them off. Departing the Caribbean for the American coast, on August 25 Hood "made the land a little to the southward of Cape Henry. . . . Finding no enemy had appeared either in the Chesapeake or Delaware, I proceeded [to] Sandy Hook."

Forty-eight hours later, de Grasse's fleet arrived at Chesapeake Bay, with twenty-eight ships of the line, four frigates, and three thousand French soldiers.

A small boat came out to meet the *Ville de Paris*. Despite seeing its fleur-de-lis flags and its sailors dressed in white, not in British blue, those in the small boat asked where Admiral Rodney could be found. The visitors were conveyed to de Grasse's cabin where they were informed that they were now prisoners. The banquet they had brought, intended for

Rodney, was eaten by the French officers while offering toasts to him. To forestall any Cornwallis exit from the peninsula, de Grasse sent some ships to block the York and James Rivers. Shortly Lafayette's associate Jean-Joseph Soubadère de Gimat came aboard with news that Rochambeau and Washington were marching down the Atlantic seaboard to link with the fleet.

Those two commanders were just then reaching Philadelphia and a profuse welcome. At Washington's request, Rochambeau loaned to Robert Morris twenty thousand dollars in specie. The term was short—one month. The French general's own troops' wages were waiting on cash that de Grasse was bringing from Cuba and the money that Laurens had carried from Versailles. Morris then gave Rochambeau a gift of flour from his warehouses—perhaps after hearing the bakery-deceit story, which Rochambeau became fond of repeating—and added ten thousand dollars of his own to the twenty thousand for Washington. The thirty thousand dollars enabled the commander to surprise his troops with a month's pay in hard cash. "This was the first that could be called money, which we had received as wages since the year '76," the diarist Joseph Plumb Martin recalled: six French crowns each, paid only to line soldiers, not to officers.

The army's poverty was reflected in its ragtag appearance as the men marched through Philadelphia in a line two miles long, stirring clouds of dust. Continental officers in handsome uniforms provided a bright contrast, though not as startling as that furnished the next day by the French. After a halt at the outskirts to powder wigs and make white uniforms glisten, the French marchers paraded through Philadelphia, resplendent far beyond the British in the 1777–78 occupation. Lauzun's Legion, riding on draped steeds, wore the most exciting multicolored garb. The Soissonnais Regiment put on a show of intricate rifle handling.

Washington smiled at the guests during the formal receptions in Philadelphia but was "distressed beyond expression," he confessed in a letter to Lafayette, at not knowing whether de Grasse had made Chesapeake Bay. In moving the land forces toward Virginia, Washington had taken a huge gamble: Should de Grasse not arrive on schedule, or be bested by the British fleet, the American and French armies, rather than Cornwallis's, might be trapped and the war lost.

By the time Washington reached Philadelphia, his emissary to de Grasse, Duportail, had boarded the *Ville de Paris* and introduced himself. The admiral was in the process of putting ashore three thousand troops, led by Claude Henri de Rouvroy, Comte de Saint-Simon to link up with Lafayette's forces, which were approaching from Jamestown. Offloading was always a time of peril since the force was not in a good defensive position and therefore was vulnerable. Saint-Simon's officers were amazed that Cornwallis did not attack. They made haste in the unloading, which stoked de Grasse's desire to use the combined troops to attack the British immediately.

Not yet, Duportail pleaded, basing his request on a Washington letter that he hand-delivered to de Grasse and likely translated for him on the spot. Washington begged the admiral not only to wait for his and Rochambeau's arrival before attacking Cornwallis but to detach ships upriver to bring the American and French troops to the Yorktown Peninsula. "I have not hesitated to open my heart to [Duportail] and acquaint him with all my resources and my orders," de Grasse wrote back, and expressed willingness to wait for a general "whose experience in the profession of arms, knowledge of the country and insight will greatly augment our resources," but protested that his short time in American waters made it unfeasible to use for transport the vessels needed to block Cornwallis's supply ships. "Come with the greatest expedition," Duportail urged Washington in his own letter. "Let us make us[e] of the short stay of the count de grasse here. we have no choice left I thinck, when 27 of line are in Chesapeake, when great americain and French forces are joined we must take Cornwallis or be all dishonored."

Duportail also wanted Washington to hurry because he feared that de Grasse might flatter Lafayette into an immediate attack. De Grasse did try, telling Lafayette, "I want to contribute everything I can to further your glory and assure you of spending a winter of tranquility [after vanquishing Cornwallis]. . . . With pleasure, I join your admirers." Lafayette resisted the pressure.

In midmorning on September 5, offloading was continuing when the scout frigate *Aigrette* signaled a press of sail arriving from the north. De Grasse hoped it was Barras, but as the number of vessels grew, the *Aigrette* soon signaled that it was the British, with so many ships that de Grasse concluded that both Hood's and Graves's squadrons had come after him.

He wanted to sail out in force to meet them. But to do so he had to wait until the Chesapeake Bay tide turned to ebb. The French exit of Chesapeake Bay began at 11:30 a.m., with Bougainville's flagship leading the vanguard. Although the fleet was anchored in proper three-column formation, it still took several hours for all the ships to exit the relatively narrow channel, which they had to do one by one, and even then de Grasse had to leave behind the four warships positioned to block Cornwallis, along with the eighteen hundred sailors and ninety officers who had been offloading troops. Thus de Grasse's fleet for this action off the Virginia Capes was smaller than it had been, and shorthanded; and he faced a formidable enemy, in attack formation, that had the weather gage.

At that very same hour, Rochambeau and his retinue were floating down the Delaware River from Philadelphia toward Head of Elk. They had passed Forts Mercer and Mifflin and other important sites of the war. Washington and his retinue had set off overland to meet them at Head of Elk; the commander loved to ride his steed and did not much like being on a boat. As the French approached the town of Chester they saw on the bank an American officer waving wildly at them with a hat in one hand and a white handkerchief in the other. Nearing, they realized it was Washington. "I never saw a man so thoroughly and openly delighted," Lauzun recalled. What happened next amazed everyone. Washington, upon conveying to Rochambeau that de Grasse had made

Chesapeake Bay, enveloped Rochambeau in a full-body embrace. Each general, Closen observed, had reason to be ecstatic, as did the young officers, "burning with the desire to try their strength against the enemy and avid for *gloire*, as we all were." There was a sense of everything coming together at last, of a moment to be savored for its melding of American and French hearts and wills in an ultimate conjoint endeavor.

The British fleet facing de Grasse's was not in as good shape as it first appeared to the spyglasses of the French. When Hood had reached Sandy Hook, he had been insistent on leaving immediately to counter de Grasse, but Graves protested that his New York fleet was not ready to go. His ships were in poor repair and to obtain four hundred able bodies press-gangs had recently had to roust men from their beds. After taking three days to ready his vessels, Graves still left behind five capital ships—and Hood was appalled. At sea it was Graves's turn to be annoyed, as Hood's vessels were "the shadow of ships more than substance," slowing the fleet to three knots per hour. The nineteen ships of the line included only three recent additions, a tenth of the ships the Admiralty had retained in European waters to counter French and Spanish initiatives in the Mediterranean and Dutch ones in the North Sea. By deciding to keep the bulk of British ships in European waters in 1781, a naval historian writes, "The Admiralty had finally sacrificed the parity in naval strength on which the safety of the scattered British army [in America] depended."

At the start of the Battle of the Virginia Capes, in the early afternoon of September 5, 1781, the British fleet was three miles north of the French, "in a position almost beyond the wildest dreams of a sea-commander," a naval analyst later wrote, since Graves's "whole fleet was running down before the wind and his enemy was . . . working slowly out of harbor. He had only to fall on their van with full force and the day was his." But standard Admiralty fighting orders decreed that attacking ships had to be in line-ahead formation, a maneuver that took Graves ninety minutes to achieve and that allowed the French to get wholly out of the bay. Only at 3:46 p.m. did Graves give the signal to engage, and shortly issued a different order, with the result that only some British ships, rather than the whole line, were positioned properly.

Both sides then began to blast away.

"Thunder, foam and fire," Bougainville wrote of that day; "Those few testing moments for which an entire naval officer's life has been built and for which so many arms have toiled, so much sweat has been poured out in the shipyards to get together all that timber, that iron, those sails." The foretop bowline of his ship was twice shot off, and sailors repairing it were killed by enemy fire. But his *Auguste*, while taking sixty-seven casualties, managed to riddle the British *Terrible* and nearly sank it. The *Auguste* also put three other British ships out of action.

After ninety minutes had gone by and Graves saw that the French were continuing to advance, he signaled his ships to cease the attack and sail away. By 6:30 p.m. the firing ended for the day. The British ships had suffered more than the French ones, although the French had lost more men. Bougainville had gained new respect for de Grasse, with whom he had been feuding, and de Grasse lauded him, saying, "That's what I call fighting." On the British side, Hood became enraged at Graves's missed opportunities, although analysts also later faulted Hood for dilatoriness in carrying out the commander's orders.

Through the night the two fleets drifted southeast, in parallel. The morning revealed that the French ships were less damaged than the British. The wind remained negligible, making it impossible for either side to do more than maintain relative positions. On the third day rainsqualls and a British wish to avoid action and complete repairs also resulted in no skirmishes. French naval corporal Simon Pouzoulet marveled in his diary at his commanders' dexterity in maneuvering for the weather gage, and regretted his ship's not being close enough to the British to send cannon shot at them. Early on September 8 Graves gave orders to sail to the windward of the French and be ready to attack, but was only able to use the weather gage for a short period, as de Grasse by well-executed maneuvers made Graves cede it. Even so, very little fighting ensued. Another night passed. The next morning, September 9, de Grasse's men spotted a fleet on the horizon and, thinking it was the British, gave chase. They never caught it, but Graves chased de Grasse, and by day's end both fleets were nearer to Cape Hatteras, North Carolina, than to Cape Henry, Virginia. That allowed the unknown fleet, which was Barras's, to slip un-opposed into the Chesapeake Bay anchorage.

Barras managed this partly because the British did not expect him—they presumed he had already combined with de Grasse and was not sailing independently—but mostly due to his own initiative. With the craftiness imbued in him by a long career in the French navy, where pres-ervation of assets was always highly regarded, and knowing that he car-ried precious cargo, to avoid encountering the British Barras had chosen a circuitous route. From Newport he sailed east around Long Island, and then due south until he reached a position lateral to Chesapeake Bay, where he turned sharply west and by rapid sailing made it into Chesa-peake Bay unopposed. Upon arrival he immediately offloaded the heavy artillery, provisions, and troops from Newport.

Thus, before shots were fired on land at Yorktown, the two French admirals, de Grasse and Barras, had immensely assisted their army breth-ren's pursuit of the common objective, the defeat of Cornwallis's army.

Washington was then in Baltimore, unaware that there had already been a decisive Battle of the Virginia Capes, and also ignorant that Bar-ras had invested the bay. That evening he rode the sixty miles to Mount Vernon, alone but for his personal servant and one aide. He had not been home since May 4, 1775. The next morning he wrote to Lafayette, "I hope you will keep Lord Cornwallis safe, without provisions or forage, until we arrive."

De Grasse was on his way to the Chesapeake to do just that, having reasoned that the British might lay off the sea action and try to beat him into the anchorage, and not knowing that Barras was already there. A modern French admiral writes that in the seminal Virginia Capes sea battle, while de Grasse was not as aggressive as a Suffren or a Rodney might have been, *"la prudence et le sang-froid"* (prudence and coolness under fire) had produced the essential victory—complete control of Chesapeake Bay.

Upon de Grasse's arrival in the bay, Barras, although more senior and entitled to command, graciously yielded it. Appreciative of the gesture, de Grasse quickly did what Washington had wanted but that he had not earlier felt able to oblige: sent ships to fetch French and American troops and matériel, using Barras's transports and some captured British ones that were able to operate in shallow waters.

The Battle of the Virginia Capes concluded when a Graves reconnaissance frigate reported that the French were all over Chesapeake Bay. The British commanders then agreed, as Graves wrote to London, that due to the enemy's superior position, the poor condition of the British ships, the impending hurricane season, "and the impracticability of giving any effectual succour to General Earl Cornwallis," they must return to New York and refit. With some luck they would return before Cornwallis was starved out and forced to surrender.

The French victory in the sea battle was not yet known at Williamsburg when Lafayette rode in at a gallop, dismounted, "hugged [Washington] as close as it was possible, and absolutely kissed him from ear to ear . . . with as much ardour as ever an absent lover kissed his mistress on his return," wrote the lawyer St.-George Tucker, who stood no more than six feet from the general. Lafayette and Washington were celebrating what was already old news, that de Grasse had arrived, and both believed him to be still at sea, fighting the British. Washington was so worried about the outcome of the sea battle that he had sent word to the Continental and French armies to halt in place, pending further news. That evening, while Washington was a guest of Saint-Simon's, news of the sea victory arrived, and he wrote to de Grasse, "felicitating your Excellency on the Glory of having driven the British Fleet from the Coast." On September 17, Washington, Rochambeau, and their retinues sailed out on a captured ship to meet de Grasse on the flower-bedecked *Ville de Paris*. Here

Washington had his third passionate embrace of the fortnight, with de Grasse, replete with the requisite triple kissing of right, left, and right cheeks. De Grasse chortled and addressed Washington as *"mon cher petit général,"* although the two of them were the same size, about six foot two, and taller than Rochambeau, whose many wounds caused him to stoop.

Washington had brought with him Lafayette, Duportail, Knox, and Chastellux, as well as Benjamin Harrison, slated to become Virginia's next governor. As with many of the Virginia signers of the Declaration of Independence, Harrison had had his property burned by Benedict Arnold, to the point of having all images of the signers and their families deliberately destroyed. Even Banastre Tarleton had not been so vicious in his raids.

The celebration on the *Ville de Paris* was enlivened by a sense of impending action, as the senior allied commanders knew that they could not simply wait out Cornwallis—they would have to force matters. The British were ensconced at a narrow place in York River, in two strongholds on opposite sides, Yorktown and Gloucester. From those points they could shell attacking French ships with land cannons and from the ships that Cornwallis had positioned upriver. Command of that river to the west also gave him escape routes.

What most worried Washington and Rochambeau, however, was not an attempted escape but that Cornwallis might hold out past the day when de Grasse had to sail for the West Indies. "The season is approaching when, against my will, I shall be obliged to forsake the allies for whom I have done my very best and more than could be expected," de Grasse once again warned. While he agreed in writing to extend his and Saint-Simon's stay beyond his October 15 deadline, he insisted that on November 1 he would have to sail, whether or not Cornwallis had surrendered. Washington, in response to this possibility, eloquently summed up the stakes:

The measures which we we are now pursuing, are big with great events; the Peace and Independence of this Country, and the general tranquility of Europe will, it is more than probable, result from our Compleat success, disgrace to ourselves, Triumph to the Enemy, and probable Ruin to the American Cause, will follow our disappointment. The first is certain, if the powerful Fleet, now in Chesapeak Bay . . . can remain to the close of a regular operation, which, from various unforeseen causes, may be protracted beyond our present expectation, The second is much to be apprehended, if from the Fear of loosing the Aid of the Fleet, the operations by Land are precipitated faster than a necessary prudence & regard to the lives of Men, will warrant—the first may be slow, but sure, the second must be bloody & precarious.

The next five days were a blur of bad weather. Washington and Rochambeau's trip back to Williamsburg was so beset by wind and rain that it took until September 22. At 11:00 p.m. on the twenty-first, de Grasse was alerted that the British were going to send fireships—ships deliberately set ablaze for the purpose of burning the enemy's—from upriver at 2:00 a.m. "In the dark night, it was a beautiful and at the same time devastating sight to observe five burning ships under full sail floating down the stream past our eyes," a naval lieutenant noted. Only by dint of good maneuvering and timely rain was de Grasse's fleet able to avoid extensive damage.

That evening at Williamsburg Washington and Rochambeau received word that British admiral Robert Digby was expected in New York momentarily with three more ships of the line, and would set out soon with Hood for the Chesapeake. Closen, sent to the *Ville de Paris* with this news, reported in his diary that it "alarmed and disquieted these excitable gentlemen of the navy, who think only of cruises and battles and do not like to oblige or to cooperate with the land troops." De Grasse wrote to Washington that it would be "imprudent of me to take a position from which it would be impossible to counter such forces," and so proposed moving some ships out of the bay to fight the British fleet and leaving others to protect the armies.

"I cannot conceal from Your Excellency the painful anxiety under which I have labored" since receiving his letter, Washington responded. Contending that the outcome of the coming campaign "is as certain as any Military operation can be rendered by a decisive superiority of strength and means—that it is in fact reducible to calculation," he charged that anything that allowed Cornwallis an escape route or a chance of resupply, such as de Grasse leaving the Bay,

> would frustrate these brilliant prospects—and the consequence would be not only the disgrace & loss of renouncing an enterprise upon which the fairest expectations of the Allies have been founded—after the most expensive preparations and uncommon exertions & fatigues—but the disbanding perhaps the whole Army for want of provisions. . . . If the present opportunity shd be missed . . . no future day can restore us a similar occasion—for striking a decisive blow . . . and that the epoch of an honorable Peace will be more remote than ever.

To emphasize this message Washington sent it with Lafayette, who was still recovering from a fever that had left him shaking. Rochambeau, also apprised of the potential move out of the bay, similarly sent de Grasse a plea against it. These emissaries, along with judicious reflection and the refusal of his captains to abandon the bay, brought the admiral to the conclusion that he ought not to chase phantoms.

"You are the most amiable admiral that I know," Rochambeau congratulated de Grasse on the decision: "You meet all of our wishes and I believe we are going to do good work." But thereafter, every day, Rochambeau sent an aide to the edge of the York River to report on whether the de Grasse fleet remained in position. Washington's heartfelt thank-you to de Grasse—"A great Mind knows how to make personal sacrifices to secure an important general Good"—was followed by his order to the armies to start the march to Yorktown at five the next morning.

The watchword of the day was "Virginia," and the countersigns "York" and "Gloucester" as the troops marched from Williamsburg thirteen miles to the vicinity of Yorktown. There the Americans would array on the right and the French on the left, but the manner in which they would be used in the siege would be up to Rochambeau, Washington acknowledging that the French general was far more expert at sieges, having been involved in fourteen earlier ones. Washington would not get in the way of the French using their expertise and their desire for *gloire,* understanding that any victory at Yorktown would ultimately be America's, and his.

For the French the siege of Yorktown was a fairly ordinary military task, neither very large nor terribly complex. At the same moment, some forty thousand French and Spanish troops, and fifty of France and Spain's warships, were conducting a long-term siege of Gibraltar. At Yorktown, Rochambeau had the requisite supplies for entrenching and cannonading, a sufficiently large workforce, the cooperation of a naval squadron, and as a target a fortified town rather than a fortress. To help his American partners understand siege operations, Rochambeau distributed to them, in translation, Vauban's fifty-two principles for conducting sieges, adapted from his *Traité de l'attaque des places* of 1703.

On the south side of the York River, facing Yorktown, the French were on the west and the Americans on the east, arrayed in a broad semicircle whose farthest point was about 1.5 miles from Yorktown. At the midpoint of that semicircle, the large French artillery pieces were emplaced and, to their rear, the headquarters of Rochambeau and Washington. On the north side of the river, in a smaller semicircle around Gloucester, the Montbarrey rules had the French positioned on the east flank and the Americans on the west.

The three American columns facing Cornwallis were led by Lafayette, Steuben, and Lincoln. Rochambeau's forces, consisting of the Soissonnais, Bourbonnais, Deux-Ponts, Saintonge, Agénois, Touraine, and Gâtinais Regiments, were under the command of the Baron de Vioménil, the Comte de Vioménil, and Saint-Simon. Across the river, near Gloucester, facing troops led by Lt. Col. Thomas Dundas and Tarleton, were the

Virginia Militia, the infantry brought by de Grasse, and Lauzun's Legion, all commanded by the Marquis de Choisy.

The Continental army at Yorktown and Gloucester included nearly all of the French and European officers who had previously played important roles in the Revolutionary War: Lafayette, Duportail, Steuben, Fleury, du Bouchet (who had hot-footed it down to Yorktown once the big field pieces had gone ahead with Barras), du Plessis, Armand, Gimat, Gouvion, and L'Enfant. Du Ponceau's frail constitution had failed him and he had returned to Philadelphia, where, since he had finally turned twenty-one, he took the oath of allegiance to the United States and became an assistant to the new secretary of state, Robert Livingston. Most of the American veteran officers were also at Yorktown—Knox, Lincoln, Wayne, and even Laurens, who had hastened from Boston and had been once again serving as an aide-de-camp until the British captured the major in charge of a regiment, whereupon Washington awarded part of that command to a grateful Laurens. The only serving senior American officers not at Yorktown were General Heath and a small army guarding West Point, and General Greene and his contingent, who were closing in on the coast of South Carolina. Washington and his staff knew very well that it had been the work of Greene and Marion, in keeping other British forces occupied, that had made possible the encirclement of Cornwallis at Yorktown.

In the French army's ranks were officers who had sought for years to serve in the American Revolution, including Lauzun, Chastellux, and Noailles, who had already seen action with d'Estaing. These visitors too were imbued with a sense of mission beyond the achieving of personal *gloire*; all had been impressed by the Americans and their zeal for independence, and had embraced the American cause as their own. Moreover, they had become admirers of the ragtag American army whose soldiers continued to fight despite conditions that would have made any European professional soldier refuse to carry on.

In the lower ranks were such long-serving soldiers as Joseph Plumb Martin, the diarist whose work under Fleury at Fort Mifflin had spurred

him to volunteer for the "sappers and miners" of Duportail's corps; he
and that corps would be at the forefront of the digging of trenches for
the siege. Also in the ranks were such stalwarts as the First Rhode Island
Regiment, composed mostly of blacks, who had acquitted themselves well
at Newport and ever since. Closen estimated that a quarter of the American troops at Yorktown were black.

For all of these French and American officers and soldiers, there was
a tremendous sense of approaching culmination, of all the roads and the
ups and downs of the war having finally led to this juncture, this once-
in-a-lifetime opportunity to achieve the decisive victory and to win not
only a war but also, and even more important, the full emancipation of
a country dedicated to republican principles.

"If the Enemy should be tempted to Meet the Army on its March" from
Williamsburg to Yorktown, Washington's order of September 27 said:

> the General particularly enjoins the troops to place their principle
> relyance on the Bayonet—that they may prove the Vanity of the
> Boast which the British make of their particular pains in deciding
> Battles with that Weapon—He trusts that . . . the french whose
> National Weapon is that of close fight; and the troops in General
> that have so often used it with success will distinguish themselves
> on every Occasion that offers—the Justice of the cause in which
> we are engaged and the *Honor* of the two Nations must inspire
> every breast with sentiments that are the presage of Victory.

Facing almost no opposition, although they took some fire, on the twenty-
eighth the allied troops made it into position around Yorktown. They
were next set to work making thousands of sharpened-stick fascines and
earth-filled gabions. A few wondered when the trench-digging would begin; the answer was not until completion of the fascines and gabions,
which would serve as barriers so that the trenches were not over-run by

the enemy. While the troops worked, the British began bombardment. Their cannonading was kept up at all hours. A single ball could do tremendous damage—one killed four Americans.

On the twenty-ninth the combined French and American army engineers made a reconnaissance of the grounds to be enfiladed with trenches, and recognized formidable obstacles in the manned British emplacements and the redoubts on the perimeter. A French engineer reported to his journal:

> They had encamped part of their troops between the redoubts and the batteries, and the main town, in a way that indicated they could extend them and defend them with the advantages of the lay of the land and of the high ground. We would be obliged to attack them with great force, and we should not have been able to do this without great loss.

But that night Cornwallis abruptly withdrew his forces from the perimeters of Yorktown and, across the river, from outside Gloucester. He was hunkering down because Clinton had assured him that British troops would come to his rescue, and would depart New York for the Chesapeake by October 5.

Cornwallis's withdrawal presented an opportunity, Washington reported to Congress: "By this Means we are in possession of very advantageous Grounds, which command in a very near Advance, almost the whole Remaining Line of their Defence. All the Expedition that our Circumstances will admit, is using, to bring up our heavy Artillery & Stores, & to open our Batteries—this Work I hope will be executed in a few Days, when our Fire will begin with great Vigor."

As these preparations were being undertaken, new units continued to arrive and augment the Continental forces. One was commanded by Alexander Hamilton. Since Hamilton's break with Washington in the spring, he had worked assiduously to obtain a command, and on July 31 Washington had relented and allowed him that of a New York light infantry battalion. Marching separately from the main armies, Hamilton's battalion made it from New York to Yorktown just as the siege was being readied.

On October 3, as Choisy was moving closer to Gloucester, Tarleton's cavalry charged out. Lauzun would recall that it was three times the size of his own, but he nonetheless ran at them. "Tarleton saw me and rode towards me with a pistol raised. We were about to fight single-handed . . . when his horse was thrown by one of his dragoons pursued by one of my lancers." The intercession of other British troops kept the two commanders apart, and the encounter ended with the British unable to deter the allies from tightening the circle around Gloucester.

That day Washington received a dispatch from Greene telling of the battle of Eutaw Springs a month earlier; in it Greene had lost ground but captured five hundred British soldiers and prevented further British progress; British troops in the south, confined to Savannah and Charleston, would be unable to assist Cornwallis. As Greene wrote to his friend Knox, "We have been beating the bush, and the General has come to catch the bird. Never was there a more inviting object to glory."

On the night of October 5–6 the second stage of the siege began—on schedule and with tremendous force and very precise instructions. Those from Washington covered fifty-five different matters, from the exact size of the fascines to the position of flags to be planted to what to do if the enemy attacked the diggers while they were at work. Shifts of the fifteen thousand men available from both armies enfiladed trenches at a distance 2,800–3,200 feet from the British lines, and parallel to them. The right end of the works was flanked by the river escarpment, the left was anchored on a small ravine. Most of the picks and shovels used were French—Rochambeau had brought along four thousand. The trenches were deliberately situated outside the range of Cornwallis's grapeshot, though not beyond that of his cannons. The diggers threw the dirt above the trench and onto the side closest to the British to screen them from enemy fire; some was thrown into the newly made gabions, which were three feet higher than the embankment. The trenches were made four feet deep and ten feet wide, allowing soldiers to course through without being overly exposed to enemy fire. Redoubts at each end, and some in the middle, housed guards to defend the diggers. Zigzag side trenches were dug to bring troops even closer to the British. A diversion was made by having a number of campfires, well off to the side, in front of which men constantly passed; the diarist Martin reported that "the British were led to imagine that we were about some secret mischief there, and consequently they directed their whole fire to that quarter, while we were entrenching literally under their noses."

"Before Morning the Trenches were in such forwardness as to cover the Men from the enemys fire," Washington wrote after that first night. "The work was executed with so much secresy & dispatch that the enemy were, I believe, totally ignorant of our labor till the light of the Morning discovered it to them." Duportail supervised the work to the point of exhaustion, relying more and more on his subordinate officers, particularly Gouvion, who laid out the path of the trench.

That evening the entrenchers were subjected to concentrated enemy fire on a single position, producing casualties—the result, they learned, of an allied deserter having told the British the trench's location. Saint-Simon's troops created a diversionary attack that allowed more progress. British deserters told of famine and pestilence thinning the British ranks. Moreover, everyone could smell the results of one desperate Cornwallis move, the killing of four hundred horses whose carcasses were then dumped in the river.

On October 7, when a Pennsylvania unit sought to parade with flags and drums in the trench, Hamilton stepped in. Citing Vauban, he decreed the classical way of doing so, which culminated in the marchers climbing out of the trench and flaunting their power by performing the "manual of arms"—rifle-handling maneuvers—in full view of the enemy. Fortunately, none of the show-offs was killed.

At various points in the entrenching process, Rochambeau and Washington, emulating Shakespeare's *Henry V*'s "a little touch of Harry in the night," separately, and in Washington's case incognito in an overcoat that hid his uniform, visited the front to speak quietly with their sappers. When Martin heard a superior officer whisper to the visitor, "Your Excellency," he deduced it was Washington. "Had we dared, we might have cautioned him for exposing himself too carelessly to danger at such a time, and doubtless he would have taken it in good part if we had."

By midafternoon on October 9, the trench was close enough to the British lines to allow the commanders to bring forward fifty-two big guns, plus mortars and smaller-bore cannons. The allies were several days ahead of the siege schedule due to the lightness of the soil to be moved and the relative absence of British harassment of the diggers. Many of the American cannons had originally been French and were a generation older than the heavy pieces brought across the Atlantic by Rochambeau. The largest had even more recently been brought from Newport by Barras, and by ox teams provided by Virginia's governor that had appeared at Williamsburg just in time to haul the big guns overland to Yorktown.

As dusk approached, at an agreed-upon signal—an American flag hoisted atop an American emplacement and a French one atop one of theirs—allied cannon fire began. Washington granted Saint-Simon the first shot, from a French twenty-four. Knox lit the flame for the second, and then handed it to Washington, who ceremoniously touched off the initial American fuse. As with virtually everything done at Yorktown, the cannonades were conducted in equal measure by American and French forces, even when, as with the quality and accuracy of the cannons, the French troops' equipment was far better than that of the Americans. In charge of the French artillery was François-Marie, Comte d'Aboville, an expert who had worked out the theory of concentrating masses of fire on a single objective, a theory he had occasion to put into practice at Yorktown. The French naval corporal Simon Pouzoulet, after fighting at sea with de Grasse, had come ashore to serve with the artillery, and marveled to his diary at how well-coordinated were the salvos of d'Aboville and Knox. D'Aboville and his lieutenants—among them, du Plessis—had more experience than the Americans; but Chastellux noted, in regard to Knox:

One cannot sufficiently admire the intelligence and activity with which he collected from different places and transported to the batteries more than 30 pieces of cannon and mortars of large caliber for the siege. . . . The artillery was always very well served, the general incessantly directing it and often himself pointing the mortars; seldom did he leave the batteries.

Within hours Washington was able to record in his diary that the combined forces' cannons had "good effect as they compelled the Enemy to withdraw from their ambrazures the Pieces which had previously kept up a constant firing." That day, 3,600 allied balls were lobbed at Yorktown, virtually destroying it above ground. A blazing ball, heated in a French oven especially constructed for that purpose, hit the HMS *Charon*, which caught fire and burned completely. All through Yorktown soldiers and civilians were dying in the streets, their limbs cut off or otherwise grievously wounded, but the incessant bombardment preventing the injured from being brought indoors for medical attention.

Cornwallis could not help but be appalled. On the tenth there were two other discouraging matters: His attempt at embarking eighteen barges loaded with British troops to land on the Gloucester side was foiled by Choisy's use of his cannons to blast them and force their return to the Yorktown side. Also, a messenger in a whaleboat, rowed all the way from New York by men who on the last leg managed to slip through de Grasse's fleet, handed Cornwallis precisely the message from Clinton that he had dreaded: No British rescue expedition had yet started out.

As the allied land forces tightened the circle around Yorktown and the siege neared its climax, in the harbor de Grasse was becoming irritable at fellow senior commanders who asked him for everything—more troops, more vessels to ferry them and their supplies, and even more flour. "You're taking my flour, that's pulling the covers off me too far," he wrote to Rochambeau. "How happy I will be when I'm out of the Chesapeake." Rochambeau apologized and offered to replace the flour. In refusing Washington's request to station ships above Yorktown to facilitate communications, de Grasse asked him to furnish rowboats to tow the French ships out of danger of fire ships, but the next day he apologized. "I am a Provençal and a sailor. Those are sufficient reasons for being impulsive. I admit my guilt and depend on your friendship."

By October 11 the Franco-American bombardment had done so much damage and disabled so many enemy cannon that Rochambeau began the next step of the siege, the digging of a second trench, within 1,152 feet of the city—nearly half a mile closer to it, a bold leap forward, as decreed by the Vauban principles. Great progress on that new trench was made by morning. But during the next day it became apparent that two redoubts, numbers Nine and Ten, were preventing the second trench from being extended farther. These redoubts were on the eastern side of Yorktown and were extremely well-fortified, in essence mini-forts, each with a moat, abatis and other sharpened sticks, and defended by determined, well-trained British regulars. For the allies to reach within storming distance of the town itself, those British redoubts had to be taken. Plans were made to do so on the night of the 14th.

Here were prime opportunities to achieve *gloire*, and everyone knew it and wanted to take part in storming these particular barricades. The Baron de Vioménil proposed that his grenadiers, his most elite troops, do the honors. Washington and Rochambeau said no, for while the grenadiers were the most experienced fighters, the tasks needed to be divided equally among the armies. Washington assigned redoubt Nine to the French and Ten to the Americans.

Both assignments caused difficulties in the ranks. First, Washington, in awarding the task to Lafayette, had to pass over Steuben. The baron acquiesced without objection because he owed Lafayette, who had protected him earlier in the year from Virginia politicians angered at his reluctance to attack a powerful enemy force. Then Lafayette wanted to award command to Gimat, now a battalion leader. Hamilton, learning of this, erupted. After all, the soldiers to be led were Americans, and he had more seniority. He also demanded command because it would be his last—indeed his only—chance for battlefield glory. Should he remain on the sidelines and the fighting end soon, he would have been through the war without a command. Washington overruled Lafayette and gave Hamilton command, with Gimat leading one of its battalions. Laurens headed another, which would attempt to prevent the British from retreating without being captured. At nearly the last minute, Armand de la Rouërie, who had ridden to Yorktown on his own after serving elsewhere in the South, pleaded with Washington and Hamilton to be allowed to take part in the assault on redoubt Ten. They accepted the marquis and some of his men as volunteers.

The password of the night was "Rochambeau," which to some American soldiers sounded like "Rush on, boys," a phrase they deemed highly appropriate. Also among Hamilton's men that night were the First Rhode Island, and Duportail's sappers and miners, one of them Martin. When the diarist saw officers affixing their bayonets to the ends of staves that were much longer than rifles, he knew the fighting was going to be intense, close, and dangerous.

On the French side were two regiments, the Deux-Ponts and the Gâtinais, both under the Comte de Deux-Ponts. Many of the Gâtinais, originally from the Auvergne region, were unhappy at having to fight in a regiment not named for their birthplace. Rochambeau solved this. "My children, I have need of you to-night," he later recalled saying to them. "I hope that you have not forgotten that we served together in the brave regiment of 'd'Auvergne sans tache' [Auvergne without reproach], an honorable name. . . . They replied that if I permitted them to win back their name they would go to the death to the last man." Rochambeau promised that if they fought well, he would petition the king to change the regiment name.

Closen, part of the Deux-Ponts, commanded fifty men for the attack. The signal to commence was three shells lofted in rapid succession. These were sent up, and the French and American units advanced. At the same time, as a diversion, Choisy began firing into Gloucester.

The French ran through the trench and emerged close to redoubt Nine, where they were met by rifle fire. Some French were cut down, but because the French force was triple or quadruple the size of the defending British, they were able to reach the outer defenses of the redoubt and have their sappers and miners start to hack through the abatis while the riflemen covered them. Things did not go well for a time. Some of the French heard, above the fray, Rochambeau's voice urging them on, shouting "Auvergne sans tache!"

The American attack on Ten featured Hamilton, Gimat, and Armand in the lead, with Laurens going around the side, and Martin and his fellow sappers and miners jumping over a moat and then hacking away at the abatis and tearing at its stakes with their bare hands. He and the other sappers evaded enemy fire, Martin realized, because they had fallen into deep shell holes produced by allied cannon fire. The first man over the top of the redoubt gave a shout that echoed Fleury's at Stony Point: "The fort's our own!" At virtually the same time Laurens was able to capture the British commander of the redoubt. In the endeavor the Americans had not fired a single gun.

The American attack was successful, and accomplished in less time and with far fewer casualties than the French one. A military expert later suggested that the French took more casualties because their soldiers hung back and let their unarmed sappers and miners work the abatis before joining them—most of the dead were from those sappers or from the Gâtinais Regiment, a third of whom perished—while the American soldiers and officers joined the sappers and made short work of the abatis.

The overall tally of the French dead continued to mount. A later accounting of Frenchmen who died in actions in defense of the United States during the Revolutionary War identified 2,112 individuals by name, several hundred of whom perished at Yorktown. Moreover, since the total American casualties in the war, according to official estimates, were approximately 6,800 dead on the battlefields, another 6,100 who succumbed to wounds or illnesses contracted while under arms, and as many as 8,000 to 10,000 more who died as prisoners of war—the number of French who lost their lives in the service of the American Revolution was highly significant.

As soon as the redoubts were taken, Cornwallis's forces opened fire on them. "It seemed as if all that side was in flames," Closen reported, and he worried that some of his comrades had been killed or injured; they had been, including a lieutenant and the Vicomte de Deux-Ponts, nearly blinded and made deaf by an incoming ball. Rochambeau awarded two days' extra pay to the soldiers, and bonuses of two *louis* for the surviving sappers. The historian Edward Lengel, summing up the attacks on the redoubts, describes them as a "little masterpiece of tactical cooperation" between the allies. Taking them allowed Washington and Rochambeau to bring forward shorter-range weapons, howitzers, and mortars, and to use the formerly British redoubts as platforms from which to lob deadly missiles into Yorktown.

In Washington's general orders the next morning, he articulated the meaning of the successful attacks: "The General reflects with the highest degree of pleasure on the Confidence which the Troops of the two Nations must hereafter have in each other. Assured of mutual support he is convinced there is no danger which they will not chearfully encounter—no difficulty which they will not bravely overcome."

The British still held out. The allied lines were pervaded by a postbattle cockiness, including a bantering Hamilton and Knox atop a captured redoubt. Their argument was over whether, when a missile came their way, anyone who saw it should shout "A shell!" rather than "A shot," the former preferred by Knox because shells did not explode until after they hit the ground and therefore could be warned against, while there was no avoiding a cannonball. Then two shells entered the redoubt. Both men took cover, Hamilton behind the copious body of Knox. After they managed to avoid being killed, Knox needled Hamilton to accept calling a shell a shell, and also "not to make a breastwork of me again."

On October 15 Cornwallis advised Clinton: "The safety of the place is . . . so precarious that I cannot recommend that the fleet and army should run great risque in endeavouring to save us." At dawn on the sixteenth he sent out 350 men who overran part of the extended allied trench, killed guards, spiked batteries, and threatened to do much more until Noailles, recognizing the British accent of their commander, directed his men to repel the force, killing a few, taking some prisoners, and causing the rest to flee back to Yorktown. Washington wondered, in a note to General Heath—then still guarding West Point—why Cornwallis had bothered with such an attack. The French did not; they recognized it as a *baroud d'honneur*, the final gesture of a soldier who knows he must soon capitulate.

Cornwallis planned one last try at escape, to extract his forces over the river to Gloucester and then away, using the British boats and command of the upper river. He and Dundas figured they could get everyone across in three trips. On the night of the sixteenth, the first trip was successfully launched and reached Gloucester. Then the rain became so torrential that it drove some boats downriver, toward the French ships, and the maneuver was halted and the troops returned to Yorktown.

In the morning the allies began a new, incessant bombardment, and a few hours later Cornwallis sent out the white flag of capitulation. At that signal the allied batteries were ordered to stop firing, and did.

It was October 17, 1781, four years to the day after the surrender of Burgoyne's army at Saratoga. As Washington and his officers knew in their hearts, while that victory at Saratoga had been an American one, albeit due in significant part to the arms, cannon, and ammunition sent by France, the victory at Yorktown was a joint one, as much a result of France's military as of that of the United States of America.

19

"The English are purchasing the peace rather than making it."
—Comte de Vergennes

John Laurens and Noailles handled the surrender negotiations for the allies, but the tone and basic terms had been fixed by Washington in a note to Cornwallis: "The same honors will be granted to the Surrendering Army as were granted to the Garrison of Charleston." This was revenge, for it meant that the defeated army would march out with flags furled and with their bands not permitted to play a tune of conquest. Laurens had been among the humiliated officers at Charleston, and as far back as 1777 had been aware of Cornwallis's "barbarous treatment of the inhabitants" near Philadelphia; he also knew that in the more recent ravaging of Virginia, Cornwallis had been as guilty as Tarleton of unnecessary violence. Thus Cornwallis, having repeatedly behaved as anything but a gentleman, was doubly ineligible for the good treatment usually granted to vanquished warriors.

The British dragged out the talks for two days, mainly to use the time to destroy some armaments, scuttle two warships, and turn loose the remainder of the several hundred black slaves lured into their service with promises of freedom. Many of the released were ill with smallpox.

At 11:00 a.m. on October 19, the articles of capitulation, already signed by Cornwallis, were countersigned by Washington, Rochambeau, and Barras, the latter also for de Grasse, who had taken ill with asthma. At 2:00 p.m. the British marched out, wearing newly issued uniforms, to a tune that was later identified as "The World Turned Upside Down," although it probably was another song whose cadence was more amenable to slow marching. As the British paraded between the ragtag American and the spiffed-up French troops, they fixed their eyes only on the French. Some accounts have Lafayette then asking the American band to play "Yankee Doodle Dandy" to turn curious British heads toward the Continentals; other accounts say that the playing of that particular tune had been forbidden. Sapper Martin thought that the marching British had stared with malice at the French, while Closen thought the British had gazed scornfully at the Americans. A New Jersey officer wrote that the British officers "behaved like boys who had been whipped at school. Some bit their lips; some pouted; others cried." Across the river at the same time, the British marched out of Gloucester to surrender to Choisy.

Cornwallis was absent from this carefully choreographed scene. He claimed illness and sent his second in command, Charles O'Hara, who in an attempt at a deliberate slap rode to the allied chiefs' enclave and asked for Rochambeau. O'Hara was about to offer his sword to the French commander when a Rochambeau aide interposed his horse between him and the French general and directed him to Washington, as Rochambeau also did by a gesture. Washington might have accepted surrender from the hand of Cornwallis but he would not do so from a subordinate, and so by his own hand gesture he further redirected O'Hara to Lincoln—the general who had had to surrender at Charleston. Lincoln accepted the sword, held it for a symbolic moment, and returned it to O'Hara. The British regulars and their allies, Hessians and Bavarians from Anspach, continued marching through the gauntlet and laid down their arms, some of the British doing so with enough force to break the firelocks, until O'Hara ordered them to stop doing that.

Washington in his report of the surrender to Congress devoted most of his letter to detailing his gratitude to the French forces: "Nothing could exceed this Zeal of our allies," he wrote of Rochambeau and his army, and "I wish it was in my Power to express to Congress how much I feel indebted to The Count de Grasse and the officers of the Fleet under his command."

A month after the surrender, as Louis XVI was visiting Marie Antoinette, who was recovering from the birth of the long-awaited Dauphin, the Duc de Lauzun entered and reported the victory at Yorktown. This news was not unexpected, as progress bulletins had long been filtering in. The king ordered a Te Deum. Lauzun then visited his longtime mentor, Maurepas. He found the first minister dying but responsive, and delivered to him a letter from Lafayette about Yorktown, which began: "The play is over, Monsieur le Comte, the fifth act has just come to an end." A few days later, Maurepas died.

In the streets of Paris the three-night celebration of the victory at Yorktown intermingled with the festivities for the birth of the Dauphin. The conjunction made it impossible for the French not to wonder, now that the Americans had been liberated, when their turn at liberty might come, since the arrival of a Dauphin, with its promise of extending the monarchy far into the next century offered scant hope of Louis XVI ever giving his people America's sort of freedom.

In London the rumor of Cornwallis's surrender arrived on November 21 and on November 26 copies of the articles of capitulation were printed in the newspapers. There was rampant speculation that Parliament, when it reopened the next day, would produce a change in ministers, and that the next government would begin peace talks in earnest. George III said no to both ideas, telling the cabinet that the loss of America "would annihilate the rank in which this British Empire stands among the European states," and therefore that the war must continue and that Lord North must remain in office.

North conveyed the message to the legislators, telling them, "A melancholy disaster has occurred in Virginia. But are we, therefore, to lie down and die? No, it ought to arouse us to action. . . . By bold and united exertions everything may be saved; by dejection and despair everything must be lost!" Yet privately North advised George III: "Peace with America seems necessary, even if it can be obtained on no better terms than some Federal Alliance, or perhaps even in a less eligible mode." He sent Nathaniel Forth to Vergennes to see if a separate peace could be made with France.

Vergennes quickly rejected this effort by a disgraced messenger, but he believed that the British would tell the Americans anyway that the French were negotiating a separate peace, in a ploy to separate the allies.

Silas Deane added fuel to that fire by advocating in British newspapers an American reunion with Great Britain, based on what he viewed as contemptuous French treatment of the United States. His articles crossed the Atlantic and brought him further vilification: Congress revoked the name of the Continental navy frigate *Deane* because "the person after whom she was called has by his perfidy and defection forfeited all title to every mark of honor or respect."

In the Commons, votes to oust Germain and Sandwich, the ministers who were deemed most responsible for losing the war, failed but damaged the North government. In late February 1782, General Henry Seymour Conway introduced in the Commons a motion that summed up British public feeling:

> That it is the opinion of the House that the further prosecution of offensive war on the continent of North America for the purpose of reducing the revolted Colonies to obedience by force will be the means of weakening the efforts of this country against her European enemies, and . . . by preventing a happy reconciliation with [America], to frustrate the earnest desire graciously expressed by His Majesty to restore the blessings of public tranquility.

The resolution lost the first time around but when reintroduced passed by a vote of 234 to 215. Its directive to cease offensive operations meant that peace must now be offered to America, if not to France, Spain, or the Netherlands. Accordingly, North resigned on March 20, 1782.

The Cornwallis surrender at Yorktown and the fall of the North government did more than set the stage for peace negotiations: they radically changed the relationships of the war's major participants. Those current enemies, the United States and Great Britain, now had to look beyond the end of the war and embrace the idea that each must become the other's principal trading partner. As for those current allies, America, France, and Spain, their realization was the opposite one: they understood that henceforth in the scramble to end the war they were competitors for territory and resources, and that each must defend its rights against the others' claims.

George Washington had predicted that there would be no peace so long as New York remained in British hands, and it did, along with Charleston, Savannah, and Wilmington, North Carolina. Washington's certainty about peace still being far off was reinforced when, despite his pleas for de Grasse's help in retaking Charleston or Savannah, the admiral left for the Caribbean in early November.

In February 1782 Florimond du Bouchet, with Rochambeau's troops in Virginia, was assigned to make a French-British exchange of ailing prisoners. Some British ones, then in a hospital near Gloucester, were to be traded for French soldiers and sailors held on the prison ships in New York Harbor. Du Bouchet transported his ailing British charges to New York, and with them entered the office of the provost marshal. It was William Cunningham, the same Tory who had run the prison ships four years earlier when du Bouchet had been aboard one, and whose cruelty had resulted in the deaths of thousands of prisoners. "Major, you give me the idea that I've seen you before," Cunningham said to him. Du Bouchet knew all too well where and when Cunningham had seen him before, but denied any such encounter and deflected the conversation to issues of the exchange. Many French prisoners were released into his custody. They were so ill that after they reached Rochambeau's winter quarters in Newport, Virginia, they all died. Du Bouchet also became quite ill and was hospitalized for months. For du Bouchet's feat in rescuing the French prisoners, Rochambeau appointed him a major general.

In winter camp Rochambeau received some new French troops, two million livres to pay his men, and some officers who had long sought to participate in the American conflict, among them the young Ségur.

Elsewhere in the world, British war losses continued to mount. In the early months of 1782 Spain captured Minorca, France captured the Caribbean islands of Nevis, Montserrat, and San Cristóbal (later renamed St. Kitts), and off India Suffren's squadron bested a British one. Hood's fleet arrived in the Caribbean too late to prevent the French governor of Martinique from retaking Saint Eustatius, its garrison of 750 British soldiers, and four million livres that Rodney had collected. Deducting from the total 170,000 pounds that Rodney had planned to keep as his share, the governor distributed that to his own officers and gave the rest back to the Dutch.

Since George III would not accept as replacement for Lord North any of the more radical Opposition leaders, in March Lord Rockingham was appointed as first minister, a position he had held in 1766. Rockingham's new government became quite popular for promising to reduce the expense of maintaining the royal family, for taking steps to appease the Irish, for rejecting new taxes on soap and salt as too great a burden for the poor, and for opening negotiations to end the Revolutionary War.

Charles James Fox, now chief of the Northern Department, insisted that such matters were his concern because he handled foreign affairs; long an advocate for American independence, Fox considered independence as a precondition to negotiations, as it would enable Great Britain to withdraw troops and ships from America and be in a better position to fight against and negotiate with France, Spain, and the Netherlands.

Lord Shelburne believed that the negotiations were his to conduct since his brief was colonial affairs and in his view the Americans were still colonists; his strategy was the opposite of Fox's—to withhold recognition of America's independence, granting it only in exchange for territory and concessions from the various belligerents.

Shelburne now dispatched to Franklin Richard Oswald, seventy-seven, a Scottish merchant; and to Adams he sent Henry Laurens, paroled from the Tower (Oswald provided the bail), in the belief that Laurens was anti-French and still had affection for Great Britain. Oswald and Laurens, once partners in the slave-trading business, crossed the Channel together in early April. Meanwhile Fox decided to send his own man to Paris, Thomas Grenville, son of a former first minister.

Adams and Laurens were old friends. Stung by learning that he was no longer the sole American commissioner in charge of making peace, Adams had the perfect excuse for remaining in the Netherlands: to complete arrangements for a Dutch loan. It was desperately needed by the United States since British ships, now unopposed in the western Atlantic, were blockading American ports and killing American commerce. Laurens informed Adams that Great Britain was thinking about ceding Canada and Nova Scotia to America. What might be demanded in exchange was unclear, so Adams was skeptical. He was also unwilling to negotiate without consulting his fellow commissioners. To Franklin and to Congress, Adams touted what he construed as his major accomplishment of this period, Dutch recognition of U.S. sovereignty and independence. Actually recognition was a by-product of the French ambassador's machinations, but that did not diminish its utility in future negotiations with Great Britain.

From Paris, Franklin soon reported to Laurens: "I told Mr. Oswald that I could make [no propositions] but in Concurrence with my Colleagues; and that if we were together we should not treat but in Conjunction with France." To Adams he wrote drily that Oswald was "selling to us a Thing that is already our own"—independence. Meanwhile

Franklin pleaded with Jay to come to Paris. "You would be of infinite Service [here]. Spain has taken four Years to consider whether she should treat with us or not. Give her Forty. And let us in the mean time mind our own Business."

From America, Foreign Secretary Livingston advised Jay to threaten Spain with the U.S. marching its army and militias to the Mississippi to defend American claims. Jay was prepared to do so. Recounting to Livingston an unexpected summons from Floridablanca after more than two years of being kept at arm's length, Jay said that he would now argue to the Spanish minister that since the United States and Spain were at peace, "Why then should we be anxious for a Treaty with her, or make Sacrifices to purchase it? . . . Why therefore not postpone it?"

With the Dutch now on board, the Spanish stiff-armed, and Great Britain pledged to negotiate, it was no wonder that in the spring of 1782 Jay and Adams refused to adhere to their year-old congressional instructions not to negotiate without Vergennes nor to agree to any settlement until Louis XVI had approved it. Franklin was somewhat shaken by his colleagues' willingness to disregard congressional instructions and pointedly asked Jay whether he would do so deliberately. Jay responded:

> Unless we violate these instructions the dignity of Congress will be in the dust. . . . Our honor and our interests are concerned in inviolably adhering to [the Franco-American treaties], but if we lean on [France's] love of liberty, her affection for Americans, or her interested magnanimity, we shall lean on a broken reed that will sooner or later pierce our hands.

Jay and Adams were willing to wait to complete the settlement until France had a chance to ratify it, but wanted to begin separate negotiations. Franklin had to agree, as did Vergennes, lest such negotiations proceed to his country's detriment.

Separate negotiations! Here was incontrovertible evidence that the

Franco-American connection was coming apart. The breakup wasn't France's fault and it wasn't America's; it was simply the final stage of a relationship whose halcyon days were past. Together the allies had had a grand victory; but what had initially impelled them to get together and enabled them to act jointly—their aligned self-interest—now mandated that they go their separate ways. And the break-up underscored that their conjoining had always been little more than an alliance of convenience.

The approach of the alliance's end was hastened by circumstances beyond the control of parties—revolts in Geneva and the Crimea. In Geneva, then under French control, revolutionaries took over the city and French troops were summoned to put down that revolt in concert with the forces of other European nations. Another insurrection, in May, drove the Russian-installed leader from Crimea. The Crimeans then applied to the Ottoman Empire for recognition as one of its provinces, which led Russia and Austria to trigger previously agreed-upon plans to dismember what remained of the Ottoman Empire. "I can see clouds on the European political horizon which demand all our attention," Vergennes wrote to Montmorin. "We will probably succeed in dissipating them if peace [with Great Britain] is not too far away, but . . . it will take a lot of skill and care to prevent some violent convulsion in the system as a whole." Reasoning that a Russian/Austrian attempt to take over the Ottoman Empire would upset the balance of power that France, Britain and Spain wanted to maintain, Vergennes concluded that it also discredited any Russian or Austrian offer to function as neutral mediators of a peace among France, Spain, Great Britain, and the United States.

Louis XVI had a more personal upset at a Russian intervention that spring, as in Paris the Empress Catherine's son put on a private reading of Beaumarchais's play, *The Marriage of Figaro*, which Louis had banned for its deprecations of the administration, its pointing up of the chasm between rich and poor and nearly every other problem encountered by the downtrodden.

Then the news arrived from the Caribbean of the defeat and capture of Admiral de Grasse.

Having gone to the West Indies for the purpose of completing the second part of the Saavedra plan, the taking of various British islands and then a large Franco-Spanish assault on Jamaica, de Grasse had had initial triumphs and managed in several encounters to get the better of Hood's fleet. But he was unable to capture Hood's swifter copper-bottomed warships. Then Rodney arrived back in the Caribbean, suffering mightily from gout and often confined to a deck chair, and steaming with anger at the French seizing of his stash on Saint Eustatius. Rodney concealed his anger when he and Hood sent de Grasse some choice provisions for a Martinique celebration of the birth of the Dauphin—de Grasse returned the favor with a present of two chests full of island liqueurs—but in early April Rodney saw an opportunity to make a crushing blow, and took it.

Learning that de Grasse was to shepherd a convoy in the Canal de Saintes passage between Dominique and Guadeloupe, Rodney and Hood positioned their fleets so as to force de Grasse to break off that task and confront them. The ensuing Battle of the Saintes lasted for several days; unlike the Battle of the Virginia Capes, it featured fighting each and every day, and in a relatively confined passage rather than on the open sea. On April 22, because the *Ville de Paris* had become so riddled through its three decks and had exhausted its ammunition, de Grasse felt that he had no choice but to surrender the vessel. His second, Vaudreuil, disobeyed standing orders never to abandon the flagship and chose instead to flee, with the majority of the French warships and the convoy, to a Spanish-protected port.

But the *Ville de Paris* was taken, the *César* sank when an accidental fire exploded its magazine, killing four hundred Frenchmen and a British prize crew of fifty, and five more French warships were captured. Six French captains died and de Grasse was wounded; later estimates put the full total of captured and wounded at fourteen to fifteen thousand. "Oh France," Rodney wrote his wife, "what joy it gives me to humble thy pride, and lower thy haughty insolence!" De Grasse was headed for captivity in London.

Vergennes downplayed to Louis the seriousness of the defeat, arguing that while this "check" in the Antilles was "very unfortunate, it is not irreparable," because the lost vessels could be replaced within the year. He began a patriotic public relations campaign, in part so that France would not seem to be impacted during the peace negotiations.

Congress, wanting to help France after this debacle, offered the newly completed seventy-four-gun *America*; France accepted the offer—which had the unexpected side result of sidelining its captain, John Paul Jones, who had looked forward to continuing his raids with the new ship.

In mid-May 1782 Grenville returned to Versailles. On May 26 he offered to the foreign minister, "without being provoked to it . . . threw at my head, so to speak, the Cession of New York, Charleston, and Savannah," Vergennes confided to Montmorin. The American cities constituted quite a bribe, but since he still considered France bound by the Franco-American alliance, Vergennes rejected the Grenville offer.

France's refusal led to arguments within the British cabinet that culminated in a vicious showdown on June 30 over a Fox desire to preemptively offer independence to America. Fox lost that vote. The next day, July 1, Rockingham died, and on hearing that news Fox resigned. George III then appointed Shelburne as first minister and allowed him also to retain the portfolio of foreign minister.

Shelburne had always seen himself as a modern Oliver Cromwell, and according to a recent biographer his assumption of full power gave to him, as it once had to Cromwell, the chance to "save the nation in direst straits, constitution corrupted, dominated by the inept and self-serving, and threatened by powerful and hostile forces abroad." But Shelburne would first have to get rid of that sticky problem, the war in America.

He had been convinced of the path to doing so, in part, by his reading of his friend Adam Smith's *An Inquiry into the Nature and Causes of the Wealth of Nations*, published in 1776, whose last chapters argued that Great Britain could be saved from the economic disaster of the Revolutionary War only by granting independence to the United States and then embracing it as the best British trading partner. Shelburne was keenly aware that the idea had also been championed by British trade organizations, whose antipathy to the North government had assured its fall. Addressing Parliament now as first minister, Shelburne declared that "if the sun of England would set with the loss of America, it [is my] resolution to improve the twilight, and to prepare for the rising of England's sun again." Few understood his ulterior meaning—that the new rise was not to be warlike but rather an ascension to the position of trading colossus, with America as Britain's main partner.

By then, Jay had joined Franklin in Paris. Although both were quite ill, over the course of four days they drew up a list of American demands that on July 10 Franklin read to Oswald. It consisted of "necessary" and "advisable" elements of any peace between Great Britain and the United States. "Necessary" were the full and complete independence of the United States and the withdrawal of all British troops; the settling of "the boundaries of *their Colonies*"—meaning the western colonies of the original thirteen states; a confinement of Canada to its boundaries prior to the 1774 expansion; and fishing rights off Newfoundland and Nova Scotia. "Advisable" were Great Britain's acknowledgment of war guilt; indemnification for damages; the ceding of Canada to the United States; and a waiving of customs duties for U.S. goods entering the British Isles. Oswald had previously reported to Shelburne Franklin's remark "that the more we favoured them [the Americans] . . . the more they could do for us in the conclusion of the separate treaties." The Franklin-Jay list showed that the Americans were quite willing to distance themselves from France: "The Doctor did not in the Course of [our] Conversation hesitate as to a

Conclusion with [us], on account of any Connection with those other states [France, Spain, and the Netherlands]."

In Philadelphia, the Franco-American alliance was still intact, and celebrating. La Luzerne had readied a large gala in honor of the birth of the Dauphin. The guests included Washington, Rochambeau, many members of Congress, governors, and fifteen hundred others.

Rochambeau attended because his army was on the move. During the winter the weather in Virginia had been unseasonably cold—enough to freeze wine, which distressed the French—but when it had turned warmer Rochambeau had brought his troops northward. He had done so slowly, taking an entire month to reach Baltimore. Towns by the wayside were delighted at his leisure because at every stop he spent a lot of hard cash to buy provisions and accommodations. By the time he reached Baltimore, word had arrived of the British resolution forbidding new offensive operations, and of the fall of the North government. Rochambeau then prepared his army to return to France from Baltimore. But the next news, of the de Grasse defeat in the Caribbean, returned the Rochambeau army to its slow march, which brought them to Philadelphia in time for the July 15 celebration.

Rochambeau discussed with his American hosts what to do with a Vaudreuil fleet that suddenly appeared in Chesapeake Bay long after his own forces had left that area; some American politicians wanted to use it to attack Canada. The idea went nowhere, among other reasons because Washington did not want to invade Canada—and no one was happier at the quashing than Vergennes. He confided to La Luzerne that whatever "hinders the conquest of that country [Canada] enters essentially into our designs. But you will understand, of course, that this way of thinking must remain an absolute secret to the Americans. It would be an offense [for which] they would never forgive us."

The main battle action in America during the summer of 1782 was near Charleston, where Greene led the American forces. John Laurens had gone to participate in it and he created a network of spies, many of them black, to keep Greene informed of British maneuvers. At a moment when the British high command was considering the abandonment of Charleston without a fight—something that Greene did not know— Greene sent a battalion to counter a British foraging expedition. The battalion was ambushed near Beaufort, and in the first volley Laurens was shot off his horse and died. He was twenty-seven.

In mid-July, Shelburne advised Oswald that he could tell Franklin Great Britain would accept American independence. Oswald conveyed the news. At last! Yet as the Franklin scholar Jonathan R. Dull emphasizes: "Franklin won this victory not because America's bargaining position was so strong but rather because Shelburne was anxious for peace."

John Jay was not convinced that independence had been won, since the structure of the dual negotiations would allow Great Britain to con- strue independence as conditional, to be resolved only when all the trea- ties were signed. With Franklin sidelined by illness, Jay insisted to Oswald that if Great Britain truly accepted American independence, Oswald's instructions must be changed to state definitively that he was dealing with the United States of America—currently, his commission referred to "Colonies or Plantations." Franklin, as always eager for unanimity among his colleagues, agreed with Jay. Since Oswald would not consent to the change, Jay canceled their next meeting. In the Netherlands a few days later, Adams learned that the commission of another British diplomat also presumed he was dealing with colonies rather than with an independent country. Direct U.S.–Great Britain negotiations were put on hold.

A new negotiator then came to the fore: de Grasse. Since his capture, the British had treated him very well, and after landing at Portsmouth he had been taken to meet the king and queen—the king used the occasion to return de Grasse's sword to him—and he was visited in his rooms at a hotel by several members of the cabinet and high government officials. De Grasse also sat for his portrait, wearing the sash of the Croix de Saint-Louis. Before his departure for France on parole on August 12, de Grasse held peace discussions with Shelburne. On August 17 the gist of those discussions was conveyed to Vergennes by de Grasse's nephew: American independence was to be complete and absolute; France would get back Saint Lucia and give back Dominica and Saint Vincent; Dunkerque would be restored to French control; France would be guaranteed fishing rights off Newfoundland, as well as the African slave-trading post in Senegal and some additional trade space in India. Spain, in this formulation, would hold on to West Florida and receive either Minorca or Gibraltar, providing that Great Britain kept the other as a fortified base.

Vergennes thought that these terms represented substantial concessions for the British, and had they not come from a messenger of such probity as de Grasse he would have wondered if they were a ploy. He forwarded the terms to Madrid.

In Paris, Jay had been dealing with Aranda, Spain's long-serving ambassador, and they were very far apart on America's boundaries. Spain claimed all of what was then known as the Northwest—Michigan, Illinois, Indiana—and the Southwest, meaning the Mississippi Delta and the Floridas. Jay insisted that the American western boundary be the western bank of the Mississippi River. They were so deadlocked that Aranda asked Vergennes to help, and Vergennes gave that task to Gérard de Rayneval, brother of Conrad Gérard.

The results of Rayneval's assistance were nearly disastrous for America. On September 6, 1782, he handed Jay a paper. It repeated the Aranda line, which La Luzerne had also been trying to hammer home to Congress: that America "cannot extend its territories beyond the bounds of its conquests." Therefore all the lands south of the Ohio River would be

Spain's, while the "fate" of the lands north of the Ohio "must be decided by the Court of London." Jay and Franklin—and Adams, when he learned of this—were stunned, as this assertion by Spain confirmed all their suspicions of betrayal by their French allies, especially when Rayneval, after handing Jay this paper, left for London.

There Rayneval's ostensible task was to discover whether what de Grasse had orally conveyed was an accurate reflection of British thinking. Shelburne told him it was not precisely so but was close. The two men quickly realized that they were of like mind about ending the war. "I not only wish to contribute to the re-establishment of peace between our sovereigns, but also to bring about a cordiality which will be to their reciprocal advantage," Shelburne told Rayneval. "If we join together and are truly in agreement, we can lay down the law to the rest of Europe." That matched what Rayneval knew to be the fondest visions of Vergennes and Louis XVI.

Shelburne wrote to George III that Rayneval "appears a Well-Instructed, Inoffensive Man of Business, and makes the most decided Professions on the part of Mons. De Vergennes, whom he states as desirous to expedite everything which can contribute to an Instant and final conclusion." The king protested: "I owne the Art of Monsr. De Vergennes is so well known that I cannot think he would have sent [Rayneval] if he was an inoffensive Man of Business," and warned Shelburne that he, George III, would not be the instrument of a "bad peace." Shelburne pressured the king by dropping hints that ratified George's belief that the British navy was disintegrating.

While Shelburne and Rayneval had been meeting, on September 13 a combined Spanish and French force of great size began an assault on Gibraltar. The attacking force included new floating batteries carrying 138 guns, and more than five thousand men, supported by thirty thousand on land and in sixteen ships of the line, and by sixty-six cannons firing from Spanish territory. Those taking part included Louis XVI's brother and cousin, an indication that France and Spain expected a victory. But British flaming cannonballs sank the floating batteries and exploded Franco-Spanish magazines with such violence that the roar could be heard twenty miles away, deafening the royals for several days, as well as most other members of the Bourbon armed forces. It became clear that Gibraltar would remain in British hands.

In Great Britain this was welcome news, but it upset Shelburne's peace efforts because it firmed the king's resolve, and that of the public, to have Great Britain henceforth take a harder line in negotiations with the French and the Americans. Parliament was due to reopen in late November and there was a strong possibility that the MPs would vote out Shelburne's ministry, and with it the determination to end the war. Before facing a confidence vote, Shelburne wanted a peace treaty in hand.

Gibraltar's loss was also a problem for the Americans because it could push Madrid to demand recompense for not obtaining Gibraltar—such as lands in the American South and West.

On September 28 Jay wrote Adams that the British had finally changed Oswald's commission and were now eager to deal with the Americans, and urged Adams to come to Paris. In the interim before he arrived, Jay, pushing hard, got Oswald to initial a paper on which the American southern boundary was fixed, at Jay's insistence, at the thirty-first parallel north latitude, that is, at the St. Mary's River border of Georgia and Florida. Similarly the western boundary was put at the Mississippi and the northern boundary at the Nipissing Line, just south of Ontario. The document also deferred the settling of America's eastern boundary to a joint commission. But it did affirm America's right to fish off Newfoundland and, of equal importance, its right to dry the fish ashore.

Jay and Franklin were delighted with the document but nervous about its reception in London. They were correct to worry. The proposed treaty arrived just after the good news about Gibraltar's resistance of the siege, and so the Shelburne cabinet rejected it. A new emissary was sent to Paris along with Oswald. Henry Strachey was thirty years younger than Oswald and a former colonial administrator in India, MP, and high treasury official—a man of broad governmental experience and energy. Strachey's instructions were to reject American positions on the flashpoints.

Adams arrived in Paris spoiling for a fight. He was so angry at Franklin and Vergennes for prior slights—some real, most imagined—that he delayed visiting Franklin for some days, and Vergennes for three weeks. He wasn't sure what to expect from Jay, with whom he had had frequent and vehement disagreements in Congress. He mused in his diary, "Between two as subtle Spirits, as any in this World, the one malicious, the other I think honest, I shall have a delicate, a nice, a critical Part to Act. F.s cunning will be to divide Us. To this End he will provoke, he will insinuate, he will intrigue, he will maneuver. . . . J. declares roundly, that he will never set his hand to a bad Peace."

On October 28 Adams and Jay met, alone, for three hours, and Adams was impressed to learn how obstinately Jay had stood up to both Vergennes and Franklin. As Jay would shortly write to Livingston, he and Adams recognized that "It is not [in France's] interest that we should become a great and formidable people, and therefore they will not help us become so." It was in the light of this understanding that Adams and Jay prepared to resume talks with Oswald and Strachey.

They began on November 2 at a dinner at the Hôtel du Roi, with Adams, Jay, Franklin, Oswald, and Strachey. The next day Adams brought a smile to Strachey's lips when he said that he had no intention of cheating anyone out of his property, and certainly not Loyalists. Shortly Adams made a proposition, with Jay and Franklin's concurrence: to have Congress recommend to the states just compensation for Loyalists. "The English Gentlemen . . . were much pleased with it, and with Reason, because it silences the Clamours of all the British Creditors, against the Peace, and prevents them from making common Cause with the [Loyalist] Refugees."

In his diary Adams repeated the old tale of the eagle and the cat: in a farmer's yard, the eagle spots what he thinks is a rabbit, and grabs it; once aloft, however, the cat manages to get his claws and teeth around the eagle's neck. "The Eagle, finding Herself scratched and pressed, bids the Cat let go and fall down. No says the Cat: I wont let go and fall, you shall stoop and set me down."

Now it was Lafayette's turn to be involved. Empowered by Congress to aid in any negotiations, so far he had failed to insert himself into the peace talks. But he smoothed the way for Adams to reconnect with Vergennes. Despite their mutual disdain, at this critical juncture they behaved themselves. Adams gave Vergennes a straightforward account of the unilateral negotiations with Great Britain and the three matters of contention, the fisheries, the northeastern boundary, and reparations. He might well have boasted of the research that he had done on those points prior to leaving the United States. When Vergennes seemed to back the British in their call for restitution of property, Adams was able to counter by saying that the British had taken property in Ireland without similar restitution.

Decorum prevailed and Vergennes, in the company of Lafayette at a dinner with Adams, promised the Americans another six million livres. Adams knew he had done something right because he was seated next to Vergennes's wife and got along well with her, even in his execrable French. Moreover, at this dinner other French nobles paid him what he regarded as the ultimate compliment: *"Vous êtes le Washington de la negotiation."*

Adams eventually came to think it was Jay who deserved that accolade, as after that dinner Jay became the leader of a united trio of Americans in the parlays with the British. Franklin, who understood that he would be outvoted if he objected too strongly, was content to play the illness card and agree to his comrades' strong positions. Meanwhile the parallel negotiations between France and Great Britain continued, with Rayneval making another trip to London. From that city Henry Laurens, now fully free, having been exchanged for Cornwallis, agreed to come to Paris and take up his post as commissioner, as Adams had begged him to do. Laurens's motivation: "Thank God, I had a son, who dared to die for his Country!"

When Strachey brought back to Paris the British refusal to accept the American ideas on the boundaries and the fisheries, Adams offered a spirited argument: that the haddock so prized by Great Britain and France were spawned on American soil and spent many months in American territorial waters before migrating to the Newfoundland banks. "I said it was the Opinion of all the Fishermen in America that England could not prevent our Catching a fish without preventing themselves from getting a Dollar. . . . That neither the English nor French could have it. It must be lost if We had it not." Adams also had research materials showing that Americans had used the banks since the 1763 treaty, with permission, and were not now about to give up that right.

Franklin had a similar killer fact to use in the reparations battle. He was willing, he said, to have America compensate the Loyalists, but contended that Great Britain must be equally willing to compensate Americans for freeing slaves and needlessly burning towns and property. Franklin pointed out that his own library in Philadelphia had been looted. He also warned that if the British pushed too hard on compensating the Loyalists—or on the fisheries—or on the United States having free access to navigation on the Mississippi—the American Congress was likely to reject the treaty.

By then Oswald and Strachey had become convinced of the correctness of the American positions, and pledged to urge them on Shelburne. When Laurens joined the talks on November 29, he ratified what Jay, Adams, and Franklin had agreed to and added only one codicil—that Americans had the right to later add to the list of what property had been taken. It was this proposition that, in effect, wedded the final settlement to the continuing right of American citizens to own slaves and for the owners to sue for their loss if the slaves had been lured or taken from them. Adams was grateful for Laurens's participation, and in his diary also had a few good words for Franklin's "sagacity." Actually the final document was the product, almost equally, of efforts by Franklin, Jay, and Adams, a reflection of their willingness to put aside personal antagonisms and concentrate their considerable intelligences on securing for their country the best settlement obtainable in the circumstances.

On November 30 Franklin, Jay, Adams, Laurens, and Oswald all signed the preliminary accord, thus ending the war between Great Britain and the United States.

Acceptance of the preliminary accord by all the combatants, however, had to wait on the conclusion of the parallel British negotiations with France and Spain. These became as complicated as three long-established monarchies could make them.

Vergennes was amazed at how much the British had conceded to the Americans, telling Rayneval: "The English are purchasing the peace rather than making it. Their concessions in fact . . . exceed all that I had thought possible." He urged Rayneval to hasten France's negotiations with Great Britain, fearing that if the Bourbon kingdoms did not move quickly enough, the generosity of the British settlement with America could turn the combined might of the English-speaking nations against them.

Frederick the Great believed that there was a simple reason why the Europeans had to come to a peace agreement quickly: "The king of Spain needs money and can get none from Holland. The new *vingtième* [additional tax] France has imposed on the people is not bringing in half what was expected . . . and as one cannot make war without money, it is to be expected that the end of their resources will be an effective motive for the belligerent powers to want peace." Louis's finance minister disagreed with that estimate, writing, "The government's credit has been maintained beyond all expectations" because the assistance extended by creditors during the war "has given us the means of bearing the burden and making the credit of France more extensive and more solid than it was during the years of peace which preceded the war." As for Spain, the more significant motivator was their defeat in the attempts to take Gibraltar by force. Spain now said it would give up its claims to Gibraltar only if France and Great Britain proffered something in exchange. "Thank God for Carlos giving up Gibraltar without France ever asking him to do so," Vergennes sighed with relief. Reinforcing Spain's continuing power to make war if the new condition was not met was the presence in Cadiz of Admiral d'Estaing at the head of a very large Spanish and French fleet that had plans, drawn by Saavedra, to reinstate the expedition against Jamaica; Lafayette was to join.

A potential Gibraltar trade set off a final six-weeks of negotiations. To reach a comprehensive, three-sided agreement, Rayneval, Aranda, Montmorin, Vergennes, Floridablanca, and Shelburne all had to exceed their instructions and make compromises. In the horse-trading, Gibraltar remained British, while Minorca and the Floridas were left in Spanish hands and British and French recent conquests in the Caribbean were mostly restored to their prewar ownership. France also received back Pondicherry in India and the islands of Saint Pierre and Miquelon off the coast of Newfoundland.

In Paris the Americans learned on December 14 of a preliminary agreement between France and Great Britain, and later in the month of details involving Spain—and of a final six-million-livres loan, given at a time when the French treasury was contemplating default on some of its own obligations.

On January 20, 1783, at Versailles, the American commissioners signed the final accords, along with the representatives of Great Britain, France, and Spain, the latter two also on behalf of the Netherlands. With these signatures, and even though the treaty, including some last-minute alterations, would not be ratified by Congress until the following December, the American Revolutionary War came to a close.

So too did the American connection with France. It had done more for the United States of America than either party to the alliance had initially imagined. France had sustained America by dint of its friendship when most other nations would have little to do with it, and by loans and gifts at times of serious financial difficulties. France had further made possible America's most significant battlefield victories, the ones that won the war, and had been of enormous help in assuring that the integrity and the independence of the United States of America would continue well into the future.

Epilogue

"After my head falls off, send it to the British, they will pay a good deal for it."
— Comte d'Estaing

1783–1844

Concerning the later lives of the French who were of central importance to the Franco-American connection during the Revolutionary War:

Comte de Barras. After taking Nevis and Montserrat in January 1782, Barras fell ill on Martinique during the Battle of the Saintes. Returning to France in 1783, he was awarded the Croix de Saint-Louis and retired with a pension of four thousand livres a year. As did many of his fellow captains and admirals, he became a founding member of the French branch of the Society of the Cincinnati, the American-based, honorary association of officers who had served during the Revolutionary War. In the early days of the French Revolution, his nephew Paul Barras protected him from the retaliation taken by the new government against the nobility and former high military officers. In 1792 he was promoted to vice admiral and died shortly thereafter.

Caron de Beaumarchais. In 1784 Louis XVI lifted the ban on production of Beaumarchais's *The Marriage of Figaro,* which became a commercial success and the basis of a Mozart opera. Beaumarchais lost money publishing Voltaire's complete works but made a fortune providing drinking water to Paris. Making common cause with the Revolution as it began, he obtained recognition of the rights of authors, something he had sought for a dozen years. Elected to the commune of Paris, he nonetheless came under suspicion of trying to profit too much from buying arms for the military, and was imprisoned in 1792. Freed, and while out of the country ostensibly seeking arms for the revolutionary forces, he was declared an enemy of the state and not permitted to return until 1796. He died in 1799, possibly by suicide. The debts he incurred in the service of the American Revolution were partially repaid to his family years later.

Achard de Bonvouloir. In India, after settling the disposition of his papers and taking a final communion, the chevalier died of a tropical illness in 1783.

Florimond du Bouchet. Initially denied membership in the Society of the Cincinnati because he had not served long enough as a field officer, du Bouchet crossed to America and in a special pleading won admission. He continued in the French military. When the French Revolution began, he blamed it on the bad example provided by the American one. His family property was confiscated and his relatives were executed. Upon the defeat of his royalist army, he went into exile. Returning under an 1802 amnesty, he served as Napoleon's commandant of the Belgian fortresses of Ypres and Breda. In 1814, during the restoration of the French monarchy, he was confirmed as a marquis, promoted to lieutenant general, and retired to complete his memoir. He died in 1826.

Le Ray de Chaumont. The American Revolution bankrupted Chaumont, because the money and credit he had advanced to the Americans, and to France for participation in it, was not repaid properly by either country. To meet obligations he sold his Passy home; his son, with Franklin's help, did extract partial recompense from the American government. Using some of that repayment the Chaumonts purchased vast tracts in the Adirondacks that the son proceeded to develop, initially as a retreat for the nobility who were under attack in France in the early part of the French Revolution. During that revolution, many remaining Chaumont family assets in France were seized, but Chaumont himself was spared the guillotine despite his continuing close connections with the royal family. He also survived Napoleon's ascension to power, and died in 1803.

Thomas Conway. Through the intercession of Lafayette, Conway, while serving in India, was included in the French branch of the Society of the Cincinnati. After serving as governor general of the French territories in India until 1787, he was appointed head of all the French forces east of Africa, but in 1791 was deemed insufficiently noble-born to be considered for further promotion. Remaining a royalist during the French Revolution, he fought alongside others in southern France. In 1791, when their group was defeated, he escaped to Ireland, land of his birth, where he was made commandant of the Sixth Regiment of the Irish Brigade, a division of the British army. He died in 1795.

Louis Duportail. In 1783 Duportail drew up plans for an American peacetime engineer corps, including an "academy" at West Point modeled on Mezières, and then returned to France. There, transferring to the infantry, he was appointed a brigadier general and later a *maréchal de camp*, manager of the installations in several important areas. In the early stages of the French Revolution, Duportail occupied a middle ground between the royalists and revolutionaries, and was appointed minister of war, completing a remarkable rise for a man not born to the nobility of the sword. During his tenure as minister he instituted some important reforms in the armed services. Forced out in 1792 by the more radical leaders, he recrossed the Atlantic, bought a farm near Valley Forge, and helped draw up the initial engineering curriculum at West Point. In 1797, during the second Washington Administration, the

United States argued that its debts to France had been incurred under a previous French regime and refused to honor them any longer. Outraged, Duportail sought to return home, and in 1802, when Napoleon extended an amnesty offer to all former French military officers, he took ship toward France, but he died while at sea.

Pierre L'Enfant. After designing the badge and insignia for the Society of the Cincinnati and overseeing their production in France, he returned to New York and began an architectural practice. His Federal Hall became so renowned that when a new capital city was decreed for the banks of the Potomac River, he was chosen to design it. His supervision of the construction brought him into conflict with many stakeholders. He lost control of the project, although his basic design and some specific buildings remained. His later life was filled with difficulties that even overwhelmed his stint teaching engineering at West Point. He died, impoverished, in 1825. In 1902 his District of Columbia plan was readopted and the "grand avenues" he had imagined were constructed. In 1909 his remains were reburied in Arlington National Cemetery.

Comte d'Estaing. At war's end d'Estaing was in Cádiz, in charge of a Franco-Spanish fleet that peace robbed of the chance to sail. He returned to his Passy home. The American state of Georgia granted him land as thanks for having attempted to relieve Savannah. In 1789 he published a play in verse, *Les Thermopyles,* and soon after was appointed commanding general of the Versailles National Guard. But because he overzealously defended Marie Antoinette and others of the royal family, and because he had in his possession medallions representing them, the Revolutionary council sentenced him to die. Before being guillotined in 1794, he reportedly said, "After my head falls off, send it to the British, they will pay a good deal for it."

François de Fleury. Serving in India, Fleury rose to *maréchal de camp*, and then returned to France and took part in the Revolution as an army officer of the king, participating in battles at Montmédy, Givet, Cambrai, and Valenciennes. In many of these he was at the side of Rochambeau, his mentor since 1780. In a 1792 battle Fleury was grievously wounded. Resigning from the army, he lived as a pensioner until his death in 1799. In 1989 the U.S. Army Corps of Engineers named its most prestigious medal for him; the medal's face repeats the device on Fleury's original medal from Congress, a helmeted Roman-era soldier standing in the ruins of a fort, holding in his right hand an unsheathed sword, and in his left, the staff of the enemy's flag, which he tramples underfoot.

Conrad-Alexandre Gérard. Upon his return to France he only partially recovered his health. He ceased diplomatic work to perform other services for Louis XVI, including membership in the council of state. Offered the leadership of an Illinois and Wabash Land Company with a domain of three million acres, he felt unable to endure the rigors of another Atlantic crossing and life in frontier America. The king rewarded him with a lucrative appointment, the chief administrative post in Strasbourg, and he was granted membership in the Society of the Cincinnati. Tortured by advancing illnesses, he and his wife became patients and patrons of Franz Anton Mesmer and his "animal magnetism." In 1790 he was replaced at Strasbourg by a mayor whom the Revolution selected. He returned to Paris, where he died the following year.

Comte de Grasse. Court-martialed at his own request in 1784 for having lost the Battle of the Saintes—the first sitting general of the French armed forces ever to be tried—de Grasse was readily acquitted. He then retired to Tilly and became a charter member of the French branch of the Society of the Cincinnati. He married for a third time but died shortly thereafter, in 1788. Of his later years, Washington wrote to Rochambeau, "It seemed as if an unfortunate and unrelenting destiny pursued him, to destroy the enjoyment of all worldly comfort." During the French Revolution his Tilly home was sacked and the cannons presented to him by Congress were carried away, melted down, and made into coins. His four daughters escaped, settled in Charleston, and were awarded a thousand dollars each for their father's service to America.

Marquis de Lafayette. After a triumphal tour of the United States in 1784, Lafayette settled in Paris as an adviser to French and American governments and a leading abolitionist. Appointed to the Assembly of Notables and the Estates-General, he advocated reforms and occupied a middle ground between revolutionaries and royalists. When the Bastille fell, he sent its key to Washington, "as a Missionary of Liberty to its Patriarch." Commander of the National Guard, he rescued Louis XVI and Marie Antoinette from certain death at Versailles, but thereafter found it increasingly difficult to defend them from the Revolution. Blamed when the royal couple briefly escaped custody, he denounced the Jacobins in 1792, which earned him a warrant issued for his arrest. Captured by Austrians, he was imprisoned outside France until 1797. Upon his release he refused to cooperate with Napoleon and was too prominent a national hero for the emperor to execute. After the death of his wife in 1807, Lafayette withdrew from national affairs until the restoration in 1815, and after it had an adversarial relationship with the new monarchy as he involved himself with revolutionary movements in Greece and elsewhere. In 1824–25 he made a last, triumphal tour of the United States, and on his return to France continued to speak out for reform and to be a thorn in the side of the monarchy until shortly before his death in 1834. He was buried with soil that he had brought back from America for just that purpose.

Duc de Lauzun. Commandant of the French troops in America once Rochambeau had departed, Lauzun returned to France and to a series of romantic affairs at court. Raised to *maréchal de camp*, in 1788, upon the death of his uncle, he succeeded to the title of Duc de Biron. In 1789 he was appointed a deputy to the Estates-General. Sufficiently revolutionary despite his noble titles, he was named head of the Army of Flan-

ders, reporting to the new National Assembly. He continued in that and in other senior posts for the Revolution's military arm until his forces were defeated in 1793. Chastised for losing, he resigned, but was then arrested, charged with showing too much leniency toward the Revolution's opponents, and sent to the guillotine. He offered his executioner a glass of wine.

Louis XVI. The king's modest attempts to liberalize France were compromised by the indebtedness incurred during the American Revolution. There was no peace dividend because the expense of maintaining the military to protect France, primarily from Great Britain, continued high. In 1786 his government's receipts were 457 million livres but expenses were 587 million. He sought viable ideas for liberalizing his rule, but there were few presented to him that did not entail considerable curtailment of the culture of Versailles, and so most of the ideas were rejected or made little impact. Classism became progressively more deeply embedded in the military and in governance, as the nobility lobbied for and won more influence over the increasingly angry and oppressed proletariat—until on July 14, 1789, a mob stormed the Bastille and began the Revolution. The mob continued on to Versailles and nearly succeeded in assassinating Marie Antoinette; the royal couple was conveyed to the Tuileries Palace in Paris, where they remained under house arrest. What had been an absolute monarchy became a limited one, until in 1791 Louis hastened the end of that arrangement by his unsuccessful attempt to flee to the protection of Prussia. The royal couple's flight changed the minds of those in the revolutionary leadership who had previously thought that Louis had been cooperating with the Revolution. In 1792 he was accused of treason and on January 21, 1793, was guillotined. His death brought to a close more than a thousand years of continuous French monarchy. Marie Antoinette survived her husband, but in the Reign of Terror of April 1793 she too was executed. In 1815 the bodies of the king and queen were exhumed and reburied alongside his ancestors at Saint-Denis.

Vicomte de Noailles. Continuing to believe in the tenets of equality and fairness embodied in the American Revolution, as a member of the Estates-General Noailles proposed the abolishing of ancestral titles. However, his own nobility forced him to emigrate to escape the guillotine, and he settled in Philadelphia. His wife and parents, left behind, were soon executed. In America his monetary capital, access to foreign credit, and closeness to Lafayette helped him amass a new fortune as a partner in William Bingham's bank. After the 1802 amnesty, Rochambeau asked Noailles to take command in Saint-Domingue, which he did. He escaped the British several times, once by replying to a query in perfect English that he, too, was seeking General de Noailles; but in a fight at the head of twenty grenadiers he was fatally wounded, and died in Cuba in 1804.

Mauduit du Plessis. Upon first returning to France, he wrote to Washington that his "zeal" for the American cause remained undimmed and that for it he would "always be ready to Lose my Life." In 1787 he was posted to Haiti as commandant of the Port-au-Prince Regiment, and there became much more of a royalist. In 1791 he resisted orders from the revolutionary government in Paris, among them, to free Haiti's slaves. He also arrested the Haitian revolutionary officials. When revolutionary regiments from France reached Saint-Domingue, they convinced du Plessis's men that he had acted wrongly, and they seized and executed him.

Pierre du Ponceau. Remaining in Philadelphia, du Ponceau studied law and began a law practice. He married, started a family, and took his place among the foremost U.S. intellectuals. As a lawyer he argued cases before the Supreme Court and wrote legal articles. He was a champion in the United States for the French Revolution and for French legal cases. Elected to the American Philosophical Society in 1791, he became its president in 1827 and held that post at the time of his death in 1844. His close friendships included Presidents Monroe and Jefferson, with whom he shared a passion for Native American languages. One of the world's foremost linguists, he won a prestigious European prize for his book on Native American grammatical systems, and was among the first Westerners to understand that written Chinese characters represented spoken words rather than ideas.

Comte de Rochambeau. Louis XVI appointed Rochambeau governor of Picardy, and in 1791, the last *maréchal de France* authorized by royalty. During the early phase of the Revolution he served as commander of the Royal Army of the North; when his forces suffered reverses he was sacked and replaced by Lafayette. A charter member of the Society of the Cincinnati, he continued in friendly correspondence with Washington, who never ceased to refer to him and to de Grasse as the "co-adjutors" of Yorktown. In 1793, during the height of the Terror, Rochambeau was arrested, and the two British cannons that Congress had presented to him were confiscated. As he was entering the cart to be taken to the guillotine, the executioner said, "Withdraw, old marshal; thy turn will come." It did not do so soon, as after the fall of Robespierre the new revolutionary council consisted of officers that Rochambeau had trained, and who revered him. Pensioned by Napoleon, he died in 1807.

Comte de Ségur. Appointed minister to Saint Petersburg in 1784, he made commercial treaties and wrote plays for Empress Catherine II's theater. Sufficiently republican despite his nobility, he joined the Revolution early and became its ambassador in Berlin. Leaving there abruptly after a duel, he went into retirement until the advent of Napoleon, then served in legislative and administrative posts. He was still enough of a noble in 1814 to be a member of Louis XVIII's Chamber of Peers, but joined Napoleon again for the emperor's Hundred Days in 1815. Forgiven for this lapse by the monarch in 1819, he served him and his successor, Charles X, until the short-lived Revolution of 1830, when he joined the insurgents. He died less than a month after France's first constitutional monarchy began.

Baron von Steuben. Steuben was intimately involved in the last stages of the American Revolution, overseeing the demobilization of the army in 1783, and the establishment of the Society of the Cincinnati. Its first meeting was held in his home, and he then served as its acting head. His fame in Europe having become considerable, he sought to return to France with honor and to receive money, but his applications were rejected. In the United States, in the postwar atmosphere, his public advocacy of a standing army did not help him. He obtained what he had been promised, a modest pension, enabling him to winter in New York City and to spend summers in the Mohawk Valley. He became steadily more enfeebled until his death in 1794.

Charles-Armand de la Rouërie. Returning to France after disbanding his legion, Armand raised Virginia tulips and kept a pet monkey. He solved his indebtedness by marrying a neighbor who brought a considerable dowry. He became involved in the politics of Breton. While in Paris to discuss the region's grievances, he was briefly imprisoned in the Bastille, which increased his heroic status. He formed the Bréton Association, civic-minded nobles whose motto, "live free or die," echoed American ideals and who signed their compact in blood. They embraced personal freedom for their poorer neighbors but rejected the radical tenets of the French Revolution. They became hunted men. In 1793, shortly after learning of the death of Louis XVI, Armand died. His enemies exhumed his body and threatened fellow Bréton rebels with his severed head.

Comte de Vergennes. His efforts on behalf of the United States went mostly unrecognized in America in the self-congratulatory climate of the post–Revolutionary War, and in France those efforts were blamed for the country's continuing debts. Such attitudes obscured the degree to which Vergennes's actions had assured the establishment of the United States and helped to restore France to a position of prime influence in European affairs, the main aims of his and Louis's foreign policy. Thanks to his adroit maneuvering, and even as the royal hold on power became more difficult to sustain, his tenure as foreign minister continued, and Louis also appointed him president of the Royal Council of Finances. Vergennes counted as one of his accomplishments the signing of a commercial treaty with Great Britain in 1786 that was remarkable for its liberality. He remained fully involved in the governance and politics of France until his death, in office, in the spring of 1787. On learning of Vergennes's passing, Louis XVI lauded him as "the only friend I could count on, the one minister who never deceived me."

Acknowledgments

I thank the following institutions and librarians for their assistance during the research and writing of this book: the New York Public Library and librarian Melanie Locay for use of the library's Frederick Lewis Allen Room; the New-York Historical Society Library; the Scoville Library of Salisbury and librarian Sara C. Woloszyn; the Charleston Historical Society collection at the Addlestone Library of Charleston; and the Cornell University Library. In Paris, the Bibliothèque Nationale de France, the Bibliothèque Historique de Paris, the Centre des Archives Diplomatiques de La Courneuve, the Service Historique de la Défense, and the Bibliothèque Mazarine.

Books are written alone but always benefit from the insights provided by early readers. Among those who assisted me with their suggestions on this book in manuscript are Larry Bader, Mark Boonshoft, Lee Dembart, David Burke, Thomas Key, Glenn Moots, Edward G. Nickerson, Constance Rosenblum, Thomas Schindler, and Jon Wilkman, and I thank them all.

At St. Martin's Press I benefited from the enthusiasm and professionalism of editor Charles Spicer, assistant editor April Osborn, and copy editor Susan H. Llewellyn.

This book was researched and written as I recovered from near-fatal injuries, and so I must express my gratitude for particular encouragement on it to, in addition to those listed above, my longtime agent Mel Berger, his associate David Hinds, Bruce McEver, colleagues on the board of the Writers Room in New York, my neighbors who listened to my stories in the coffee shops of Salisbury, Connecticut, and Millerton, New York, and especially to my wife Harriet, sons Noah and Daniel, daughters-in-law Elizabeth and Julia, and grandchildren Leo, Giovanni, and Francesca.

—Salisbury, CT, September 2016

Notes

Sources cited several times in these notes are identified in abbreviated form below and fully in the bibliography, while those cited just once are fully identified in the notes but are not in the bibliography. Where sources are available both in print and on-line, I have cited the on-line version as being more readily accessible to interested readers. Most of the cited correspondence to and from founders such as Washington, Franklin, Adams, and Deane can be found at founders.archives.gov, or at franklinpapers.yale.edu or at masshist.org/ publications/apde2/, and for brevity's sake is cited below only by date.

Prologue

1 *"Our want of powder."* Washington to Joseph Reed, Dec. 25, 1775.

2 *"A Proclamation for Suppressing Rebellion and Sedition."* George III, Aug. 23, 1775, www.archives.gov/historical-docs/todays-doc/?dod-date=823.

2 *"Friends . . . in other parts of the world."* Establishment of the Committee of Correspondence, Nov. 29, 1775.

4 *"Toute l'Europe nous souhaite le plus."* C. W. F. Dumas to Franklin, letter lost but likely July 8, 1775, as quoted in Franklin to Dumas, Dec. 9, 1775.

4 *"While we profess ourselves."* Thomas Paine, *Common Sense*, 1776, www.ushistory .org/paine/commonsense/.

5 *"Elderly, lame gentleman."* John Jay, in Carl G. Karsch, "The Unlikely Spy," www .ushistory.org/carpentershall/history/french.htm.

7 *"We admire . . . the grandeur."* Vergennes to Guines, Aug. 7, 1775, Wharton, vol. 1, 333.

7 *"Gentlemen, I shall take care of my head."* Bonvouloir, quoted by Jay, in Louise V. North, "Franklin and Jay," johnjayhomestead.org/wp-content/uploads/Franklin -and-Jay.pdf.

7   *Often-repeated plea.* See for example Washington to Hancock, July 10–11, 1775.

7   *Set up a chessboard.* Cook, Charles, and Nancy Cook. *Blueprint for a Revolution: The Spies at Carpenter's Hall.* ushistory.org/CarpentersHall/history/blueprint5 .htm.

8   *"Monsieur Bonvouloir is begged to examine."* Bonvouloir to Guines, Dec. 28, 1775, Doniol, vol. 1, 267–269, 287–292.

9   *Knew of the chevalier's mission.* Hamon, 25.

1. "The true science of a sovereign."

13   *"Two bottles of the Ratifia."* Penet/Pliarne to Washington, Dec. 18, 1775.

14   *"Tyranny, usurpation, fatal errors."* Samuel Cooper, *A Discourse on the Man of Sin.* (Boston: Greenleaf's, 1774), 12, 40–41.

14   *"A form of spiritual and intellectual 'slavery.'"* Michael S. Carter, "A 'Traiterous Religion': Indulgences and the Anti-Catholic Imagination in Eighteenth-Century New England," *Catholic Historical Review* (Jan. 2013): vol. 99, issue 1, 52–77.

14   *"Anti-Catholic rhetoric was more."* Glenn A. Moots, "Samuel Cooper's Old Sermons and New Enemies: Popery and Protestant Constitutionalism," *American Political Thought* 5 (Summer 2016): 391–420.

14   *Dismissed Americans as lower forms.* Echeverria, *Mirage;* see also Shachtman.

15   *"It is amazing that America has not yet."* Raynal, *Histoire philosophique.*

15   *"An innate taste for liberty."* Gazette de France, Apr. 4, 1774, Faÿ, *Revolutionary Spirit,* 22.

16   *"Under the auspices of liberty."* Chastellux, Echeverria, 35.

16   *"It is necessary, Sire."* Turgot to Louis XVI, Aug. 24, 1774, Stephens, *Turgot,* 87.

16   *"There was something said."* Pacheco, *French Secret Agents.*

17   *"Acquaint himself with the greater."* Choiseul to de Kalb, Kapp, *Kalb,* 47.

18   *"Value to the mother country."* Ibid., 53–55.

18   *"More vigorous policies."* D'Aiguillon/Louis XV to George III, Brecher, 23.

19   *"Never let people read your mind."* Hardman, 21.

19   *Sexual ineptness.* Ryan N. Fogg and Stephen A. Boorjan, "The Sexual Dysfunction of Louis XVI: A Consequence of International Politics, Anatomy, or Naïveté?" *Authors Compilation Journal,* Apr. 2010, Wiley Online Library.

19   *"Obscured by inglorious idleness."* Ségur, 17.

19   *"Louis le Sévère."* Jean-Christian Petitfils, *Louis XVI* (Paris: Perrin, 2005), 167.

19   *"Resurrexit."* Hippeau, *Paris et Versailles,* 93.

20   *"By a long-drawn-out process of subtle blackmail."* Price, 17.

20   *"Sagacious and capable."* List of Le Dauphin, Soulavie, vol. 1, 282–285.

22   *"The true science of a sovereign."* Louis XVI, introduction to Fénélon, *Maximes morales et politiques tirées de Télémaque,* in Crout, 367.

23   *Vergennes's first* tour d'horizon. "Mémoire de M. de Vergennes à Louis XVI sur la situation politique de la France relativement aux différentes puissances," Annales Nationales, K164, no. 2, 1774.

23   *"Spirit of revolt . . . dangerous."* Vergennes to Guines, June 23, 1775, Lever, 302.

23   *"Perhaps there has never been."* Louis XVI to Carlos III, Aug. 7, 1775, Dull,
      French Navy, 30.

2. "Arrogance and insults against which my heart revolted."

25   *"Persona of the prince."* Louis XVI, in Soulavie, vol. 2, 52–53.

26   *"No Bankruptcy."* Turgot to Louis XVI, Stephens, *Turgot*, 87.

26   *Matched the color of her hair . . . 176,000 livres.* Hippeau, 110–115.

27   *"The most mortal enemy."* Saint-Germain, Mention, *Saint-Germain*, xxiv.

27   *Gulf between the blue-uniformed nobility.* Blaufarb, *French Army*, 12–45.

27   *"The first class instantly obtains."* Saint-Germain, *Mémoires*, 120–121.

28   *"The choice of horses."* Soulavie, vol. 3, 70.

28   *"Arrogance and insults."* Vergennes, *"Mémoire sur la politique extérieure de la
      France depuis 1774 adressé au Roi,"* 1782. Archives des Affaires Étrangères, Mé-
      moires et Documents (hereafter cited as AAE-MD), France, 446.

29   *"Vergennes gobe-mouches."* Lucien Taupenot, *Vergennes, Un Bourguignon instigateur
      heureux de l'indépéndance des États-Unis* (Précy-sous-Thil: Éditions de l'Armançon,
      2000), 39–40.

31   *"Girl, man, woman."* D'Éon to Beaumarchais, Jan. 7, 1776, Kates, 233.

31   *"Army of infuriates."* Beaumarchais to Vergennes, Nov. 1775, Murphy, 233.

33   *"Famous quarrel between America and England."* Beaumarchais to Louis XVI,
      Feb. 29, 1776, Morton and Spinelli, 34.

34   *"Pact with the Insurgents."* Vergennes, *"Considerations."* Mar. 12, 1776, Doniol,
      vol. 1, 273–78. Translation in Giunta, *Documents*, 18–24.

3. "The want of experience to move upon a larger scale."

37   *Less than thirty rounds.* Washington to John Augustine Washington, Mar. 31,
      1776.

37   *1.5 million pounds.* Neil C. York, "Clandestine Aid and the American Revolu-
      tionary War Effort, a Reexamination," *Military Affairs* (Feb. 1, 1979): vol. 43,
      no. 1, 28.

37   *"I can hardly express."* Washington to Congress, July 10–11, 1775.

38   *"Who am I to blame."* Washington to Richard Gridley, Apr. 28, 1776.

38   *"His wants are common to us all."* Washington to Hancock, June 17, 1776.

39   *Books that he brought from his home.* Amanda C. Isaac, *Take Note! George Wash-
      ington the Reader* (Mount Vernon, VA: 2013), 14.

39   *"Must be subdued or relinquished."* Burgoyne to Lord Germain, Aug. 1775, Mackesy,
      72–73.

39   *"The most distinguished birth."* Saint-Germain, *"Ordonnance du roi,"* Mar. 25, 1776,
      Blaufarb, 31.

40   *"L'instrument de leur gloire est celui du supplice."* Mention, 120.

40   *"Persuaded that the surest way,"* pamphlet by Monsieur in Soulavie, vol. 3,
      107–108.

40 *"I am grieved."* Louis XVI to Turgot, in Stephens, *Turgot,* 133.

41 *"Nothing can hinder the course."* Turgot memorandum, Apr. 6, 1776, translated in Wharton, vol. 1, 339.

41 *Réflexions.* Rayneval/Vergennes, n.d., Doniol, vol. 1, 278–286 (contemporaneous with other spring 1777 critiques); translation in Giunta, *Documents,* 24–29.

42 *"Our peace with England is nothing."* Vergennes to Aranda, May 3, 1776, Doniol, vol. 1, 376.

43 *"Defend the principle of liberty of the seas."* Petitfils, 374.

43 *"Well instructed in the Military Art."* Barbeu-Dubourg to Franklin, Mar. 24, 1776.

44 *"Treachery and Ingratitude."* Washington to Baron de Calbiac, July 23, 1776.

44 *"You cannot conceive."* Washington to Hancock, Feb. 11, 1777.

45 *"Foreign powers could not be expected."* Adams, *Autobiography,* part 1, sheet 22.

46 *"It is probable that the Court of France."* Committee of Secret Correspondence: Instructions to Silas Deane, Mar. 3, 1776, Giunta, *Documents,* 5–7.

47 *Sign a "partition treaty."* Hutson, "The Partition Treaty."

47 *"Do not the tyrants of Europe think."* *Pennsylvania Evening Post,* Apr. 16, 1776, in ibid., 891.

47 *"Therefore resolved that it be recommended."* Congressional Resolution, May 15, 1776, Stevens, no. 572.

48 *"Swift sailing well escorted vessels."* The Committee of Secret Correspondence Instruction to William Bingham, June 3, 1776, Giunta, *Documents,* 7–8.

48 *"Free and Independent States."* Declaration of Independence, July 4, 1776, www .archives.gov/exhibits/charters/declaration_transcript.html.

48 *"Mary Johnston."* Arthur Lee to Beaumarchais, 1776, Morton and Spinelli, 44.

48 *File off the* fleurs-de-lis. Dubourg to Vergennes, June 19, 1776, Stevens, no. 570.

49 *"Very pleased that my country."* Dubourg to Franklin, July 5, 1776.

50 *"Their Lordships will perceive."* Young to Philip Stephens, Aug. 10, 1776, in Clark, *NDAR,* vol. 6, 142–143.

4. "Dukes, marqueses, comtes and chevaliers without number."

53 *Vergennes, who did not want the British to know.* Bancroft, "A Narrative," Aug. 14, 1776, Stevens, no. 890.

53 *Commercial pact with America.* See for example Deane to Vergennes, Aug. 15, 1776, AAE-CP États-Unis (hereafter cited as É-U), vols. 1–2, 1774–1778.

54 *"The incontestable, hereditary enemy."* Vergennes, Aug. 31, 1776, ibid.

54 *"If we are forced to make war."* Louis XVI to Vergennes, Oct. 18, 1776, Hardman, 94.

55 *"A levee of officers."* Deane to Jay, Dec. 2, 1776, Idzerda, vol. 1, 13–14.

56 *"Considering the importance of having."* Deane to Congress, Sept. 11, 1776, in George I. Clark, *Silas Deane: A Connecticut Leader in the American Revolution* (New York: G. Putnam's Sons, 1913), 76. The original letter, seen by Clark, was later destroyed in a fire and no copies have been found.

57 *"A Rousseau Republican."* Du Bouchet, *Journal d'un émigré,* n.p.

58   *"That if the war between England."* De Kalb to Dr. Frederick Phile, Dec. 26, 1775, Zucker, 85.

58   *"A military and political leader,"* De Kalb to Deane, Nov. 11, 1776, Kapp, 95; fuller version, Dec. 17, 1776, Stevens, no. 604, and Doniol, vol. 2, 65–69. The British knew of the de Broglie command project by January 25, 1777.

60   *"An extreme ardor for* gloire." Du Bouchet, *Journal.*

60   *"It became impossible not to indulge."* Ségur, 127–130.

60   *"His high birth, his Alliances."* Lafayette agreement with Deane, Idzerda, vol. 1, 17.

61   *"I think the game will be pretty."* Washington to Lund Washington, Dec. 10–17, 1776.

62   *"These are the times that try men's souls."* Paine, "The American Crisis," no. 1, www.ushistory.org/paine/crisis/c-01.htm.

62   *"If France Desires to Preclude."* Committee of Secret Correspondence to the American Commissioners, Dec. 21–23, 1776.

63   *"I have not yet taken any Publick."* Franklin to Hancock, Dec. 8, 1776.

63   *"Is a subtle artful Man."* Stormont, *NDAR,* vol. 7, 587.

63   *"Without intelligence, without Orders."* Deane to Jay, Dec. 3, 1776.

64   *"We beg leave to acquaint."* American Commissioners to Vergennes, Dec.23, 1776, Giunta, *Documents,* 30.

5. "The arrival of these great succours raised the spirit of the Rebels."

65   *"Found her so much Lumbered."* Wickes to the American Commissioners (Franklin), Jan. 11, 1777, Franklin Papers.

66   *"Well-dispos'd towards us."* Franklin to Committee of Secret Correspondence, Jan. 4, 1777.

66   *"We may possibly."* American Commissioners to Vergennes, Jan. 5, 1777.

67   *"France and Spain, in allowing."* Louis XVI: Answer to the American Commissioners, Jan. 13, 1777, Giunta, *Documents,* 32.

67   *"Let Old England see how they like."* Committee of Secret Correspondence to Wickes, Oct. 24, 1776, *NDAR,* vol. 6, 1400–1403.

67   *"Nothing Certainly can be more Contrary."* Stormont to Weymouth, Feb. 22, 1777, *NDAR,* vol. 7, 589.

68   *Bancroft never considered himself a traitor.* Schaeper, *Edward Bancroft,* 56–64; Bancroft's first report on Deane, Aug. 16, 1776, in Stevens, no. 890.

68   *Written a treatise on the game.* Franklin, "The Morals of Chess."

69   *His time in Edinburgh.* Michael Atiyah, "Benjamin Franklin and the Edinburgh Enlightenment." *Proceedings of the American Philosophical Society* 150, no. 4 (Dec. 2006): 591–606.

69   *"Nothing could be more striking."* Ségur, 101.

70   *Pledged an "immortal hatred."* Chaumont to Stormont, Schaeper, *Chaumont,* 64.

70   *"The military consistence."* Duportail, in Le Pottier, 43.

71   *"Construction of fortifications proper."* Janis Langins, *Conserving the Enlightenment: French Military Engineering from Vauban to the Revolution* (Cambridge: MIT Press, 2004), 155, 215.

71   *"It is certain that if my going to America,"* Duportail to Franklin, Kite, 14.

72   *"Unaccountable folly."* Stormont to Weymouth, Apr. 2, 1777, Stevens, no.1504.

72   *"On the whole . . . this affair."* Lafayette to Carmichael, Apr. 19, 1777, Idzerda, vol. 1, 50.

73   *"Much superior to any that I have."* Heath to Washington, Apr. 26, 1777.

73   *"The arrival of these great succours."* Stormont to Weymouth, July 9, 1777, Van Alstyne, 128.

74   *"Altho no one will dispute."* Washington to R. H. Lee, May 17, 1777.

74   *"The strongest obligations rest upon us."* R. H. Lee to Washington, May 22, 1777.

6. "France has done too much, unless she intends to do more."

77   *"The glory of conquering kings."* Vergennes to Louis XVI, Apr. 12, 1777, Crout, 383.

78   *"Irrevocably loose the most favourable."* "Memoir to induce France to declare openly for America," spring 1777, in Stevens, no. 149 (underscored in original).

78   *"And continue said war for the Total."* American Commissioners to Aranda, Apr. 7, 1777, Chávez, 62.

79   *"Feeling ourselves assisted."* American Commissioners to Committee for Foreign Affairs, May 25, 1777. Dull, *Diplomat*. 16.

79   *"Surrender to the Congress,"* Conyngham, McGrath, *Fast Ship*, 135.

79   *"The Capture . . . is a complete Refutation."* London Public Advertiser, June 5, 1777, *NDAR,* vol. 9, 604.

79   *"It is extremely mortifying to proud Britain."* Franklin. *NDAR,* vol. 8, 810–811.

79   *London Chronicle . . . St. James Chronicle.* Lutnick, 150.

80   *"As the Self Love."* Bingham to Congress, June 29, 1779, Alberts, 454–463.

80   *Four British West Indies trading companies.* O'Shaughnessy, *Empire Divided*, 158.

81   *"That part of cargo."* Bingham to Congress, Alberts, 458.

81   *"Either to abandon America."* Vergennes, *"Mémoire communiqué au roi le 23 juillet 1777 et approuvé le même jour par Sa Majesté,"* Doniol, vol. 2, 460–469.

82   *"Will have the effect."* Vergennes to Louis XVI and council, Aug. 23, 1777, Stevens, no. 706.

82   *"Carrying consideration as far."* Vergennes to Noailles, Sept. 6, 1777, Stevens, no. 1679.

83   *"You have compromised my reputation."* Du Bouchet.

83   *"As to the situation."* Coudray to Pennsylvania Supreme Executive Council, July 1777, Walker, *Engineers of Independence*, 148–153.

84   *"Was unmasked, and it was proven."* Idzerda, vol. 1, 79.

84   *"I would not wish Monsr. Portail."* Washington to Gates, July 29, 1777.

85   *"Though I ardently desired."* De Kalb, Kapp, 115.

86   *"The friendship with which he has honored."* De Kalb to Pierre de Saint-Paul, Nov. 7, 1777, Idzerda, vol. 1, 145–146ff.

86   *"Has endeavoured to throw contempt."* Stirling to Washington, Aug. 1777.

87   *Resistance to panic.* Michael C. Harris, *Brandywine, A Military History*. El Dorado Hills, CA: Savas Beatie, 2014, 392–404.

87 *"Never saw so close and severe a fire."* Conway to Sullivan, Patrick H. Hannum, "New Light on Battle Casualties: The Ninth Pennsylvania at Brandywine," *Journal of the American Revolution* (Oct. 20, 2015).

88 *"Take care of him as if he were my son."* Lafayette, Unger, 46. While this line is in Lafayette's *Mémoires,* it is not in his Oct. 1, 1777, letter to his wife, in which he reports other instances of Washington's early closeness.

89 *"Soupçons of presumption, vanity, and egoism."* Magnin, *Mottin de la Balme,* 270.

89 *"Self-disciplined, intelligent, fair to their superiors."* Durand Echeverria and Orville T. Murphy, "The American Revolutionary Army, A French Estimate in 1777: Part II—Personnel," *Military Affairs* 27, no. 4 (Winter 1963–64): 156.

90 *"The fact that the soldiers."* Ibid., 155.

90 *"The most amiable, kind-hearted and upright."* De Kalb to de Broglie, Sept. 24–Oct. 1777, Kapp, 129.

91 *No stomach for the fighting.* J. to H. Laurens, June 9, 1778, W. Simms, 102, *"Supernumerary,"* letter of Dec. 3, 1777, ibid., 93.

7. "If ever destruction was complete, it was here."

93 *Rochambeau's men prevailed.* Mention, *Saint-Germain,* 208.

94 *"We are very fond here."* Kościuszko to Gates, May 18, 1777, Alex Storozynski, *The Peasant Prince* (New York: St. Martin's Press, 2009), 26.

94 *Occupied that strategic high point.* Ron Morgan, "Arthur St. Clair's Decision to Abandon Fort Ticonderoga and Mount Independence," *Journal of the American Revolution,* May 2016.

94 *"Manner of taking up the ground."* Burgoyne, ibid.

95 *"Not within the Compass."* Washington to Schuyler, July 15, 1777.

95 *"One can only speculate."* Don Higginbotham, "The War for Independence, to Saratoga," Blackwell, 296.

96 *"Little effect upon the strength."* Burgoyne to Germain, Aug. 20, 1777, Commager, 577.

97 *Did have to ration ammunition.* Snow, *1777: Saratoga,* 142.

97 *"Like Robinson Crusoe."* Du Bouchet.

97 *"You know my poverty."* Clinton to Burgoyne, Michael Pearson, *The Revolutionary War: An Unbiased Account* (New York: Capricorn, 1972), 276.

98 *Distributed twelve barrels of rum.* Ketchum, *Saratoga,* 389.

98 *Conferred with Arnold in the field.* Stephen Williams, "Letters change view of Benedict Arnold, Gen. Gates," *Saratoga Daily Gazette,* Mar. 26, 2016. A newly discovered letter, written two days after the battle, alters prior conceptions of Gates as having stayed in a fortified headquarters and Arnold as having seized command on the field without Gates's permission. See also, Snow, *1777,* 158–171.

99 *"It will be as unfortunate a measure."* Washington to R. H. Lee, Oct. 16, 1777.

99 *"Heaven has been determind."* Conway to Gates, in Washington to Conway, Nov. 5, 1777.

100 *"I believe I can attest that the expression."* Conway to Washington, Nov. 5, 1777.

100 *"The perplexity of his style."* J. to H. Laurens, Jan. 3, 1778, W. Simms, 102.

101 *"Have thrown the army."* Washington to H. Laurens, Nov. 17–18, 1777.

102 *"Re-entrant salient angle."* Closen, 122.

102 *"He possesses a degree of modesty."* Washington to H. Laurens, Jan. 13, 1778.

102 *"Wants no Retreat."* Fleury to Hamilton, Oct.16, 1777, Walker, 160.

102 *"Our batteries were nothing more."* Martin, *Private Yankee Doodle*, 84–95.

103 *"Had the reinforcements arrived."* Washington to John Augustine Washington, Nov. 26, 1777.

103 *"Cost us two of the most precious months."* Sir James Murray, Jeffrey M. Dorwart, *Fort Mifflin of Philadelphia* (Philadelphia: University of Pennsylvania Press, 1998), 53–54.

104 *"To attack the Enemy in their Lines."* Duportail to Washington, Nov. 24, 1777. Kite, 37–38.

105 *Compared Washington's strategies to Fabius's.* Osman, 86.

105 *"You cannot employ [Duportail] too much."* Washington to Lincoln, Mar. 30, 1780.

105 *"There is a hundred times more enthusiasm."* Duportail to Saint-Germain, Nov. 12, 1777, Arthur P. Watts, "A Newly Discovered Letter of Brigadier-General Duportail," *Pennsylvania History* 1 (1934): 101–106.

106 *"Consider, if you please."* Lafayette to Washington, Oct. 14, 1777.

106 *"Hung on the rear of the enemy."* De Kalb to de Broglie, Dec. 12 and 25, 1777, Zucker, 154–55.

107 *"I cannot but observe."* De Kalb to H. Laurens, Jan. 7, 1778, Kapp, 145.

8. "France and Spain should strike before England can secure the advantage."

111 *"The Ministers of France still continue."* American Commissioners to the Committee for Foreign Affairs, Sept. 8, 1777. Stevens, no. 262.

112 *Used the term "peace."* Noailles to Vergennes, November 21, 1777, in Chris Tudda, "'A Messiah that Will Never Come': A New Look at Saratoga, Independence, and Revolutionary War Diplomacy," *Diplomatic History* 12, no. 5 (Nov. 2008): 779–810.

112 *"I have lost the fruits."* Beaumarchais to Vergennes, Jan. 1, 1778, Doniol, vol. 2, 686.

112 *"Sir, is Philadelphia taken?"* Franklin, in William Temple Franklin, ed. *Memoirs of the Life and Writings of Benjamin Franklin* (London, Henry Colburn, 1818), vol. 2, 56 (underscoring in original); see also Schiff, *Grand Improvisation*, 109–112.

112 *"Total reduction of the forces."* American Commissioners to Vergennes, Dec. 4, 1777, É-U, vol. 2, no. 279.

113 *"An offensive on the part of France."* De Broglie, plan of Dec. 18, 1777, Sudipta Das, *De Broglie's Armada: A Plan for the Invasion of England, 1765–1777* (Lanham, MD: University Press of America, 2009), 18.

114 *"To make it last as long as."* Vergennes, *Diary of A. Lee*, Commager, 680–681.

114 *"Fifty thousand troops have not."* *Public Ledger*, MPs, and *Evening Post*, Lutnick,

106–109; see also Brendan Simms, *Three Victories and a Defeat: The Rise and Fall of the British Empire* (New York: Basic Books, 2009), 608–612.

114 *"A gentleman who has a slender."* Wentworth to Deane, Dec. 12, 1777, Stevens, no. 719; see also Schaeper, *Bancroft*, 107–112.

115 *"General Ideas for the Preliminaries."* Wentworth, Dec. 12, 1777, Stevens, no.719.

115 *"It was manifestly in the Interest."* American Commissioners to Committee for Foreign Affairs, Dec. 18, 1777, Giunta, *Documents*, 50–51.

115 *"The destruction of the army."* Louis to Carlos III, Jan. 8, 1778, Doniol, vol. 2, 714.

116 *"These dispatches contain the resolution."* Wentworth to Eden, Jan. 6, 1778, Stevens, no. 332.

116 *"To a perpetual and everlasting."* Franklin, Schiff, 119.

117 *"I observe much eagerness."* Chaumont to Vergennes, Jan. 7, 1778. Stevens, no. 772.

117 *"Provided it would completely occupy."* North. Simms, *Three Victories*, 624.

118 *"Given the distrust."* Gérard, Report of a Conference with the American Commissioners, Jan. 9, 1778, Giunta, *Documents*, 52–58.

118 *"The immediate conclusion of a treaty."* Ibid.

120 *"If France were mad enough."* Forth diary entry, Ward, 52.

121 *"Lost the esteem."* Franklin to Hutton, Feb. 1, 1778, John W. Jordan, "Some account of James Hutton's Visit to Franklin in France, in Dec. 1777," *Penna. Magazine of History and Biography* 32 (1908): 228–256.

121 *"I abominate with you all Murder."* Franklin to Hutton, Feb. 12, 1778, ibid.

121 *"Deputy Plenipotentiary for France and Spain."* A. Lee, Potts, 193.

121 *"To give it a little revenge."* Franklin, Richard Meade Bache, "Franklin's Ceremonial Coat," *Penna. Magazine of History and Biography* 23 (1899): 444–452.

122 *"Amity and Commerce."* Benjamin Franklin and Silas Deane to the President of Congress, Feb. 8, 1778, Giunta, *Documents*, 59–60.

9. "When an Enemy think a design against them improbable they can always be Surprised."

124 *"They will laugh in France."* Lafayette to Washington, Jan. 20, 1778.

124 *"Wise . . . good officer."* Lafayette to J. Laurens, Jan. 26, 1778, Zucker, 255.

124 *"Within two days."* Lafayette to H. Laurens, Fleming, *Washington's Secret*, 172.

124 *Lists of those officers.* See for example É-U, no. 1, 132.

125 *"Mr. Dana—Congress does not trust me."* Fleming, 175.

126 *"With more warmth and obstinacy."* De Kalb to de Broglie, Zucker, 175.

126 *"I believe that of General Conway."* Lafayette to Washington, Mar. 25, 1778.

127 *"No Treaty would be entered."* Franklin to Vergennes, Feb. 22, 1778, É-U, no. 285.

127 *"It was near Nine at night."* Franklin and Deane to A. Lee, Feb. 26, 1778.

128 *The supposed affair with Mme. Chaumont.* Gallo, *John Paul Jones,* treats the affair as accepted fact; Schaeper, *Chaumont,* believes it is only conjecture.

128 *"When an enemy thinks the design."* Jones to American Commissioners, Feb.1778, Dennis M. Conrad, "John Paul Jones," *Sea Raiders,* 60.

129 *"Proceed with . . . in the manner you shall."* American Commissioners to J. P. Jones, Gallo, 40.

129 *Salute was the first officially given.* Tuchman, *The First Salute,* 5–17.

130 *"If you shall find it impracticable."* Germain to Clinton, Mar. 8, 1778, Stevens, no. 360.

130 *"WAR WITH FRANCE."* Gazeteer, Mar. 19, 1778, Lutnick, 130.

130 *"Filled with a true spirit."* Morning Post, Mar. 21, 1778, ibid.,137.

131 *"There is a Stile in some of your letters."* Franklin to Lee, three letters, drafts never sent, Apr. 1–4, 1778.

133 *"We are sailing with neither watch muster."* Bougainville, Dunmore, 234.

133 *"Warm, close, and obstinate."* Jones to the American Commissioners, May 17, 1778, Commager, 945.

134 *"Benevolent neutrality,"* Chávez, *Spain and the Independence of the United States,* 121.

134 *"For herself, Spain has no other."* Floridablanca to Aranda, Jan. 13, 1778, Chávez, 76–77.

10. "To hinder the enemy from rendering himself master."

136 *"With an Air and Manner."* Steuben diary, Lockhart, *Drillmaster,* 41.

136 *"Nearly every statement."* Ibid., 45.

136 *"The Object of my Greatest Ambition."* Steuben to Washington, Dec. 6, 1777.

137 *"With him I had lisped."* Du Ponceau, "The Autobiography of Pierre de Ponceau," *Penna. Magazine of History and Biography* 63, no. 1(Apr. 1939): 204.

138 *Du Ponceau formed his closest friendship.* Henry Ammon, *James Monroe: The Quest for National Identity* (Charlottesville: University of Virginia Press, 1990), 18.

139 *"Soldier, Sailors, Deserters from any Troops."* Mottin de la Balme advertisement, 1778, Magnin, 271.

139 *"The repeated cavils of some officers."* J. to H. Laurens, Mar. 9, 1778, W. Simms, 135.

139 *"Considering the few Moments."* Gates to Steuben, Mar. 25, 1778, Lockhart, 109.

140 *"Remaining quiet in a secure."* Washington to General Officers, Apr. 20, 1778.

140 *"We were beaten at Brandywine."* Duportail memo, Apr. 23, 1778, Kite, 60–73.

142 *"On the front seat of each pavilion."* John André, "Description of the Mischianza." Benjamin J. Lossing, *Pictorial Field Book of the Revolution, vol. 2* (New York: Harper & Bros., 1859–1860).

142 *"Nauseous . . . dancing at a funeral."* Weintraub, 155.

144 *"We trust that the inhabitants of North-America."* Carlisle Commission to Congress, June 9, 1778, and response, June 17, 1778, http://teachingamericanhistory .org/library/document/response-to-british-peace-proposals/.

144 *"Nothing but an earnest desire."* Laurens to Washington, June 17, 1778.

144 *Secret instructions, which empowered the commissioners.* Mackesy, 189.

146 *Louis objected only to language.* Soulavie, vol. 3, 396–397.

11. "Concerting my operations with a general of Your Excellency's repute."

149 *"Has been of a greater use."* Lafayette to H. Laurens, June 7, 1778, Idzerda, vol. 2, 71.

150 *"I place my honor and fortune,"* Lee to Lafayette, in *Memoir of 1779*, Idzerda, vol. 2, 10.

150 *"Nothing but the misinformation."* Charles Lee to Washington, June 30, 1778.

151 *"I find my self just able."* Conway to Washington, July 23, 1778.

152 *"The arrival of this fleet."* Lord to Lady Carlisle, July 21, 1778, Commager, 701.

152 *"Concerter mes opérations."* D'Estaing to Washington, July 8, 1778, Calmon-Maison, *L'Admiral d'Estaing*, 202 (English translation in Founders Online).

152 *"Shall then move down."* Washington to d'Estaing, July 14, 1778.

153 *"I have the honor to be as much related."* Lafayette to d'Estaing, July 14, 1778, Idzerda, vol. 2, 102.

153 *"Disaffected inhabitants."* J. to H. Laurens, July 18, 1778, W. Simms, 207–208.

153 *"Actif et aimable."* D'Estaing to Vergennes, July 19, 1778. *AE-CP-É-U Supplement, 1777–1787*, no. 40.

154 *"It has given me, much Grief."* Adams to R. H. Lee, Aug. 5, 1778.

154 *"There never was before I came."* *Adams Diary*, vol. 2, Apr. 21, 1778.

155 *"This is an ugly situation for me."* Adams to S. Adams, Aug. 7, 1778.

155 *"Cultivate a harmony."* Adams to A. Lee, McCullough, *John Adams*. 207.

155 *"The more I consider our Affairs."* Adams to James Warren, Aug. 4, 1778.

155 *"Taking eleven of the finest ships."* Keppel to Sandwich, Simms, *Three Victories*, 613.

156 *"England, too long accustomed."* Ségur, 180.

157 *"Do not my dear General Sullivan."* Washington to Sullivan, Mar. 15, 1777.

158 *"Where there was even a Probability."* Sullivan to Washington, Whittemore, *Sullivan*, 80.

158 *"A certain Northern heroe."* Greene to Sullivan, July 23, 1778, ibid., 85.

158 *"Admitted to be temperamental."* Stephens, *Neither the Charm*, 84.

159 *"Was as sudden as a change."* Laurens to H. Laurens, Aug. 4, 1778, W. Simms, 210.

159 *"Revealed difficulties, stemming as much from."* Blancpain, *L'Amiral d'Estaing*, 91.

159 *"Were the most favorable ones."* D'Estaing, *Mémoires*, in Doniol, vol. 3, 337.

159 *"Comedic . . . grand spectacle."* Lafayette to d'Estaing, Aug. 5, 1778, Calmon-Maison, 210.

160 *"Withdrew his attention wholly."* Laurens to H. Laurens, Aug. 22, 1778, W. Simms, 218.

160 *"I dare hope that Your Excellency."* D'Estaing to Sullivan, Aug. 7, 1778, in Whittemore, 94.

160 *"Much umbrage."* Laurens to H. Laurens, Aug. 22, 1778, W. Simms, 220.

160 *"Sensed the gravity of the situation."* Fleury, Calmon-Maison, 213.

161 *"I had the pleasure of seeing."* Sullivan to Washington, Aug. 10, 1778.

161 *"The British admiral maneuvered."* Edward Lengel, "Aspects Tactiques de la Coopération Franco-Américaine," in Chaline, *La France*, 173.

161 *"To combat all those difficulties."* Sullivan to Washington, Aug. 13, 1778.

161 *"Imagine the cruel situation."* J. to H. Laurens, Aug. 22, 1778. W. Simms, 221.

162 *"The express orders I have from the King."* D'Estaing to Sullivan, Aug. 21, 1778, (in French) enclosed in Sullivan to Washington, Aug. 23, 1778.

162 *"It Seems That the Captains."* Sullivan to Washington, Aug. 23, 1778.

162 *"Victim of the state."* Blancpain.

162 *"The least act of feebleness."* D'Estaing to Gérard, Doniol, vol. 3, 239.

162 *"Derogatory to the honor of France."* Sullivan and American officers to d'Estaing, Aug. 22, 1778. Stephens, *Sullivan,* 89.

163 *"Would you believe . . . they dared to summon."* Lafayette to d'Estaing, Aug. 22, 1778. Idzerda , vol. 2, 139.

163 *"Need not mean falling out."* Lafayette to d'Estaing, Aug. 24, 1778. Idzerda, vol 2, 143.

163 *"I feel myself hurt also."* Washington to Lafayette, Sep. 1, 1778.

164 *"May any comparable efforts."* Inscription, in Dunmore, 234. The monument was approved in 1778 but not built until 1917.

164 *"It having been supposed."* Sullivan, General Orders for Aug. 26, 1778. Whittemore, 103.

164 *"Become a colonel of infantry."* D'Estaing, report to Ministry of the Marine, Sep. 9, 1778. Doniol, vol. 3, 363.

164 *"America has declared herself independent."* Steuben to Gérard, Sep. 25, 1778. 40 CP É-U, 1777–1787, supplement vol. 1, No. 171.

12. "Take a bit of courage, have a bit of patience, and all will go well."

166 *"Prenez un peu de courage."* Floridablanca to Montmorin, Doniol, vol. 3, 492.

166 *"My Children the Savages of Canada."* Lafayette, Dec. 18, 1778, Idzerda, vol. 2, 213–215.

166 *"You were born French."* D'Estaing proclamation, Oct. 28, 1778, AAE MD, É-U, I, No. 216.

167 *"Should be, to gain the love."* Steuben "Blue Book," Lockhart, 195.

168 *"Un esprit de parti."* Gérard to Vergennes, July 16, 1778, Meng, *Despatches,* 157.

168 *"Neglected nothing."* Gérard to Vergennes, Nov. 1, 1778, ibid., 240.

169 *A public explanation.* Deane, "Address to the Free and Virtuous Citizens of America," http://connecticuthistoryillustrated.org/islandora/object/40002%3A379 3#page/1/mode/2up.

170 *"The stores which Silas Deane."* Paine, Keane, 175.

170 *"My full opinion is."* Paine to Gérard, Jan. 1779. 40 CP É-U, 1777–1787, Supplement vol. 1., 247.

171 *"These United States will not conclude."* Congressional Resolution, Jan. 7, 1779, excerpted in letter to Gérard, ibid., 254.

171 *"Why was not Gen Washington."* Carlisle, notes of questions, July 1778, Stevens, no. 81.

171 *"The French interference."* Carlisle to North government, Sept. 29, 1778, ibid., no. 529.

173 *"What comfort our indecision."* Bougainville diary, Dunmore, 235.

174 *"Only an hour before the plot."* Lafayette, *Mémoire of 1779,* Idzerda, vol. 2, 225.

174 *"Confines of the Hôtel."* Ibid.

174 *"Very humble and very obedient."* Lafayette to Louis XVI, Feb. 19, 1779. Idzerda, vol. 2, 232–33.

174 *"I will not dissimulate."* Vergennes to Louis XVI, Dec. 5, 1778. Murphy, 267.

175   *"Point of honor."* Montmorin to Floridablanca. Doniol, III, 521.

175   *"Useless . . . out of place."* Floridablanca, in Montmorin to Vergennes, Feb. 22, 1779. Murphy, 270.

175   *"If we succeed only."* Vergennes to Montmorin, Feb. 12, 1779, Patterson, 31.

175   *"They may be won with the bait."* Ibid.

176   *"He will recognize the independence."* Proposed Article 12, Doniol, vol. 3, 810.

176   *"All the possible advantages."* Renaut, 289.

177   *"Fortunately, England . . . has cut through."* Montmorin to Vergennes, May 17, 1779, Murphy, 276.

178   *"I do not think a Storm practicable."* Wayne to Washington, July 3, 1779.

178   *"The fort's our own."* Fleury, Edward G. Lengel, "Bayonets at Midnight: The Battle of Stony Point," *Military History* 26, no. 5 (Jan. 2010).

179   *"I would rather have included your tales."* Raynal, in footnote to "The Speech of Miss Polly Baker," Apr. 15, 1747 (Founders Online).

179   *"A mine is prepared under the foundations."* Raynal, 1779 ed., Geneva.

13. "What a wonderful opportunity is slipping from our grasp."

182   *"Ninety-five Holes."* Newspaper account, O'Shaughnessy, *Empire Divided*, 170.

182   *"If we only go to Savannah."* D'Estaing to Sartine. Perkins, 273–274.

182   *"There is every reason to believe."* Washington to Gérard, May 1, 1779.

182   *"It is necessary to defend."* Marquis de Brétigny to d'Estaing, Alexander A. Lawrence, *Storm over Savannah* (Athens: University of Georgia Press, 1951), 19.

183   *"Much will depend on a prudent."* Franklin to Lafayette, Mar. 22, 1779, Idzerda, vol. 2, 243.

183   *"I shall expect you to point out."* Jones to Lafayette, May 1, 1779, ibid., 264.

184   *"You shall not require."* Chaumont to Jones, June 1779, Gallo, 74.

184   *"The British courage failed."* Jones to Franklin, July 1, 1779, ibid., 73.

185   *"A question of a guerre de campagne."* French planning document, Feb. 1779, Patterson, *Other Armada*, 48.

186   *"Talked only of feats of arms."* Lauzun, ibid., 152.

187   *"Twenty million to support the paper."* Lafayette to Vergennes, June 1, 1779, Idzerda, vol. 2, 270.

187   *"Blackness overwhelms me."* Vergennes to Montmorin, Patterson, 165.

187   *"The disunion of the two parties."* Gérard to Vergennes, July 9, 1779, Meng, 762.

187   *"That the king is actually the only."* Vergennes, Sept. 25, 1779, ibid., 79.

188   *"The combined [fleet] is at present anchored."* D'Orvilliers to Sartine, Aug. 16, 1779. Manceron, *Wind*, 179.

188   *"Whatever is prudent."* Lafayette to Franklin, Aug. 19, 1779, Idzerda, vol. 2, 303.

189   *"He means to take as small a share."* Count Rumford, Patterson, 174.

189   *"It had exhausted England."* Lafayette to Congress, Oct. 7, 1779, Idzerda, vol. 2, 321.

190 *"Not a day passed but we are receiving."* London Evening Post, Sept. 20, 1779, Gallo, 82.

190 *"I have not yet begun to fight."* Jones, ibid., 90.

192 *"I don't know what can be done."* Vergennes to Lafayette, Sept. 16, 1779, Idzerda, vol. 2, 311–312.

192 *"America is in a state of crisis."* Fleury, Nov.16, 1779, Stevens, no. 1616.

192 *"Raise three thousand able bodied negroes."* Massey, *Laurens*, 132.

192 *"Foundation for the Abolition."* Ibid., 133.

193 *"I learn your black Air Castle."* H. to J. Laurens, Sept. 27, 1779, Massey, 143.

193 *"I know I have been disobedient."* D'Estaing to Maurepas, Blancpain, 99.

193 *"The damage done to my ships."* D'Estaing to Sartine, Perkins, 275.

194 *"Had nothing to fear from the rear."* The Siege of Savannah in 1779; as described in two contemporaneous journals of French officers in the fleet of Count d'Estaing (Albany, GA: Joel Munsell, 1874), 19.

194 *"So thoroughly cleared the way."* Douglas B. Shores, *Kazmierz Puɫaski: General of Two Nations* (San Diego: CreateSpace, 2015), 215.

195 *"Always knows how to make jokes."* Wilson, *Southern Strategy*, 134.

195 *"If I had not attacked Savannah."* D'Estaing, "Journal of the Siege of Savannah," Doniol, vol. 4, 263.

195 *"Carried away by his courage."* Siege of Savannah, 21–22.

196 *"Our imprudence in leaving our trench."* Ibid., 22.

196 *"With more vivacity than precision."* Ibid., 25.

196 *"We begin to lose confidence."* Ibid., 25–26.

197 *"Be treated at all times like whites."* D'Estaing, ibid., 65.

197 *"Great God! It would have been."* De Grasse, Lewis, 80–81.

198 *"700 mulâtres et 200 hommes levés."* D'Estaing to Gérard, Doniol, vol. 4, 269.

14. "The country that will hazard the most will get the advantage in this war."

201 *"The miscarriage of our great preparations."* Lafayette to Maurepas, Jan. 25, 1780, Idzerda, vol. 2, 345–346.

202 *"The sentiments of the people."* Bingham to Jay, July 1, 1780, Alberts, 85.

203 *"It is sorrowful for me to think."* Laumoy to Lincoln, Mar. 4, 1780, Borick, 42.

203 *"The impracticability of defending."* Washington to Laurens, Apr. 26, 1780.

203 *"In a desperate State."* Duportail to Washington, May 17, 1780.

204 *"I attached myself wherever."* L'Enfant, Berg, 47.

204 *"Attended with many difficulties."* De Kalb to Washington, Zucker, 199.

204 *"A state of inactivity,"* Laurens to Washington, May 25, 1780.

204 *"Hard captivity."* L'Enfant, Berg, 47.

204 *"How many people have reproaches."* Duportail to Marbois, July 7, 1780, Kite, 176–177.

205 *"Signal misfortune."* Bingham to Jay, July 1, 1780, Alberts, 85.

206 *"Unheard-of barbarity."* Chávez, 180.

206 *"Not to lose sight of the principle."* Reported in La Luzerne to Vergennes, June 11, 1780, O'Donnell, 101.

207 *"The medall voted for me by congress."* Fleury to Franklin, Mar. 1780.

207 *"Pride, hauteur, and almost of severity."* Kennett, 12.

207 *Rochambeau's 6,000 were just four divisions.* Claude D. Sturgill, "Money for the Bourbon Army in the Eighteenth Century: The State within the State," *War and Society* 4, no. 2 (Sept. 1986): 17–30.

208 *"The more I reflect on the fleet."* George III to Sandwich, Mar. 6, 1780, Kennett, 15.

209 *"The General to whom His Majesty entrusts."* Montbarrey to Rochambeau, Mar. 1, 1780, Keim, *Rochambeau,* 296–297.

209 *"Produced at first the most profound."* Cardinal de la Rochefoucauld and other quotes regarding the quinquennial, Kite, *Duportail,* 187.

210 *"Always occupied with his main task."* Rochambeau, *Mémoires,* vol. 1, 242.

15. "My command of the F–Tps at R Is-d stands upon a very limited state."

214 *"I am the only person."* Adams to Vergennes, Feb. 12, 1780.

214 *"While I admit, Sir."* Vergennes to Adams, June 21, 1780, Giunta, *Emerging,* 77.

214 *It concerned the future sovereignty.* Jean Bauer, "With Friends Like These: John Adams and the Comte de Vergennes on Franco-American Relations," *Diplomatic History* 37, no. 4 (2013): 664–692.

215 *"Whether something might not be done."* Adams, in Franklin to Huntington, Aug. 9, 1780.

215 *"Sentiments therein express'd."* Franklin to Vergennes, Aug. 3, 1780, Giunta, *Emerging,* 95.

215 *"This Court is to be treated."* Franklin to Congress, Aug. 9, 1780, ibid., 199.

216 *"The manner, the forms."* Floridablanca to Jay, Feb. 28, 1780, ibid., 39.

216 *"Since His Majesty's armed forces."* Miralles to Don José de Gálvez, Mar. 12, 1780, ibid., 43.

217 *"The intolerable heat."* De Kalb to wife, June 21, 1780, Zucker, 203.

217 *"I meet with no support."* De Kalb to Dr. Phile, ibid., 200.

217 *"Take care lest your northern."* C. Lee to Gates, ibid., 206.

217 *"Plenty will soon succeed."* Gates, ibid., 210.

217 *"The general's astonishment."* Otho Williams, John Buchanan, *The Road to Guilford Courthouse: The American Revolution in the Carolinas* (New York: Wiley, 1997), 162.

218 *"Threw down their* loaded *arms."* Williams, ibid., 166 (italics in original).

218 *"Gave us three days."* Rawdon, Zucker, 217.

219 *Cooper, who had recycled his sermons.* Moots, "Samuel Cooper's Old Sermons," 398–401.

220 *France had been paying 30 percent.* See Dull, *French Navy,* and Stockley, *Birth of America,* 89.

220 *Great Britain's debt service.* Patrick K. O'Brien, "The Political Economy of

British Taxation, 1660–1815," *Economic History Review,* 2nd series, 41, no. 1 (1988): 1–32; see also P. Mathias and P. K. O'Brien, "Taxation in England and France 1715–1810," *Journal of European Economic History* 5 (1976), 601–650.

220   *Producing 85 million livres but promising 105.* Hardman, 60.

220   *The loans made to America.* Robert D. Harris, "French Finances and the American War, 1777–1783," *Journal of Modern History* 48, no. 2 (1976): 233–258. Harris puts the total of loans to America at 12 million livres, the "extraordinary" (overbudget) French military outlay for the war at 125 million livres, and the total outlay at 1 billion livres, half of prior estimates.

221   *"Shall we dismiss Necker."* Louis XVI to Maurepas, Hardman, 63.

221   *Overrule precedent to accelerate.* Étienne Taillemite, "Les Officiers Généraux de la Guerre d'indépendance," Chaline, *Les Marines,* 384.

221   *"Distributed in the military."* Marquis de Ségur, Blaufarb, 35.

222   *"Have no secrets."* Rochambeau to Washington, July 12, 1780.

222   *"As a Genl Officer I have the greatest."* Washington to Rochambeau, July 16, 1780.

223   *"Permit me, my dear marquis."* Rochambeau to Lafayette, Decré, 94.

224   *"There can be no decisive."* Washington Answers to Queries by the Comte de Rochambeau and the Chevalier de Ternay, Sep. 22, 1780, translated by Hamilton from Lafayette's contemporaneous notes.

225   *"My command of the F-T-ps."* Washington to Lafayette, Dec. 14, 1780.

225   *"I will cooperate when."* Arnold to André, May 23, 1779, Commager, 748.

225   *"I have accepted the command."* Arnold to André, July 12,1780, ibid.

225   *"An object of the utmost importance."* Clinton to Lord Germain, Oct. 11, 1780, ibid., 750.

16. "Siberia alone can furnish any idea of Lebanon, Connecticut."

227   *Based on a draft of a treaty seized.* "Plan of a Treaty," Stevens, no. 936.

228   *"Inexperience in affairs."* Washington to J. Laurens, Jan. 15, 1781.

228   *"I suspect the French Ministry."* Hamilton to Laurens, Feb. 4, 1781, Massey, 176.

229   *"Cast your gaze upon the capital."* Raynal, 1781 ed., Manceron, *Wind,* 362–363.

230   *"Restored to the tyrant."* Laurens to S. Huntington, Mar. 23, 1781, Massey, 179.

230   *"Mr. Lawrens is worrying the Minister."* Franklin to Jay, Apr.12, 1781.

231   *"The homage of the most ardent gratitude."* Laurens to Louis XVI, Apr. 18, 1781, Giunta, *Emerging,* 165.

231   *"Not . . . suited to the nature."* Vergennes to Lafayette, Apr. 19, 1781, Massey, 182.

231   *"Could not put their affairs in better hands."* Franklin to Laurens, May 17, 1781. Franklin had earlier said much the same to John Jay, letter of Apr. 12, 1781.

231   *"I know John is so full of love."* H. Laurens, n.d., 1781, Massey, 187.

232   *"Des princes souverains."* Lewis, 95.

232   *"Long and troublesome campaign."* Instruction to de Grasse, Amiral Rémi Monaque,

"La Bataille de la Chesapeake ou Le Triomphe de la Concorde," Chaline, *La France*, 182.

233 *"Siberia alone can furnish."* Lauzun, *Mémoires du Duc de Lauzun* (Paris: Olivier Orban, 1986), 237.

233 *"Vegetate . . . in the most sinister."* Axel von Fersen, *Lettres d'Axel Fersen à son père, pendant la guerre d'indepéndance d'Amérique* (Paris: Firmin-Didiot, 1929).

233 *"Ignorant superstitious." Royal Gazette,* Oct. 28, 1780, Kennett, 84.

234 *"The enemmy Have Been so Kind."* Lafayette to Washington, June 28, 1781.

236 *"I saw with grief."* De Grasse to de Castries, Lewis, 110.

237 *King's brothers were laughing at Louis XVI.* Decré, 116.

237 *"Never aspired to such an important function."* Rochambeau, Keim, 378.

238 *"However desirable such an event."* Rochambeau summary, Wethersfield meeting, June 23, 1781, http://rotunda.upress.virginia.edu/founders/default.xqy?keys=FOEA -print-01-01-02-5842.

238 *"All the ungraciousness."* Chastellux, Chernow, *Washington,* 402.

238 *"May be considered a transgression."* Chastellux to Washington, May 12, 1781.

239 *"What are the operations."* Rochambeau summary,Wethersfield meeting. rotunda .upress.virginia.edu/founders/default.xqy?keys=FOEA-print-01-01-02-5842

239 *"Should the West India fleet arrive."* Ibid.

239 *"Extend our views to the Southward."* Washington, May 21, 1781, diary entry.

239 *"Fixed with Count Rochambeau."* Ibid.

239 *"Make the estimates."* Washington to Duportail, May 28, 1781.

240 *"Grand quantity of blood."* Du Bouchet.

17. "Could not waste the most decisive opportunity of the whole war."

241 *"A gentleman of the first abilities."* Whittemore, 170.

244 *"You are to accede to no treaty."* Instructions to the American Peace Commissioners from Congress, June 15, 1781, Giunta, *Emerging,* 199.

245 *"As an American I [feel]."* Jay to President of Congress, Sept. 20, 1781, Stinchcombe, 176.

245 *"No province in which the English."* Vergennes to La Luzerne, Oct. 7, 1781, Giunta, *Emerging,* 251–253.

245 *"As there is upon Earth."* Adams to Vergennes, July 13, 1781, ibid., 208–215.

246 *"Gate of Death."* Adams to Abigail Adams, Oct. 9, 1781.

248 *"Could not waste the most decisive."* Saavedra, Chávez, 201.

249 *"Without the money the Conde de Grasse."* Ibid., 202.

250 *"The spot which seems to be indicated."* De Grasse to Rochambeau and Barras, July 28, 1781, Lewis, 139.

251 *"The boy cannot escape me."* Cornwallis, Ketchum, *Yorktown,* 184.

251 *"You will immediately take such."* Washington to Lafayette, Aug. 15, 1781.

252 *"Taking Whatever is in the Rivers."* Lafayette to Washington, Aug. 21, 1781.

252 *"I have named no halting day."* Washington to Rochambeau, Aug. 17, 1781.

253 *"The seizure of some bread."* Closen, *Revolutionary Journal*, 95.

253   *"You can be sure."* Ibid., 97.

253   *"Is it not advantageous."* Duportail to Washington, Aug.15, 1781, Kite, 202.

254   *"A land of milk and honey."* Ibid., 111.

254   *"Establishing a boulangerie."* Rochambeau, "Relation," 1.

254   *"To make Clinton believe."* Closen, 109.

254   *"By these maneuvres."* Diary of Jonathan Trumbull, Jr., in fn., Washington Diary entry, Aug. 19, 1781, Founders Archive.

255   *"This maneuver prevented General Clinton."* Rochambeau, "Relation," 2.

18. "The measures which we are now pursuing are big with great events."

257   *"Made the land a little to the southward."* Hood, Lewis, *De Grasse*, 152.

258   *"This was the first."* Martin, *Private Yankee Doodle*, 222–223.

258   *"Distressed beyond expression."* Washington to Lafayette, Sept. 2 1781.

259   *"I have not hesitated to open my heart."* De Grasse to Washington, Sept. 2, 1781.

259   *"Come with the greatest expedition."* Duportail to Washington, Sept. 2, 1781, Kite, 207.

259   *"I want to contribute everything."* De Grasse to Lafayette, Unger, 154.

260   *"I never saw a man so thoroughly."* Lauzun, 246.

261   *"Burning with the desire."* Closen, 123.

261   *"The shadow of ships more than substance."* Miller, 487.

261   *"Had finally sacrificed the parity."* Dull, *French Navy*, 237.

261   *"In a position almost beyond."* William M. James, *The British Navy in Adversity: A Study of the War of American Independence* (New York: Longmans, 1926).

262   *"Thunder, foam and fire."* Bougainville diary, Dunmore, 242.

262   *Simon Pouzoulet.* Catherine Papini, *Journal Historique de Simon Pouzoulet (Castelnau de Guers 1759–1839) sur l'expédition aux Amériques avec l'Amiral comte de Grasse, 1781–1782* (Nîmes: Lacour/Rediva, 2000), 83–84.

263   *"I hope you will keep Lord Cornwallis."* Washington to Lafayette, Sep. 10, 1781.

263   *"La prudence et le sang-froid."* Monaque, 191.

264   *"And the impracticability of giving any effectual."* Graves, Lewis, 169.

264   *"Hugged [Washington] as close."* St.-George Tucker, in Chernow, *Washington*, 411.

265   *"The season is approaching."* De Grasse to Washington, Sept. 16, 1781.

265   *"The measures which we are now pursuing."* Washington to de Grasse, Sept. 19, 1781.

266   *"In the dark night."* Karl Gustaf Tornquist, Lewis, 176.

266   *"Alarmed and disquieted."* Closen, 133–134.

266   *"Imprudent of me to take."* De Grasse to Washington, Sept. 23, 1781.

267   *"I cannot conceal from Your Excellency."* Washington to de Grasse, Sept. 25, 1781.

267   *"The most amiable admiral."* S. et d. Lecomte, *Rochambeau* (Paris: Editions Lavazuelle, 1976), 124.

267   *"A great Mind knows how."* Washington to de Grasse, Sept. 27, 1781.

270 *"If the enemy should be tempted."* Washington, General Orders, Sept. 27, 1781.

271 *"They had encamped part."* Journal of Capitaine du Chesnoy, in Walker, 307.

271 *"By this means we are in possession."* Washington to Thomas McKean, Oct. 1,1781.

272 *"Tarleton saw me."* Lauzun, 250–251.

272 *"We have been beating the bush."* Greene to Knox, Sept. 29, 1781, Brooks, 157.

273 *"The British were led to imagine."* Martin, 232.

273 *"Before Morning the trenches."* Washington Diary, Oct. 6, 1781.

274 *"Had we dared."* Martin, 231–232.

274 *Pouzoulet . . . with the artillery.* Pouzoulet, Papini, *Journal*, entry 76.

275 *"One cannot sufficiently admire."* Chastellux, *Travels,* 71.

275 *"Good effect as they compelled."* Washington Diary, Oct. 9, 1781.

275 *"You're taking my flour."* De Grasse to Rochambeau, Oct.13, 1781, Kennett,148.

276 *"I am a Provençal and a sailor."* De Grasse to Washington, Oct. 1781, Lewis, 184–185.

277 *"My children, I have need of you."* Rochambeau, Oct. 14, 1781, Keim, 458.

278 *2,112 individuals.* Warrington Dawson, *Les 2112 français mort aux États-Unis en combatant pour l'indépendance américain* (Paris: Au siège de la société des Americainistes, 1936).

279 *"It seemed as if all that side."* Closen, 149.

279 *"Little masterpiece of tactical cooperation."* Lengel, "Aspects Tactiques," 178.

279 *"The General reflects with . . . pleasure."* Washington, General Orders, Oct. 15, 1781.

279 *"Not to make a breastwork."* Knox, Oct. 14, 1781, Ketchum, *Yorktown,* 237.

279 *"Safety of the place is."* Cornwallis to Clinton, Oct. 15, 1781, Kennett, 149.

280 *"Baroud d'honneur."* Ibid.

19. "The English are purchasing the peace rather than making it."

281 *"The same honors will be granted."* Washington to Cornwallis, Oct. 17, 1781.

281 *"Barbarous treatment."* J. Laurens to H. Laurens, Dec. 15, 1777, Simms, 94.

282 *Another song whose cadence was more amenable.* Tuchman, *First Salute,* 288.

282 *"Behaved like boys who had been."* New Jersey officer, Ketchum, *Yorktown,* 252.

283 *"Nothing could exceed this Zeal."* Washington to McKean, Oct. 19, 1781, copy in AAE-C.P., É.-U., Supplement, Opérations Militaire, no, 258.

283 *"The play is over."* Lafayette to Maurepas, Oct. 20, 1781, Unger, 159.

283 *"Would annihilate the rank,"* George III, Simms, *Three Victories,* 654–655.

284 *"A melancholy disaster."* Lord North, Manceron, *Gracious Pleasure,* 205.

284 *"Peace with America seems necessary."* North to George III, Jan. 21, 1782, *Correspondence of King George the Third,* vol. 5, 337.

284 *"The person after whom she was called."* Charles Thomas to Robert Morris, June 4, 1782, Patton, 214.

284 *"That it is the opinion of the House."* General Henry Conway resolution, Feb. 28, 1781, Lewis, 222.

285 *"Major, you give me the idea."* Du Bouchet.

287 *Ceding Canada and Nova Scotia.* Adams to Franklin, Apr. 16, 1782.

287 *"I told Mr. Oswald."* Franklin to H. Laurens, Apr. 20, 1782.

288 *"Selling to us a Thing."* Franklin to Adams, May 8, 1782; see also Adams, *Peace Journal*, May 9, 1782.

288 *"You would be of infinite Service."* Franklin to Jay, Apr. 22, 1782, ibid., 358–359.

288 *"Why then should we be anxious."* Jay to Livingston, Apr. 28, 1782, ibid., 363–364.

288 *"Unless we violate these instructions."* Jay to Gouverneur Morris, Oct. 13, 1782, and other letters, Sep.–Nov. 1782, Morris, 310.

289 *"I can see clouds."* Vergennes to Montmorin, Aug. 10, 1782, Stockley, 96.

291 *"Oh France . . . what joy it gives me."* Rodney to Lady Rodney, Lewis, 253.

291 *"Very unfortunate."* Vergennes to Louis XVI, Jean-François Labourdette, *Vergennes, Ministre principal de Louis XV* (Paris: Éditions Desjonquères, 1990), 205–206.

291 *"Without being provoked to it."* Vergennes to Montmorin, May 31, 1782, Giunta, *Emerging*, 415.

292 *"Save the nation in direst."* Ritcheson, 325.

292 *"If the sun of England."* Shelburne to Parliament, July 1782, Stockley, 55.

292 *"Necessary"* and *"advisable."* Oswald to Shelburne, July 10, 1782, Giunta, *Emerging*, 462–464 (italics in original).

292 *"That the more we favoured."* Franklin to Oswald, May 31, 1782, Ritcheson, 335.

293 *"The Doctor did not in the Course."* Oswald to Shelburne, July 10, 1782.

293 *"Hinders the conquest."* Vergennes to La Luzerne, Oct. 14, 1782, O'Donnell, 208.

294 *"Franklin won this victory."* Dull, *Diplomacy*, 145.

294 *"Colonies or Plantations."* Oswald Commission, July 25, 1782, Giunta, *Emerging*, 471–473.

295 *These terms represented substantial concessions.* Vergennes to Montmorin, Aug. 18, 1782. Stockley, 78.

296 *"Cannot extend its territories."* Rayneval to Jay, Sep. 6, 1782, ibid., 556–559.

296 *"I not only wish to contribute."* Shelburne to Rayneval, Stockley, 99–100.

296 *"Appears a Well-Instructed."* Shelburne to George III, Sept.13, 1782, Crout, 388.

296 *"I Owne the Art."* George III to Shelburne, Sept.14, 1782, ibid.

298 *"Between two as Subtle Spirits."* Adams Diary, Oct. 27, 1782.

298 *"It is not [in France's] interest."* Jay to Livingston, Nov. 17, 1782. Alexander De-conde, "The French Alliance in Historical Speculation," in *Diplomacy and Revolution: The Franco-American Alliance of 1778*, ed. Ronald Hoffman, et al. (Charlottesville, VA: 1981), 1–37.

299 *"The English Gentlemen were much pleased."* Adams Diary, Nov. 3, 1782.

299 *"The Eagle, finding Herself scratched."* Ibid.

299 *"Vous êtes le Washington."* Adams Diary, Nov. 10, 1782.

300 *"Thank God, I had a son."* H. Laurens, in ibid., Nov. 20, 1782.

300 *"I said it was the Opinion."* Ibid., Nov. 26, 1782.

301 *"The English are purchasing the peace."* Vergennes to Rayneval, Dec. 4, 1782, Giunta, *Emerging*, 706–708.

301 *"The king of Spain needs money."* Frederick, Oct. 24, 1782, Stockley, 89.

302 *"Thank God for Carlos giving up."* Vergennes to Montmorin, Dec. 17, 1782, Brecher, 208–209.

302 *"The government's credit has been maintained."* Jean-François Joly de Fleury, Jan. 1783, Harris, "French Finances."

Bibliography

Archives

Annales Nationales
Archives des Affaires Étrangères
Archives, Service Historique de la Défense
Founders Archive (on-line)
The Papers and Diaries of John Adams
The Papers of Benjamin Franklin
The Papers of George Washington

Printed Materials: Primary Sources

Du Bouchet, Langlois. *Journal d'un émigré, ou cahiers d'un étudiant en philosophie, qui a commencé son course des son entrée dans le monde.* Vol. 1. Paris, 1823.
Chastellux, Marquis de. *Travels in North America in the Years 1780–81–82.* New York, 1828.
Clark, William Bell, et al., eds. *Naval Documents of the American Revolution.* (*NDAR*). Washington, DC, 1964–2015.
Closen, Baron Ludwig von. *The Revolutionary Journal of Baron Ludwig von Closen,* translated by Evelyn M. Acomb. Chapel Hill: University of North Carolina Press, 1958.
Commager, Henry Steele, and Richard B. Morris, eds. *The Spirit of Seventy-Six.* New York: Harper & Row, 1975.
Doniol, Henri. *Histoire de la participation de la France a l'établissement des États-Unis d'Amérique: Correspondance diplomatique et documents.* Paris: Imprimerie Nationale, 1886–1892.

Fersen, Axel. *Lettres d'Axel Fersen à son père, pendant la guerre d'indépendance d'Amerique.* Paris: Firmen-Didot, 1929.

Fortescue, John, ed. *The Correspondence of King George III from 1760 to December 1783.* London: Macmillan, 1927–1928.

Giunta, Mary A., et al., eds. *The Emerging Nation: A Documentary History of the Foreign Relations of the United States under the Articles of Confederation, 1780–1789.* Washington, DC: National Historical Publications and Records Commission, 1996.

———. *Documents of the Emerging Nation: U.S. Foreign Relations, 1775–1789.* Lanham, MD, Rowman and Littlefield, 1998.

Idzerda, Stanley J., et al., eds. *Lafayette in the Age of the American Revolution: Selected Letters and Papers, 1776–1790.* Vols. 1–2, Ithaca, NY: Cornell University Press, 1977–.

Keim, De B. Randolph, ed. *Rochambeau, A Commemoration by the Congress of the United States of America of the services of the French auxiliary forces in the war of independence.* Washington, DC: GPO, 1907.

Martin, Joseph Plumb. *Private Yankee Doodle, Being a Narrative of Some of the Adventures, Dangers and Sufferings of a Revolutionary Soldier.* Boston: Little, Brown 1962.

Meng, John J., ed., *Despatches and Instructions of Conrad Alexandre Gérard, 1778–1780.* Baltimore: Johns Hopkins Press, 1939.

Papini, Catherine. *Journal Historique de Simon Pouzoulet (Castelnau de Guers 1759–1839) sur l'expédition aux Amériques avec l'Amiral comte de Grasse, 1781–1782.* Lacour/Rediva: Nîmes, 2000.

Rochambeau, Jean-Baptiste Donatien de Vimeur, Comte de. *"Relation, ou Journal des opérations du Corps Français sous le commandement de Comte de Rochambeau, Lieutenant-Génèral des Armées du Roi, depuis le 15 d'Août 1781."* Philadelphia: Guillaume Hampton, 1781.

———.*Mémoires militaires, historiques et politiques de Rochambeau, ancien maréchal de France et grand officier de la Légion d'honneur.* Paris, 1809.

Simms, William Gilmore, ed. *The Army Correspondence of Col. John Laurens.* New York: Bradford Club, 1867.

Ségur, Louis-Philippe de. *Memoirs and Recollections of Count Ségur.* London: Henry Colburn, 1825.

Saint-Germain, Claude-Louis, Comte de. *Mémoires.* Switzerland, 1779.

Stevens, Benjamin Franklin, compiler. *B. F. Stevens' Facsimiles of Manuscripts in European Archives relating to America, 1773–1783.* 10 vols. London, 1889–1898.

Walker, Paul K. *Engineers of Independence: A Documentary History of the Army Engineers in the American Revolution, 1775–1783.* Honolulu: University Press of Hawaii, 2002.

Wharton, Francis. *The Revolutionary Diplomatic Correspondence of the United States, vol. 1,* Washington, DC: General Post Office, 1889.

Printed Materials: Secondary Sources

Alberts, Robert C. *The Golden Voyage: The Life and Times of William Bingham, 1752–1804.* Boston: Houghton Mifflin, 1969.

Auricchio, Laura. *The Marquis: Lafayette Reconsidered.* New York: Alfred A. Knopf, 2014.

Balch, Thomas. *The French in America During the War of Independence of the United States, 1777–1783.* Vol. 2. Philadelphia: Porter & Coates, 1895.

Berg, Scott W. *Grand Avenues: The Story of Pierre Charles L'Enfant.* New York: Pantheon, 2007.

Blancpain, François. *L'Amiral d'Estaing, Serviteur et Victime de l'État (1729–1794).* Bécherel: Éditions Les Perséides, 2012.

Blaufarb, Rafe. *The French Army 1750–1820: Careers, Talent, Merit.* Manchester, UK: University of Manchester Press, 2002.

Borick, Carl P. *A Gallant Defense: The Siege of Charleston, 1780.* Columbia: University of South Carolina Press, 2003.

Brecher, Frank W. *Securing American Independence: John Jay and the French Alliance.* Westport, CT: Praeger, 2003.

Brooks, Noah. *Henry Knox: A Soldier of the Revolution, Major-General in the Continental Army and Washington's Chief of Artillery.* New York: Cosimo, 2007.

Broz, Joseph. *Histoire du Régne de Louis XVI, Les Années où l'on pouvait prévenir ou diriger La Révolution Française.* Paris: Jules Renouard, 1839.

Calmon-Maison, Jean Joseph Robert. *L'Amiral d'Estaing (1729–1794).* Paris: Calmann-Levy, 1910.

Chaline, Oliver, Philippe Bonnichon, and Charles-Philippe de Vergennes, eds. *Les Marines de la Guerre d'Indépendance Américaine, 1763–1783. Vol. 1,* Paris: Presses Universitaires de Paris (PUPS), 2013.

———. *La France et L'Indépendance Américaine.* Paris: PUPS, 2008.

Chávez, Thomas E. *Spain and the Independence of the United States: An Intrinsic Gift.* Albuquerque: University of New Mexico Press, 2002.

Crout, Robert Rhodes. "In Search of a 'Just and Lasting Peace': The Treaty of 1783, Louis XVI, Vergennes, and the Regeneration of the Realm." *International History Review* 5, no. 3 (Aug. 1983), 364–398.

Decré, Antoine. *L'indépendance américaine avec Rochambeau.* Paris: La Pensée Universelle, 1997.

Dull, Jonathan, *The French Navy and American Independence: A Study of Arms and Diplomacy, 1774–1787.* Princeton: Princeton University Press, 1975.

———. *A Diplomatic History of the American Revolution.* New Haven: Yale University Press, 1985.

———. "Franklin the Diplomat: the French Mission." *Transactions of the American Philosophical Society,* 1982.

Dunmore, John. *Louis de Bougainville: Soldier, Explorer, Statesman.* Gloucestershire, UK: Nonsuch, 2005.

Echeverria, Durand. *Mirage in the West: A History of the French Image of American Society to 1815.* Princeton, NJ: Princeton University Press, 1957.

Faÿ, Bernard. *The Revolutionary Spirit in France and America.* Translated by Ramon Guthrie. New York: Harcourt Brace, 1927.

Fleming, Thomas. *Washington's Secret War.* New York: HarperCollins/Smithsonian, 2005.

Gallo, Joseph. *John Paul Jones: America's First Sea Warrior*. Annapolis, MD: Naval Institute Press, 2006.

Gordon-Bowen-Hassell, E., Dennis M.Conrad, and Mark L. Hayes. *Sea Raiders of the American Revolution*. Oahu, HI: University Press of the Pacific, 2003.

Greene, Jack P., and J. R. Pole, eds. *The Blackwell Encyclopedia of the American Revolution*. Oxford, UK: Blackwell, 1991.

Hamon, Joseph. *Le Chevalier de Bonvouloir, premiere émissaire secret de la France auprès du Congrès de Philadelphie avant l'indépendance américaine*. Paris: Jouve, 1953.

Hardman, John. *Louis XVI*. New Haven, CT: Yale University Press, 1993.

Hippeau, C. *Paris et Versailles, Journal Anecdotique de 1762 à 1789*. Paris: Aug. Aubry Librairie, 1869.

Hutson, James H. "The Partition Treaty and the Declaration of Independence." *Journal of American History* 58 (Mar. 1972), 887–896.

Idzerda, Stanley, and Roger E. Smith, *France and the American War for Independence*. New York: Scott Limited Editions, 1979.

Kapp, Friedrich. *Life of John Kalb, Major-General in the Revolutionary Army*. New York: Henry Holt, 1884.

Kates, Gary. *Monsieur d'Éon Is a Woman*. New York: Basic Books, 1995.

Kennett, Lee. *The French Forces in America, 1780–1783*. Westport, CT: Greenwood Press, 1977.

Ketchum, Richard M. *Saratoga: Turning Point of America's Revolutionary War*. New York: Henry Holt, 1997.

———.*Victory at Yorktown: The Campaign that Won the Revolution*. New York: Henry Holt, 2004.

Kite, Elizabeth Sarah. *Brigadier General Louis Lebeque Duportail, Commandant of Engineers in the Continental Army 1777–1783*. Baltimore: Johns Hopkins University Press, 1953.

Lengel, Edward G. *General George Washington: A Military Life*. New York: Random House, 2005.

Lever, Evelyne. *Louis XVI*. Paris: Fayard, 1985.

Lewis, Charles Lee. *Admiral de Grasse and American Independence*. Annapolis, MD: Naval Institute Press, 1945.

Lockhart, Paul. *The Drillmaster of Valley Forge: The Baron de Steuben and the Making of the American Army*. New York: HarperCollins, 2005.

Luraschi, Christophe. *Conrad-Alexandre Gérard: Artisan de l'indépendance américaine*. Biarritz: Atlantica-Séguier, 2008.

Lutnick, Solomon. *The American Revolution and the British Press 1775–1783*. Columbia: University of Missouri Press, 1967.

Mackesy, Piers. *The War for America, 1775–1783*. Lincoln: University of Nebraska Press, 1993.

Magnin, Frédéric. *Mottin de la Balme, Cavalier des Deux Mondes et de la Liberté*. Paris: L'Harmattan, 2005.

Manceron, Claude. *Their Gracious Pleasure, 1782–1785*. Translated by Nancy Amphoux. New York: Alfred A. Knopf, 1989.

———. *The Wind from America, 1778–1781*, Translated by Nancy Amphoux. New York: Alfred A. Knopf, 1978.

Massey, Gregory D. *John Laurens and the American Revolution*. Columbia: University of South Carolina Press, 2000.

McCullough, David. *John Adams*. New York: Simon & Schuster, 2001.

McGrath, Tim. *Give Me a Fast Ship: The Continental Navy and America's Revolution at Sea*. New York: NAL Caliber, 2014.

Mention, Léon. *Le Comte de Saint-Germain et Ses Reformes*. Paris: A. Clavel, 1884.

Miller, Nathan. *Sea of Glory: A Naval History of the American Revolution*. Charleston, SC: Naval and Aviation Publishing Company, 1974.

Morton, Brian N., and Donald C. Spinelli, *Beaumarchais and the American Revolution*. Lanham, MD: Lexington Books, 2003.

Murphy, Orville T. *Charles Gravier Comte de Vergennes: French Diplomacy in the Age of Revolution 1719–1787*. Albany: State University Press of New York, 1982.

Osman, Julia. *Citizen Soldiers and the Key to the Bastille: War, Culture, and Society, 1750–1850*. Houndmills, UK: Palgrave Macmillan, 2015.

O'Donnell, William Emmett. *The Chevalier de la Luzerne: French Minister to the United States, 1779–1784*. Louvain/Brussels: Bibliothèque de L'Université, 1938.

O'Shaughnessy, Andrew Jackson. *Empire Divided: The American Revolution and the British Caribbean*. Philadelphia: University of Pennsylvania Press, 2000.

———. *The Men Who Lost America: British Leadership, the American Revolution, and the Fate of the Empire*. New Haven: Yale University Press, 2013.

Pacheco, Josephine Pennel. *French Secret Agents in America, 1765–1776*. Ph.D. thesis, University of Chicago, December 1950.

Patton, Robert H. *Patriot Pirates: The Privateer War for Freedom and Fortune in the American Revolution*. New York: Random House, 2008.

Patterson, A. Temple. *The Other Armada*. Manchester, UK: Manchester University Press, 1960.

Paul, Joel Richard. *Unlikely Allies: How a Merchant, a Playwright, and a Spy Saved the American Revolution*. New York: Riverhead, 2009.

Perkins, James Breck. *France in the American Revolution*. Boston: Houghton Mifflin, 1911.

Petitfils, Jean-Christian. *Louis XVI*. Paris: Perrin, 2005.

Le Pottier, Serge. *Duportail, ou le Génie de George Washington*. Paris: Economica, 2011.

Potts, Louis W. *Arthur Lee, A Virtuous Revolutionary*. Baton Rouge: Louisiana State University Press, 1981.

Price, Munro. *Preserving the Monarchy: The Comte de Vergennes, 1774–1787*. Cambridge, UK: Cambridge University Press, 1995.

Raynal, Abbé Guillaume Thomas François. *Histoire philosophique et politique des Établissements et de Commerce des Européens dans les deux Indes*. Amsterdam, 1770.

Renaut, Francis Paul. *Le Pacte De Famille Et L'amérique; La Politique Coloniale Franco-expagnole De 1760 À 1792*. Paris: Editions Leroux, 1922.

Ritcheson, C. R. "The Earl of Shelbourne and Peace with America, 1782–1783: Vision and Reality." *International History Review* 5, no. 3 (Aug. 1983), 322–363.

Schaeper, Thomas J. *Edward Bancroft: Scientist, Author, Spy.* New Haven, CT: Yale University Press, 2011.

———. *France and America in the Revolutionary Era: The Life of Jacques-Donatien Leray de Chaumont, 1725–1803.* Providence, RI: Berghahn Books, 1995.

Schiff, Stacy. *A Great Improvisation: Franklin, France, and the Birth of America.* New York: Henry Holt, 2005.

Shachtman, Tom. *Gentlemen Scientists and Revolutionaries.* New York: Palgrave Macmillan, 2014.

Simms, Brendan. *Three Victories and a Defeat: The Rise and Fall of the British Empire.* New York: Basic Books, 2009.

Snow, Dean. *1777: Tipping Point at Saratoga.* New York: Oxford University Press, 2016.

Soulavie, Jean-Louis. *Mémoires Historiques et Politiques du Règne de Louis XVI, depuis son Mariage Jusqu'à sa Mort.* Paris: Treuttel et Würtz, 1801.

Stephens, Karl T., *Neither the Charm Nor the Luck: Major-General John Sullivan.* Denver, CO: Outskirts Press, 2009.

Stephens, W. Walker, ed. *The Life and Writings of Turgot, Controller General of France 1774–6.* New York: Burt Franklin, 1971.

Stinchcombe, William C. *The American Revolution and the French Alliance.* Syracuse, NY: Syracuse University Press, 1969.

Stockley, Andrew. *Britain and France at the Birth of America: The European Powers and the Peace Negotiations of 1782–1783.* Exeter, UK: University of Exeter Press, 2001.

Tuchman, Barbara. *The First Salute: A View of the American Revolution.* New York: Random House, 1988.

Unger, Harlow Giles. *Lafayette.* New York: Wiley, 2002.

Van Alstyne, Richard W. *Empire and Independence: The International History of the American Revolution.* New York: Wiley, 1965.

Van Vlack, Milton C. *Silas Deane: Revolutionary War Diplomat and Politician.* Jefferson, NC: McFarland, 2013.

Ward, Marion. *Forth.* London: Phillimore Books, 1982.

Weintraub, Stanley. *Iron Tears: America's Battle for Freedom: Britain's Quagmire, 1775–1783.* New York: Free Press, 2005.

Whittemore, Charles P. *A General of the Revolution: John Sullivan of New Hampshire.* New York: Columbia University Press, 1961.

Wilson, David K. *The Southern Strategy: Britain's Conquest of South Carolina and Georgia, 1775–1780.* Columbia: University of South Carolina Press, 2005.

Zucker, A. E. *General De Kalb, Lafayette's Mentor.* Chapel Hill: University of North Carolina Press, 1966.

Index

List of Illustrations